Psychotherapy and Spirit

SUNY Series in the Philosophy of Psychology
Michael Washburn, editor

PSYCHOTHERAPY AND SPIRIT

Theory and Practice in
Transpersonal Psychotherapy

BRANT CORTRIGHT

STATE UNIVERSITY OF NEW YORK PRESS

Published by
State University of New York Press, Albany

For information, address State University of New York Press,
State University Plaza, Albany, N.Y., 12246

Production by Marilyn P. Semerad
Marketing by Theresa Abad Swierzowski

Library of Congress Cataloging in Publication Data

Cortright, Brant, 1949–
    Psychotherapy and spirit : theory and practice in transpersonal
psychotherapy / Brant Cortright.
        p.   cm. — (SUNY series in the philosophy of psychology)
    Includes bibliographical references and index.
    ISBN 0–7914–3465–6 (hc). — ISBN 0–7914–3466–4 (pbk).
    1. Transpersonal psychotherapy.   I. Title.   II. Series.
RC489.T75C67   1997
616.89'14—dc20   96–46518
                                                                                  CIP

                    10 9 8 7 6 5 4 3 2 1

To Zita

Contents

Part 2: Specific Approaches

Part 3: Clinical Issues

Part 4: Conclusion

Acknowledgments

There are many people I would like to thank for their assistance in the writing of this book. My wife, Jennifer, has been extraordinarily supportive in this venture, and for the many times she took our young children by herself while I worked on weekends, I am profoundly appreciative.

I am fortunate to be teaching at a truly extraordinary and wonderful school, the California Institute of Integral Studies. Many friends and colleagues here have been extremely helpful. Michael Kahn has been both an enthusiastic yet critically challenging friend. He read the entire manuscript and provided crucially valuable feedback. This book owes much to his continually asking difficult questions.

Bob Rosenbush gave much time and thought to essential sections, and our conversations illuminated important material. Sandra Kojan-Sands was a goddess-send. She brought to light several oversights and significantly improved one section. Brendan Collins and Jorge Ferrer both gave subtle and penetrating feedback at a crucial point that was much appreciated. Robert McDermott helped hone an early section and provided important feedback. Conversations with Jim Ryan, Paul Schwartz, Paul Linn, Dan Gottsegan, Jennifer Welwood and Roger Marsden were very much appreciated. Paul Herman has been a wise and supportive friend/colleague who helped in ways known and unknown.

From a distance, Dorian Schneidman helped in developmentally shaping the perspective of one chapter particularly, and Jeff Shapiro gave time, support, and stylistic feedback on one chapter.

As editor of this general series, Michael Washburn supported this project throughout and provided extremely valuable feedback on a key section.

Certainly my clients and students over the years have been more helpful than they could know in teaching me and challenging me on so many facets of this entire subject. My thanks to all.

Introduction

Transpersonal psychology is coming of age. It is bursting out every-where. New books, magazines, articles, and workshops are appear-ing daily that reflect the emerging transpersonal worldview, and it is spreading rapidly to other fields, ranging from anthropology to ecol-ogy. It is an increasing force that is touching all areas of culture, thought, and society.

Although transpersonal psychology and the perspective that emerges from it has implications for many fields of endeavor, it began with psychotherapy, and it is here that it has had greatest impact. It has spawned new approaches to healing and growth, and shed new light on many clinical issues. But while the transpersonal literature is growing rapidly, most contributions focus upon a specific viewpoint. The time finally seems right for a volume which concisely puts together the major developments in transpersonal psychotherapy as they are rele-vant to both theory and clinical practice.

That is what this volume attempts to do. Part 1 provides an overview of the theoretical framework of transpersonal psychotherapy. Part 2 takes a look at the main transpersonal approaches to psychother-apy as they have been developed so far. Part 3 examines some of the key clinical issues in the field as well as some of the clinical and ethical dilemmas that present themselves in this new endeavor. Part 4 attempts to synthesize some of the overarching principles of transpersonal psy-chotherapy as they apply to actual clinical work.

Because the focus of this book is psychotherapy, there are many influences in the larger transpersonal movement that have not been directly addressed here. Such things as 12-step programs, the self-help movement, shamanism, eco-feminism, paranormal research, and many other forces have all made important contributions, but I have focused on what most directly concerns transpersonal psychotherapy.

Much of the transpersonal literature thus far has been an enthusiastic embrace of whatever has been put forth. This seems quite natural, since during the early years of transpersonal psychology, when the field was intellectually shaky, it was developmentally appropriate to support and protect this newborn movement. But as a result, transpersonal psychology has been marked by a paucity of critical examination of the ideas and theories that comprise the field.

This book, besides being a presentation of the current state of transpersonal psychotherapy, also presents a critical evaluation of these theories, methodologies, and technologies. Such assessment seems necessary to me at this stage in the development of transpersonal psychotherapy, for now that the transpersonal field is stronger and more theoretically developed, it is ready to bear greater examination. Without challenge there can be no confirmation of what is valid or modification or elimination of what is unfruitful. I believe such critical evaluation is ultimately a sign of strength and adds to it, for only by subjecting our theories to rigorous scrutiny can the transpersonal field grow into strong, healthy adulthood and enter more fully into the larger professional discourse in the field of psychotherapy. My hope is that this book will contribute to the ongoing dialogue on some of the serious and complex issues transpersonal psychotherapy raises.

One brief note about the use of the words "ego" and "self" as they are used in the transpersonal literature and in this book. Ego and self have vastly different meanings depending upon the context. Most often in transpersonal and spiritual literature, and in Eastern spiritual systems particularly, ego and self are used interchangeably to mean the separate sense of "I" or self-consciousness. But in psychoanalysis ego and self have very specific meanings. Ego is a mental apparatus which, along with the id and the superego, organizes the psyche. The self, on the other hand, is closer to the "I" sense, sometimes defined as an independent center of initiative and experienced as continuous in time and space. Carl Jung's usage is similar, but he adds the Self, which in Jungian thought is the central archetype of the psyche, is connected to but not identical with our spiritual nature, although it cannot be experienced directly. Hinduism uses Self to indicate the atman, our non-evolving soul or ultimate spiritual being, and Hindu spiritual practice aims at enlightenment, which is the direct experience of identity with this Self. All of these various meaning can be quite confusing unless the context is clear. I have tried to make the context clear throughout this book. When I speak of ego or self in this book I generally use them to refer to the "I" sense, although in discussions of psychoanalysis or Jungian thought I specify the special context and meaning of these words.

Part 1

Transpersonal Theory

Chapter One

Basic Assumptions

Most transpersonal psychotherapists wonder from time to time (or perhaps like me wonder almost daily), What does it really mean to do transpersonal psychotherapy?

There is so much that passes for transpersonal psychotherapy, ranging from what may appear to be very traditional and mundane to the very far out and flaky. *What does a transpersonal orientation look like when it comes to actually sitting with a client?* How is it translated into action? Is it shown by what the therapist does or how the therapist is? How can a therapist be grounded in accepted psychotherapy practice and open to the realm of spirit? Are there some common principles, methods, guidelines which characterize a transpersonal approach?

Many questions arise. Some of them are practical: Is meditation helpful for therapy? What is the interface between meditation and psychotherapy? How can working with altered states of consciousness assist psychotherapy? What light does spiritual emergency shed on the psyche and on psychopathology? What implications do these issues have for healing and growth?

Other questions focus on the therapeutic relationship: What is the relationship of the therapist to the spiritual life of the client? That of detached witness? support? teacher? guru? Does the therapist provide active spiritual guidance? And if so, when and of what kind? These are tricky questions, for they take us to the boundaries of the therapist's professional identity. If the role of the therapist blends into spiritual teacher or guide, what are the implications of this for practice and training? And, more disturbing, why can we reliably produce good, competent therapists far better than anyone has been able to produce good gurus or spiritual teachers?

Perhaps the most fundamental questions in transpersonal psychology revolve around what is the relationship of the personal to the transpersonal. What is the relationship of self to spirit? And what is the nature of this relationship?

The transpersonal field is currently at an evolutionary edge in psychology, and as such it is sizzling with creative energy and aliveness. Although there is much to be said in favor of being a discipline at the frontier in which there is experimentation, pushing past traditional boundaries, innovation, and excitement, there are hazards as well, hazards better acknowledged and addressed than ignored. This book attempts to raise some of these issues as well.

DEFINING TRANSPERSONAL PSYCHOLOGY

Transpersonal psychology can be understood as the melding of the wisdom of the world's spiritual traditions with the learning of modern psychology.

It is the world's spiritual traditions and modern psychology that provide the two most interesting and compelling answers to the fundamental question human beings have asked throughout the ages, "Who am I?" In reply to this question, the world's spiritual traditions look deep within and respond, "A spiritual being, a soul," and religious practices are the means by which spiritual traditions seek to connect to this deeper identity within. On the other hand, modern psychology has arrived at a very different answer to the question, "Who am I?" Psychology looks within and gives the answer, "A self, an ego, a psychological existence," and depth psychotherapy is psychology's journey into the reclaiming, healing, and growth of this self.

Transpersonal psychology is the attempt to put these two answers together. By creating a new synthesis of these two profound approaches to human consciousness, the spiritual and the psychological, transpersonal psychology attempts to honor the learning of each. It has become a cliché in transpersonal circles that, "You need to be a somebody before you can be a nobody." While the issue is considerably more complex than this, this statement does reflect what transpersonal psychology is concerned with: developing a self while also honoring the urge to go beyond the self.

In moving beyond the confines of the self, consciousness is seen to open up into ranges of experience which go far beyond Freud's initial formulations of id, ego, and superego. Consciousness is seen to be a vast, multidimensional existence where ever new aspects of Being are manifested. This collective religious wisdom speaks of all existence as one vast, spiritual reality. All human beings (and all creatures and creation) partake of this spiritual reality.

Our self, our psychological existence, is described by these perennial traditions as the most visible, surface expression of a fundamentally spiritual essence, the ground of being. Any explanations in psychology that consider only the outward appearance of things will inevitably fall short. Just as modern depth psychology looks past the surface view of the mind to discover a dynamic unconscious of which people are generally unaware, so the teachings of religious traditions point to a supreme and ultimately spiritual source of consciousness that supports this outer psychological existence we call our "self."

No amount of study of genetics, biochemistry, or neuroscience, on the one hand, or of family systems, mother-child interactions, and early childhood development on the other hand, in other words no explanation that only considers the outward appearances of nature or nurture, will ever provide satisfactory answers to life's fundamental questions. Only by looking to the spiritual dimension that includes and transcends heredity and environment can we discover an adequate answer to the problems of human existence.

Another approach to defining transpersonal psychology takes us to the meaning of the word transpersonal. According to *Webster's Unabridged Dictionary*, the prefix *trans* is Latin for beyond or across. The first definition of *trans* pertains to "above and beyond," as in a *trans*cendent experience which takes us beyond our ordinary consciousness. The second definition pertains to "across" or "to the other side of," as in a *trans*atlantic flight which goes across the Atlantic Ocean to the other side. Both of these meanings of *trans* are appropriate in defining transpersonal psychology.

The definition of transpersonal as "beyond the personal" is the meaning which was initially emphasized during the formative years of transpersonal psychology. Indeed, sometimes transpersonal psychology is thought of exclusively in terms of what is beyond the personal, including such things as mystical experience, altered states of consciousness, kundalini experiences, various psi phenomena (such as ESP, clairvoyance, channeling, telepathy, etc.), shamanic journeying, unitive states, near-death experiences, and so on. While these phenomena "beyond" the personal form a part of transpersonal psychology, they are becoming less of a focus as transpersonal psychology has recently moved toward a more complete view that seeks to find the sacred in the daily, ordinary life and consciousness in which most people live.

The definition of *trans* as "across" also applies, since transpersonal psychology moves across the personal realm, acknowledging and continuing to explore all aspects of the self and the unconscious that traditional psychology has discovered while also placing this personal psychology in a larger framework. Thus the self is still very much the focus in transpersonal psychotherapy. But by moving across traditional personal psychology to the larger spiritual context, the individual self moves out of its existential vacuum into a wider dimension to which the world's spiritual teachings point.

So taking these two meanings of "beyond" and "across," the literal meaning of transpersonal includes both the personal and what is beyond it. Transpersonal psychology studies how the spiritual is expressed in and through the personal, as well as the transcendence of the self.

Transpersonal psychology in this sense affords a wider perspective for all the learning of conventional psychology. It includes and exceeds traditional psychology. And by holding all of conventional psychology within it, it recasts psychology into a new mold and spiritual framework.

DEFINING TRANSPERSONAL PSYCHOTHERAPY: THEORY AND PRACTICE

It is customary in psychotherapy to differentiate between theory and practice. The level of theory includes philosophical worldviews, basic assumptions about human nature, concepts about what is being studied, and a methodology which forms the bridge between theory and practice. Technology is the means by which this methodology is enacted.

Every therapeutic approach has a more or less explicit theory behind it, a methodology for producing change, and a technology or set of techniques to implement the methodology.

For example, in classical psychoanalysis, the level of theory includes notions of the unconscious, defense mechanisms, the id, ego, and superego, the theory of instincts, dreams, et cetera. The methodology (or the method by which change comes about), most analysts would agree, is the working through of the transference. The level of technology includes free association, interpretation, and dream analysis. Taking the therapeutic approach of bioenergetics as another example, the level of theory is very similar to psychoanalysis except that the body is the central focus. The methodology is the softening of the body armor, the chronically contracted muscular patterns that deaden a person's aliveness. The techniques range from the breathing exercises and cathartic expression to the stress positions used to build up a charge in the body and increase the energy flow so that the armor can soften.

In each of these, the technology flows out of the methodology, and the methodology flows out of the theory. Every technique in psychotherapy, regardless of the school, implies a theory which contains basic assumptions about human nature. So whether someone says to a person who's crying, "There, there, don't cry. It'll be okay," based on a theory received from a grandmother that sees feelings as dangerous and best suppressed; or whether the person says, "Can you stay with your tears, keep breathing, and give your tears a voice," based on a theory that sees the experiencing and expression of feelings as helpful, both imply a set of assumptions about human nature and growth which generates a particular response. This chapter and the following chapter examine transpersonal theory. The following chapter examines the methodology that emerges from transpersonal theory. Most of the rest of the book explores the implications of these for clinical application.

THEORY

Transpersonal psychotherapy is not completely encompassed by any particular writer. Ken Wilber, Carl Jung, Stanislav Grof—each of these theorists represents specific viewpoints within transpersonal psychology, which is a field much like politics or art where many viewpoints co-exist. Nor is transpersonal psychotherapy defined by Buddhist "psychology," or Christian or shamanic "psychologies," for these do not really constitute psychologies at all in the sense that this word is used today. Russell (1986) has argued persuasively that the key insights of Western psychology are absent in such spiritual systems. To call them psychologies is to miss most of what modern psychology has discovered, such as categories of differential diagnosis, a theory of childhood development, a theory of psychopathology, views of intra-psychic conflict, defense mechanisms, the dynamic unconscious, and so on. Nor is transpersonal psychotherapy defined by specific subject matter, such as meditation or altered states or spiritual emergency, although these are some of its most visible topics. Transpersonal theory goes beyond these specific viewpoints to articulate a comprehensive psycho-spiritual vision of life and its unfolding.

Transpersonal theory is not a unified, clearly demarcated, cut-and-dried approach. It is still quite new, with many different formulations and syntheses, and it has much unexplored territory. It is also important to recognize that transpersonal theory, like all theory, is but a way of organizing our experience of reality, it is not that reality itself. Commenting on this many years ago, Alfred Korzybski said cogently, "The map is not the territory." He also said, "The map does not represent all the territory." We need to remember that no matter how thorough our theoretical maps are, they will always leave something out. Korzybski's third statement, "The map is self-reflexive," reminds us of the need for map awareness and points to the need for continual reevaluation and revision of our maps as human understanding advances. Transpersonal psychology, like any field of human endeavor, will always be a "work in progress."

Despite the fact that transpersonal psychology is still in its formative stages, it has nevertheless undergone a historical development. The first two decades of writings in the field were largely focused on what might be called the "high end" of human experiencing. An excerpt from the statement of purpose of the first *Journal of Transpersonal Psychology* serves to illustrate this.

> The Journal of Transpersonal Psychology is concerned with the publication of theoretical and applied research, original contributions, empirical papers, articles and studies in meta-needs, ultimate values, unitive consciousness, peak experience, ecstasy, mystical experience, B-values, essence, bliss, awe, wonder, self-actualization, ultimate meaning, transcendence of the self, spirit, sacralization of everyday life, oneness, cos-

mic awareness, cosmic play, individual and species-wide synergy, maximal interpersonal encounter, transcendental phenomenon; maximal sensory awareness, responsiveness and expression; and related concepts, experiences, and activities. (Sutich, 1969, p. 16.)

Today such a statement may seem rather amusing, with its emphasis on things like bliss, ecstasy, awe, cosmic unity, and so on. What about suffering, pain, abuse, psychosis, war, greed? What about daily life? However, it is important to realize the context for the emergence of transpersonal psychology, namely the late 1960s, a time when bliss, wonder, and awe were in the air, revolution was in the streets, and enlightenment seemed just around the corner. Although transpersonal psychology has been criticized for being removed from the ordinary reality most people live in by its narrow focus on the high end of human life, this stage did serve a necessary historical purpose, namely to bring attention to those parts of human experience which had been neglected by the previous models of psychology and/or pathologized out of genuine consideration (such as Freud's dismissing mystical experience as being merely a return to the oceanic oneness of the womb).

By bringing attention to these experiences, transpersonal psychology has helped bring about a major paradigm shift away from the traditional scientific, materialistic, Cartesian worldview toward a more holistic, spiritual perspective. It has also affirmed spiritual seeking as an essential aspect of human motivation. Seeking for the Divine, whether called God, Brahman, Buddha-nature, Reality, Being, Truth, Love, or anything else, has been a major aspiration and force in all cultures and periods of history, yet it has been virtually ignored by traditional psychology. Transpersonal psychology brought this central motivating force into the center of psychology, rather than overlooking it or relegating it to the periphery. (In so doing, it has been important to distinguish between religion and spirituality. Religion is the organized, established structures associated with organized religion, which some people find great meaning in but which others do not. Spirituality is the soul's free quest for the divine and often is not affiliated with a traditional organized religion.)

More recently, however, there has been a shift in transpersonal psychology to how the spiritual is expressed in everyday life. It has become clear that transpersonal psychology must include the whole—not just the high end of human experience but the very personal realm of ordinary consciousness as well. Regular people with ordinary problems who are also on a spiritual path are seeking psychotherapy and growth from transpersonally oriented practitioners. They are looking for therapists who will honor their seeking for something sacred and who can respect their whole being—in its psychological and spiritual fullness—rather than belittling or minimizing their spiritual seeking, as much of traditional psychotherapy has historically done. Thus, there are emerging new approaches to seeing how, for example, meditation can interface with traditional therapy, how relationships can be used for spiritual unfolding, how a transpersonal perspective effects how we view childhood development, dreams, physical healing, and psychosomatic syndromes, as well as how it influences our understanding of the development and treatment of psychopathology.

With this larger viewpoint, we assume a different perspective even in the exploration of the "lower end" of human functioning and psychopathology. For example, psychosis can be seen to be more than just pathological flooding of the ego by the id, it also becomes a psychic opening to vast cosmic forces and presents a possibility for spiritual emergence and psychological healing.

In one of the only articles ever to seriously address the question of what constitutes transpersonal psychotherapy, Vaughn (1979) said that context (consisting of the beliefs, values, and intentions of the therapist), content (transpersonal experiences), and process (consisting of the development from identification, through disidentification, to self-transcendence), were the key elements. Within the discussion given in this book, these would all fall within the domain of theory. Vaughn also correctly noted that it is the context which defines a transpersonal approach. To this it is important to add: the consciousness of the therapist is what brings this context alive.

To borrow an idea from gestalt therapy, "meaning" can be defined as the relation between figure and ground. For example, the word "bow" (figure) can mean several things depending upon the ground (context) in which it appears—bow and arrow, to bow before the queen, the bow of a ship. It is the ground or context that determines the meaning of any given figure. Thus the figure of any given therapeutic intervention is given meaning by the theoretical ground in which it is embedded. It is this ground of transpersonal theory which gives meaning and value to the techniques used in a transpersonal approach, with consciousness forming the methodological bridge between theory and technique.

The defining character of transpersonal psychotherapy is the theoretical and methodological framework which informs the therapeutic process. It is certainly tempting to identify transpersonal psychotherapy through the level of technique, for this is the most visible expression of therapy. But transpersonal psychotherapy is not to be defined by technique. Indeed, the level of technique is the least important level of transpersonal psychotherapy. That transpersonal psychotherapy is not a specific technical modality is both a cause of some confusion and a source of strength. Rowan (1993), for example, in his book *The Transpersonal*, makes this error of identifying the transpersonal approach with certain techniques (primarily visualization, active imagination, and meditation). But all techniques could be thrown away and the transpersonal approach would remain, ready to innovate with new techniques. For all techniques can be transpersonal, given a transpersonal framework.

To be sure, there are specific techniques, such as holotropic breath work, altered state work, or psychosynthesis' guided imagery that are often identified as transpersonal, but even here it is the surrounding context that provides a transpersonal meaning. Some of these techniques, such as guided imagery, have been used in behavioral programs having nothing to do with the transpersonal. The meaning of the techniques changes given the shifting context.

In this way transpersonal psychology is more like humanistic psychology than psychoanalysis. Whereas in psychoanalysis all the various schools share a similar set of techniques, humanistic psychology has a wide range of modalities, from bioenergetics to gestalt to client-centered approaches. Similarly, the larger perspective of transpersonal psychotherapy, by not being limited to a specific approach, can be adapted to fit a number of technical variations.

The importance of theory, therefore, is that it is the overarching framework that defines transpersonal psychotherapy. Transpersonal content often never arises in transpersonal therapy, yet the meaning-giving frame provides the transpersonal orientation. A therapist may use an approach that is informed by a behavioral, psychoanalytic, or humanistic orientation (ideally a therapist is open to all theoretical models, though in practice most therapists tend to favor one), but transpersonal therapy proceeds by no set technique or formula. Transpersonal therapy lies not in what the therapist says or does, but in the silent frame that operates behind the therapist's actions, informing and giving meaning to the specific interventions. It is thus a wider container which can hold all other therapeutic orientations within it.

BASIC ASSUMPTIONS

The following chapters discuss transpersonal theory in more detail. At this point, it might be helpful to distill some of the key assumptions that define a transpersonal approach. For while there are many different perspectives within the field, there are some underlying principles that unite transpersonal therapists. These are:

1. **Our essential nature is spiritual.** Transpersonal psychology affirms that both modern psychology and the world's spiritual traditions are correct about the nature of human identity: our being is both psychological and spiritual in nature. But the transpersonal view gives primacy to the spiritual source which supports and upholds the psychological structures of the self.

2. **Consciousness is multidimensional.** Transpersonal psychology has pioneered exploration and research into other levels or states of consciousness. Within the field of psychology, such alternate states were either pathologized into irrelevance (e.g., mystical union was described as "artificial schizophrenia") or dismissed altogether as simply fantasies. Research with psychedelic compounds which radically alter consciousness, the use of non-drug techniques such as shamanic journeying, breathing, fasting, hypnosis, and meditation to induce altered states, and study of the world's religions all demonstrate that the normal, ordinary consciousness most people experience is but the most outward tip of consciousness. Spiritual experiences often catapult a person into realms and states of expanded consciousness that reveal how limited and restricted normal consciousness is.

   Other dimensions or aspects of consciousness show the truth of the wisdom traditions, the cosmic connectedness of all beings, the unity within all outward diversity, the subtle realms and levels of consciousness which are more open to the clarity, peace, light, love, knowledge, and power behind this physical manifestation. To exclude any of these dimensions from psychology leads to an impoverished theory of consciousness.

3. **Human beings have valid urges toward spiritual seeking, expressed as a search for wholeness through deepening individual, social, and transcendent awareness.** The search for wholeness, which is one way of viewing Maslow's research into the hierarchy of needs (Maslow, 1968, 1970, 1971), takes the individual into increasing levels of self-discovery, actualization, and seeking for transcendence. The transpersonal vision sees this entire psychological drama as a subset of a larger quest for spiritual union. Not only is spiritual seeking healthy, it is essential for full human health and fulfillment. The definition of mental health must include a spiritual dimension to be complete.

Spiritual seeking can become increasingly important and central in a client's life. The mystics of most religious traditions indicate that the deepest motivation for all human beings is the urge toward spirit. Maslow's map is a Western confirmation of what many religious traditions have expressed, which is that initially the growth of consciousness focuses upon building up the physical, emotional, mental structures of the self. It is just this area that most of Western psychology has studied. Traditional psychology has focused on motivational hierarchies—survival needs, sex and aggression, the need to integrate feelings and impulses, finding intimacy, developing a cohesive self, and actualizing the self's potentials through meaningful work and activities. Transpersonal psychology completes the process, putting this motivational path into the context of a spiritual journey. In this journey the individual moves from more basic needs to progressively higher needs, leading (either along the way or at the end) to the aspiration for spiritual fulfillment.

In hindsight, it is hard to understand how psychology, which tried to discover the truth of human experience, could have avoided the realm of spirituality for so long, for it has been a central preoccupation of every human culture throughout history. Yet it is also understandable given Western science's attempt to put aside all metaphysical speculation and focus only on what is experimentally observable. It is through this kind of "ordinary mind" focus that psychology has come upon its discoveries. Historically in the West, organized religion in the form of the Catholic Church stultified thought for centuries. Separating religion from science during the Renaissance powerfully liberated human inquiry. Apparently only now are we ready to bring spirituality back into scientific and psychological thought.

4. **Contacting a deeper source of wisdom and guidance within is both possible and helpful to growth.** Western psychotherapy seeks to uncover a deeper source of guidance than the conscious ego or self. Different systems describe this in different terms. Gestalt therapy speaks of "the wisdom of the organism," which knows far more than the person does, and seeks to replace ego control with "organismic self-regulation." Jungian psychotherapy tries to replace the ego as the locus of control with the Self, which is more in touch with the wisdom of the unconscious. Self psychology and object relations try to bring the "nuclear self" or the "real self" to the forefront, rather than the defensively constructed, false self. Existential psychotherapy makes the "authentic self" the true guide rather than the compromised inauthentic self. *All of modern psychotherapy may be seen to be an intuitive groping toward a deeper source of wisdom than the surface self.*

For thousands of years religious traditions have declared that our fundamental nature is a source of vast intelligence, and we can and should turn inward in the search for real wisdom. Some psychological systems explicitly deny this unseen dimension (e.g., psychoanalysis and gestalt), while other systems make no mention of it. Still others (e.g., Jungian and psychosynthesis) specifically acknowledge this spiritual level.

Transpersonal psychotherapy, in line with traditional psychotherapy, aims at assisting people in accessing their inner wisdom for greater emotional and psychological integration but makes clear that whatever any particular system or psychology calls it, it is a deeper, spiritual reality that is the source of the self's or the organism's wisdom. Transpersonal psychology makes explicit what western psychology has only vaguely pointed toward.

5. **Uniting a person's conscious will and aspiration with the spiritual impulse is a superordinate health value.** Affirming the infinite ways in which the spiritual impulse may express itself is a primary value in transpersonal psychotherapy. It is not that setting out on a spiritual path clears up all psychological problems. Nor does it mean that people should be pushed, however gently, toward entering a spiritual path. Rather the assumption is that this cognitive set and, more fundamentally, this spiritual orientation, puts one into greater alignment with the healing forces of the psyche and the universe, expressed variously as the Tao, Divine Will, et cetra. This creates optimal conditions for psychological integration. Thus transpersonal psychology supports the spiritual urge. It also is alert for ways clients misuse the spiritual impulse to avoid dealing with neurotic patterns. This misuse has been called "spiritual by-passing" and will be examined in a later chapter.

   In spiritual seeking it is crucial for the therapist to honor all spiritual paths. Dogmatic clinging to any particular spiritual practice is severely limiting to transpersonal practice. If there is one thing to be dogmatic about, it is the importance of not being dogmatic. There is no one way to the Divine, the paths are as varied as there are individuals, and a broad knowledge of and respect for these varied paths (including atheism) is crucial.

6. **Altered states of consciousness are one way of accessing transpersonal experiences and can be an aid to healing and growth.** From its beginnings transpersonal psychology has been influenced by altered state research in general and psychedelic research in particular. It is clear that for many people psychedelic compounds have been a significant awakener. They can open a door to the infinite, profoundly touching the foundation of our being, disclosing new possibilities of consciousness that had been entirely unseen or merely abstract. In the Hindu text the Bhagavad Gita, Sri Krishna gives a boon to the hero of the story, Arjuna, in the form of a vision of the divine universal. This divine vision has powerful and life-changing effects upon Arjuna. The experience of altered states of consciousness can serve as a modern equivalent of Krishna's

vision to Arjuna, opening up new realms of experience with great power and intensity. While not for everyone, the judicious induction of altered states of consciousness has a respected place in transpersonal work, and altered states have significant implications for psychological and physical healing. (See later chapter on altered states of consciousness.)

7. **Our life and actions are meaningful.** Our actions, joys, and sorrows have significance in our growth and development. They are not merely random, pointless events. Moving beyond a purely scientific, materialistic, or existential perspective allows us to view life from a broader vantage point. The strict existential position is that health results from creating meaning in a meaningless world. The spiritual position, by contrast, is that health comes about as we uncover the meaning inherent in what is. A transpersonal synthesis would see both our need to continually discover deeper meaning and acknowledge our contribution to continually constructing and interpreting this deeper meaning. The transpersonal perspective is that discovering this meaning is extremely therapeutic and accords with Victor Frankl's observations that a person can cope with anything if it is meaningful, no matter how terrible it may appear.

Modern psychology has taught us a great deal about the importance of honoring our pain, of going into it, feeling and exploring it rather than avoiding or repressing it. As we relate to our pain it reveals its story, taking us to deeper levels of our being. As we become more vulnerable to our own depths, this expanding awareness heals.

Often it is the wounds and tragedies of life that provide the impetus to make the inward journey. And in the darkest, most painful area of the psyche, there may be discovered a redeeming light, a source of solace, healing, and new growth. Psyche is Greek for soul, and to open our psyche is to open to the transforming power of the spirit. A transpersonal perspective views our spiritual ground as the source of this healing. One common example occurs in Alcoholics Anonymous (AA) meetings where people sometimes refer to their alcoholism as the best thing ever to happen to them, for it was this that launched them on their path of renewal and spiritual seeking.

This perspective results in a more expansive view of the client in his or her growth toward a higher, more encompassing self. This shift from the local scene to the big picture allows a person to see that the outer, surface show is not the only perspective, and that there is a larger process of transformative growth occurring.

8. **The transpersonal context shapes how the person/client is viewed.** Much of traditional diagnosis and therapy tends toward seeing the client as "other." But a transpersonal approach (in agreement with the humanists) views the client, just like the therapist, as an evolving being and fellow seeker. This translates into a therapeutic stance of compassion toward the client, moving the therapist toward becoming more heart-centered in psychotherapy practice, while walking that fine line of maintaining appropriate boundaries.

PRACTICE

When the goals of therapy are limited, the techniques must necessarily be limited. But when the goal is the expansion of consciousness and widening the entire range of human experiencing, then the techniques are limitless. Active as well as traditional techniques can be used within this defining transpersonal context.

Techniques are simply ways of accessing the self and its depths. They are not ends in themselves. Each person can enter the inner world more easily in some ways than in others. The appropriate use of techniques is the matching of client capacities and preferences to these ways.

Some of the possible techniques are: interpretation, reflection, focusing, exploring cognitions, confrontation, role-playing, guided imagery and fantasy, dreamwork, bodywork approaches (such as bioenergetics, sensory awareness, yoga, tai chi, aikido, biofeedback, and other mind/body disciplines), breathwork, expressive arts techniques, expanding expressiveness, meditative practices, journal work, voice work, and altered state work (such as hypnosis, psychedelics, holotropic breathwork, and shamanic journeying).

In general, any area of life that the therapist has assimilated and which can enhance consciousness can be used. Growth in the skillful use of techniques continues throughout a therapist's life.

Regardless of the goal of therapy, a transpersonal orientation may be used to achieve this. For example, the work of Jon Kabat-Zinn at the University of Massachusetts shows how the very behavioral goal of stress reduction can be worked with in a transpersonal way, using yoga and mindfulness meditation to enhance a person's awareness and promote healing of the mind/body split.

CHALLENGES FOR TRANSPERSONAL PSYCHOTHERAPY

At present, transpersonal psychotherapy evokes rather fuzzy images about actual therapeutic work with clients. As the second section of this book will show, transpersonal psychotherapy is usually identified with specific techniques associated with a specific school or approach. Yet transpersonal psychotherapy is far wider and more inclusive than any of these particular schools. And while in practice most transpersonal therapists tend to blend either a humanistic or, less commonly, a psychoanalytic approach with a transpersonal framework, this still tends to perpetuate a separatist, exclusive way of working.

It is a contention of this book that transpersonal psychotherapy will never reach its full stature until it has synthesized into itself the most powerful insights and techniques that the behavioral, psychoanalytic, and humanistic schools have discovered. Then the transpersonal approach will begin to realize more definition, while allowing for flexibility and innovation, and to come ever closer to actualizing its potential of being both an integrative and creatively original way of working.

Transpersonal psychotherapy views all psychological processes against the backdrop of spiritual unfolding. The psyche is no longer seen as an endpoint or final term, rather it opens into a vaster spiritual reality, a spiritual existence which exceeds and contains this process of psychological development. It is this changed perspective—the figure of the psyche against the supporting ground of the spirit—that typifies a transpersonal approach.

Much of transpersonal psychotherapy during its first two decades was simply an additive mixture—adding psychology to spirituality without changing either one very much. But more recent formulations see this as a new synthesis in which both are changed and modified as part of a new whole. The challenges for transpersonal psychology are to be rigorous in developing and testing theory, to be steeped and grounded in both western psychological theory and spiritual tradition, and to carefully attempt to put these two deep sources of wisdom together in a bold new vision. The hope is that this will result in a more psychologically-informed spirituality and a spiritually-based psychology.

Chapter Two

The Psycho-Spiritual Framework

If transpersonal psychotherapy is the integration of spirituality and psychology, it becomes important to delineate the overall framework of these two domains. What assumptions about human nature and consciousness do they make? And what implications are there for human growth?

Psychology and spirituality have each produced different languages and metaphors for describing the human condition. The word "metaphor" does not mean that these approaches are merely fantasies or poetic images, for in one sense all of science and philosophy are metaphors. The contemporary philosopher Richard Rorty (1989), for example, refers to the development of scientific thought as the continual re-creation of new languages and new metaphors for describing anew what one seeks to understand. In postmodern language, the language and metaphors that science and philosophy have produced are constructions.

Spiritual and psychological systems, then, are but those abiding descriptions and metaphors that have resonated most deeply with human experience over time. Both spiritual and psychological traditions speak to what we are, to what is wrong with the human condition, and to the transformative possibilities open to us. A comprehensive theory of transpersonal psychology strives to integrate the world's spiritual and psychological approaches into a new whole and tries to find a common, underlying methodology for producing growth and change. This chapter attempts to articulate the broad outlines of this theory. I believe this psycho-spiritual framework provides the widest, most inclusive theoretical framework for transpersonal psychology, within which more specific approaches such as Wilber, Jung, Washburn, Grof, and other theorists, can be situated. First the spiritual dimension will be examined, followed by the psychological dimension of the theoretical framework.

THE SPIRITUAL DIMENSION

Searching for the most thorough understanding of the wide variety of spiritual experience that has been recorded throughout history and across different cultures has led to the formulation of the "perennial philosophy." Perennial philosophy, a phrase first coined by Aldous Huxley, refers to those core areas of agreement between the world's spiritual traditions. It has assumed its most sophisticated exposition by the renowned philosopher Huston Smith, who has written on this subject for over 30 years. Although widely accepted within the transpersonal field, it should be noted that there is not universal agreement that the spiritual underpinnings of transpersonal psychology can be fully explained by the perennial philosophy (see Walsh & Vaughn, 1993), and given the nature of philosophical discourse it seems unlikely there will ever be universal agreement about such a matter. Nevertheless, it is clear that the map of spiritual experience that the perennial philosophy provides is extremely large. At the very least it must be accounted for, if only to make room for the different *interpretations* of the perennial philosophy in the transpersonal field.

By way of introduction it is worth noting the distinctions between the two major expressions of spirituality in the world's religions—those that emphasize the Personal Divine, theistic or theistic-relational traditions (which includes most of western spirituality) and those that emphasize the Impersonal Divine or nondual traditions (which includes much of Eastern spirituality.)

Spirituality in the West has been guided by a view of the individual soul seeking for a relationship with the Divine. Mainstream Christianity, Judaism, and Islam are examples of theistic-relational traditions that focus on discovering a personal relationship to the Divine and stress the reality of the soul. That is, the individual soul is not viewed as entirely separate from or independent of the Divine. The soul exists in relationship to the Divine, and when it cuts itself off from the Divine, existential alienation, emptiness, or in Christian terms "fallenness," result. The answer to this condition is to seek spiritual freedom, wholeness, "salvation" by reestablishing this connection with Spirit through spiritual practice. Or, rather than being personified, the Divine may be viewed as a Power or Presence within the person ("the Lord seated in the heart of every creature," in the language of the *Bhagavad Gita*). Here also the goal is for the person to enter into deeper communion with this spiritual Power or Presence.

Spirituality in much of the East, on the other hand, has been guided by an emphasis on pure spirit and a seeking for a merging of the individual into the Impersonal Divine. Buddhism, Advaita Vedanta, and Taoism are examples of nondual traditions that stress the illusory nature of the self and the existence of a formless, nameless, impersonal spiritual reality which is ultimately revealed as the ground of being.

Although both theistic and nondual approaches can be found in most religious traditions, the main body of each tradition tends to emphasize one or the other. Thus, the mystical traditions in Christianity, Judaism (Kabbalah), and Islam (Sufism) articulate the Impersonal, nondual dimension of spiritual experience, but in these traditions as a whole the nondual experience has been made secondary to the relational, theistic dimension of spiritual experience. Similarly, experiences of the soul and the Personal Divine are encountered in Vedanta. Actually, contrary to popular belief, most of India and most schools of Vedanta *are* theistic. But in the West what is better known is Advaita Vedanta, and in Advaita the theistic-relational experiences have been made secondary and are viewed merely as steps toward the nondual experience of Brahman. Buddhism, however, is one tradition that firmly maintains there is no soul and that reality is completely and ultimately nondual and impersonal.

For completeness it is worth noting that there are also traditions which do not emphasize either theism or nondualism and hold both aspects of the Divine equally. Hinduism in particular offers this view, and it can be found as well by individuals in most any of the other traditions.

Two other points are worth noting. First, the perennial philosophy sees both immanent and transcendent aspects to the Divine, while many religious traditions only focus on one or the other. Second, acknowledging the feminist, ecological, and third world critiques of the hierarchical way in which the perennial philosophy is often presented leads to two possible responses. The first, favored by Eisler (1987), Wilber (1995), and Rowan (1993), is to try to rescue hierarchy from its current political incorrectness by showing that the way hierarchy has been used destructively represents a fundamental misuse and distortion of this philosophy. The second possibility is to see the different levels as dimensions of experience that coexist simultaneously, that interpenetrate and comingle. As Rothberg (1986) has noted in an excellent review of this subject, hierarchy is but one way of presenting or organizing the perennial philosophy and does not inhere in the perennial philosophy itself.

With this as background, let us turn to Huston Smith to fill out the spiritual framework. Smith (1976) states that at its simplest level, the perennial philosophy recognizes four levels or dimensions of identity:

1. body
2. mind
3. soul (the "final locus of individuality")
4. spirit (the atman that is Brahman/Buddha-nature)

The levels of body and mind (which includes feelings) are fairly self-evident to most people and are the levels studied by conventional science and psychology. But the dimensions of soul and spirit need more explanation. Soul in this view refers to that aspect of us which transcends birth and death (and in Hinduism reincarnates) and is a vehicle through which the transcendent expresses itself in personal terms in the world. It is our spiritual nature which is particular to each of us.

While soul is that aspect of identity that relates to the Divine, spirit is identity with the Divine. In Hinduism this is the atman which is Brahman, eternal and non-evolving. In Buddhism this is Buddha-nature. The realm of spirit transcends the subject-object duality. No longer is there duality or multiplicity: everything in existence is seen to be but manifestations of the One. Hence the term nondual to describe these traditions.

In describing cosmology the perennial philosophy also speaks of four levels or dimensions of existence:

1. the terrestrial plane
2. the intermediate plane
3. the celestial plane
4. the infinite plane

The *terrestrial* plane is the most familiar to us and consists of that reality given to our physical senses and mind. It is this earth plane of sensible experience and mental constructions.

The *intermediate* plane is sometimes referred to as the psychic plane. It is a realm of subtle energies, refined perception, and subtle physical processes and beings. This is the level of clairvoyance and psychic phenomena (e.g., ESP, predictions of future events, knowing what happened in a person's past, etc.). This is also the domain of different types of discarnate entities such as good spirits and evil spirits (*devas* and angels, *asuras* and titans), nature spirits, ghosts, and souls recently departed from the terrestrial plane. It includes our subtle body, often called the astral body or etheric body, as well as the perception of auras, *chakras*, and subtle energy fields. This is also the world of shamanism, a realm that houses both good or higher domains and evil or lower domains, and the journeys of the shaman are into the various regions of this plane.

It is interesting to note that in traditional societies, insanity is often viewed with both awe and respect, for insane people are seen to be caught in the grips of psychic forces that mix together this intermediate plane with our own terrestrial plane. The best example of this is possession, which will be examined further in the chapter on spiritual emergency.

Another feature of the intermediate plane is that it is the realm of Jung's archetypes. These are universal patterns that make up the collective unconscious and shape psychological life into the forms we see. These universal patterns are also responsible for mythology, universal symbols, and the recurrent motifs in stories and legends that occur in cultures around the world.

The *celestial* plane Smith correlates with the realm of the Personal Divine, the spiritual reality that the world's theistic-relational traditions refer to. This Divine Presence may be with or without form. When viewed in terms of form, the world's religious traditions abound with the many forms this Divine Being may take, for example, Tara, Krishna, the Divine Mother, the Divine Father. Western theistic traditions tend to image this as a single Divine Being: classic monotheism. Hindu theistic conceptions have a whole pantheon of gods which are but various forms that the Personal Divine assumes. This is sometimes wrongly called polytheism. Actually the various Hindu gods (e.g., Shiva, Brahma, Vishnu, Kali) are but different reflections of the one Personal Divine, different masks or personalities of the one Divine Being.

As mentioned previously, this Divine Presence may either be seen to be within the aspirant (where the individual soul is a portion or spark of the Divine Being), or there may be the perception of the total otherness of the Divine without (as in Judaism), or both of these simultaneously (as in Hinduism).

It is the goal of spiritual practice in theistic-relational traditions to establish a relationship with the Divine. Our soul longs for union with the Divine, and as we approach this, the various powers of the soul begin to manifest: peace, light, love, joy, strength. The infusion of these soul qualities into our life brings the solution to our confusions and pain. While the intermediate plane is the realm of the archetypes, the celestial realm is the source of the archetypes.

The *infinite* plane is what Smith calls the level of the Impersonal Divine. At this level of spiritual experience there is nothing but the Divine—oneself, others, and the world all are forms of the one spirit that is the same essence in all. While the Personal Divine is often experienced in terms of form, the Impersonal Divine is always experienced without form. Indeed, many times it is referred to only in negative terms. In the Hindu Upanishads it is *nirguna Brahman* (Divine without qualities) or spoken of as *neti, neti* (not this, not that). In Mahayana Buddhism it is *sunyata* (emptiness, void). In Taoism it is the Tao that cannot be spoken. It is a realm beyond all distinctions.

When positive qualities are attributed to the infinite it is with the qualification that such descriptions are only close approximations. There are three recurrent aspects of Brahman that Hinduism uses to describe the indescribable: *Sat, Chit,* and *Ananda* (Being or Existence, Consciousness, and Bliss). The Divine or Brahman is Being, not *a* being. Brahman is viewed as a vast impersonal consciousness, and all this vast creation of the universe is seen to be nothing but the play (*lila*) or movement of consciousness. Brahman or atman is our ultimate identity and forms the ground of our own consciousness.

The appeal of the perennial philosophy is due to its completeness and wide range. It would be difficult to find a spiritual experience that does not fit somewhere into this framework. This model also provides a context for understanding the competition that exists among many traditions, something that is rarely commented upon when discussing such high philosophy. There is a long running dispute among the followers of theistic-relational approaches and followers of nondualism. Many theistic-relational adherents claim moral superiority of their view and suggest that followers of Buddhism and Vedanta, for example, simply want to escape from the world, get off the wheel of reincarnation, and merge into the absolute. On the other hand many adherents of nondualism firmly reject any idea of soul or personal god and believe such experiences are either total ignorance or are merely initial steps toward a higher Truth. And adherents of theism and nondualism both tend to denigrate shamanism as a more primitive approach to spirituality (although shamanistic traditions have traditionally located themselves in the theistic-relational camp).

The world's spiritual traditions each believe they have the most complete map and that the maps of competing traditions are more fragmentary. Part of the value of the perennial philosophy is that it provides a wide enough framework for understanding these competing claims. This discussion also gives us a context for understanding some of the disputes in the transpersonal literature, such as that between Wilber and Washburn, for this can be seen as differing interpretations of the perennial philosophy. Although individuals may have preferences for one or another, it would be premature for the field of transpersonal psychology as a whole to choose one view over another or to make a judgment about what constitutes the fundamental nature of spiritual truth.

Spiritual Models of Transformation

All spiritual systems, whether theistic-relational or nondual, describe our identity as spiritual in nature. Our fundamental identity is a spiritual being or essence or soul. Further, spiritual language and metaphors explain that what is wrong with the human condition is due to impurity and unconsciousness (or ignorance due to conditioning). We are unconscious or ignorant of our true spiritual nature because we have been conditioned to identify with our outer nature, that is, the levels of body and mind (as the perennial philosophy would term it). Impurity is our continued identification with our unregenerate feelings, gross desires, sensations, body habits, et cetra. that prevent us from a more subtle, refined perception of who we are. Our true nature is spiritual awareness, but we cling to and are conditioned to identify with the *contents* of this awareness. Entranced by the outward looking mind and senses, our identification with the contents of consciousness, our feelings, sensations, and thoughts, keeps us ignorant of our true nature, pure spirit. This lack of consciousness or ignorance is the source of suffering and pain.

If what is wrong from the spiritual perspective is ignorance and impurity, then the remedy or transformational possibility offered by spiritual systems is purification and freedom from our conditioning, a waking up to what is real. Spiritual practice is designed to bring about an increasing purification of the being and awakened consciousness. The various ethical and moral rules are helpful aids in quieting, calming, and purifying the surface mind.

In theistic-relational traditions, practices such as *bhakti*, love, and devotion are designed to open our being to the higher, purifying power of the Divine, to reestablish and to deepen the soul's relationship with Spirit. In this union or sacred "marriage" with the Divine the soul finds fulfillment, love, peace, and beatitude.

In the nondual traditions, on the other hand, meditation practices aim at bringing awareness to the mechanical, unconscious conditioning that normally operates in daily life. As consciousness deepens and perception refines, the empty and ultimately illusory nature of the self is seen. This truth liberates the seeker from the bondage of the habitual identifications with the outer self, and there is a release into the pure vastness of spirit. Individual identity merges into the perfect peace and bliss of Brahman or Buddha-nature, which brings freedom from these habitual identifications and awareness of a deeper, spiritual reality.

THE PSYCHOLOGICAL DIMENSION

There are numerous schools of psychotherapy that have produced different models of human growth and experience. Psychological traditions define our identity as psychological in nature and use specialized language and metaphors for describing what is wrong with the human condition and why people are in pain. All of these models provide windows into dimensions of human experience. Or, to switch metaphors, the different schools of psychotherapy are lenses which organize our perceptions and allow different aspects of human experience to come more clearly into focus.

One way of organizing these different schools has been to cluster them into historical and conceptual forces in the development of psychology, referred to as the First Force (behaviorism), the Second Force (psychoanalysis), the Third Force (humanistic psychology), and the Fourth Force (transpersonal psychology.)

First Force

The First Force in psychology was behaviorism. Beginning with Pavlov in the late 19th century and culminating in the thousands of experiments with rats for which American psychology became famous in the 1940s and '50s, the focus was the scientifically observable, namely learning and behavior. Behaviorism had a profound effect on American psychology. Even today most American introductory psychology textbooks begin by defining psychology as "the study of behavior." Behavior therapy and cognitive therapy are the two most widely known clinical outgrowths of behaviorism, and each has led to some important therapeutic advances. For instance, behavior therapy is the treatment of choice for phobias. But behaviorism is a very limited view of the psyche because it has restricted itself to the outwardly observable. More recently, cognitive therapy has begun to examine how thinking influences feelings. This has now been deemed theoretically justifiable by reconceptualizing thinking as an internal behavior (i.e., how people talk to themselves or "self-talk"), and cognitive therapy has been shown to be a helpful approach in trying to eliminate specific symptoms, particularly certain kinds of depression.

The Behavioral Model of Transformation. Surprisingly, behaviorism comes the closest to the spiritual language, for it attributes pain to the conditioning that people receive. People learn or are conditioned into faulty and irrational ways of perceiving, thinking, and responding to situations, which in turn generate negative feelings, depression, anxiety, and pain.

The remedy for poor conditioning in the behavioral model stresses new learning over old. Whereas spiritual systems emphasize the importance of freedom from all conditioning, behaviorism does not even consider this to be a possibility. Instead the best that can be accomplished from this view is new, better conditioning which is more adaptive and flexible. For example, rather than being phobic of bridges, a person learns to be relaxed. Or rather than failure triggering thoughts of being the worst person in the world and becoming suicidally depressed, a person might simply recognize the inevitability of mistakes and merely feel mildly depressed.

Second Force

However much behaviorism has discovered about learning, it was the Second Force in psychology—Freud's psychoanalysis—that charted the first maps of the interior of the psyche. Psychoanalysis opened up a profound understanding of the psyche. It was the first enduring depth psychology, that is, it considers the unconscious as well as the conscious. It is hard to overestimate the revolutionary impact of Freud's insights and how thoroughly they have permeated modern psychology. The idea that who we are as adults is significantly determined by our childhood, that our dreams are meaningful, that there are feelings and impulses that shape our lives beyond our rational, conscious ego, and that we have unconscious defenses against these feelings—these are notions we now take for granted but which were virtually unthinkable before Freud.

Yet all genius is still a product of its time, and Freud is no exception. Just as Darwin's ideas about evolutionary conflict for survival of the fittest were in vogue during Freud's time, so many other of the scientific metaphors of the early 1900s are embedded in Freud's psychology. Classical psychoanalysis is sometimes referred to as a conflict model, for it abounds with psychic forces that are ever in conflict—between impulse and defense, mind versus body, self versus society, forces tending toward maturation versus regression, id versus superego, sex versus aggression. The psyche is viewed as a battleground, and psychic conflict is the central feature of psychological life. Freud's theory was also quite pessimistic, something which many of his followers, such as Jung, Rank, Adler, Horney, and Reich, objected to. Freud once said that the goal of psychoanalysis was to reduce neurotic suffering to common unhappiness—not a particularly inspiring or ennobling goal for human existence.

Psychoanalytic Models of Transformation. Depth psychology, pioneered by psychoanalysis and with humanistic psychology in full accord, agrees with spiritual systems that unconsciousness is the problem, but it employs different language to describe this process. The psychoanalytic descriptive metaphors center primarily upon the emotional wounding people suffer growing up. People are hurt as children, and their adaptations to that hurt prevent these wounds from healing. A complementary metaphor of defenses augments the wounding metaphor. In order to cope with the pain of this wounding, people defend against it by pushing this pain away. The vocabulary of defense mechanisms, with terms such as repression and disavowal, is employed to describe how people cope with the pain of this wounding, that is, they turn their attention away from it and become unconscious of it.

So, since the parents, due to their own wounding, cannot deal with the child's wounds, the child (needing to maintain its place in the family system) holds down or holds in the feelings and pain, and after awhile becomes unconscious of them. The child then grows up in a chronically contracted stance derived from innumerable repetitions of similar incidents and as an adult still walks around with the same defensive postures he or she employed as a child. Repression and other defensive avoidances of inner states then becomes the source of inner fragmentation, psychic pain, and conflict.

The proposed remedy consists of healing through remembering, reexperiencing, releasing, and working through the old wounds. Depth psychotherapy is the process of seeing how current suffering is a replay of old patterns of wounding: a person reconnects to the old hurts, and then feels and expresses what he or she was not allowed to feel or express as a child. Through feeling these old wounds much more fully than before, being with these wounds in many different ways and giving verbal expression to this experience, the person begins to heal.

The process by which these old wounds come into consciousness again is through lifting the defenses that keep them unconscious. Through psychotherapy the resistances begin to lift, allowing the person to re-own these lost feelings, impulses, experiences. The inner fragmentation and splits are healed in reclaiming these lost energies through fuller expression, and new aspects of the person emerge along with greater energy (since energy is no longer being expended keeping large portions of the self unconscious) and self-awareness.

Another metaphor that comes from psychoanalytic self psychology relates to the above metaphor of wounding and the defenses against this wounding but adds another dimension. Because of the wounding and defensive attempts to cope with this pain, the self never fully develops, leading to deficits or gaps in the very structure of the self. This faulty self structure causes the person to relate through a false self (defensive structure), depriving the person of healthy vitality, self-esteem, and the capacity for genuine intimacy. So structural deficits and false or defensive self structures are the major metaphors of this approach.

This metaphor of locating the human problem in terms of precarious or inadequate self structure proposes the remedy of building new self structure. That is, through the therapy process, as wounds are uncovered and worked through, defensive or false structures give way as the nuclear self emerges. Within the therapeutic relationship, that is via the transference, the developmental derailments are remobilized and the thwarted developmental needs reactivated. Over time the archaic forms of the self undergo a developmental process by which they are modified, refined, and new structures of the self develop. Healing and growth of the self involves more than simply reowning disowned parts in this model. The self needs to grow and develop new structure to manifest fully. As this proceeds, the self becomes cohesive, resilient, more capable of intimacy, self-esteem, and able to realize its destiny or "nuclear program."

Third Force

During the 1930s, '40s, and '50s, there were a number of other forces percolating within psychology, such as Reich's work with the body, existentialism, phenomenology, and gestalt therapy. Two of the most influential psychologists of the '50s were Carl Rogers and Abraham Maslow, who helped forge the beginnings of humanistic psychology, the Third Force. Maslow, who coined the term *humanistic psychology*, criticized Freud for studying pathology and instead decided to study healthy people. In so doing, he created the first map of human growth, one which has been essentially validated by subsequent research.

Maslow discovered a hierarchy of needs within people. As lower needs were met, higher needs emerged, taking the individual on a journey of increasing self-actualization. For example, as basic needs for food, clothing, safety, and belonging are met, higher needs for self-esteem, meaningful work, and the development of unique capacities arise, which propel the person to actualize what is potential and bring forth new dimensions of creativity and self-expression. The underlying movement is one of growth, the unfolding of new capacities and talents as the individual flowers into greater differentiation and individuation. This perspective emphasizes the holistic, organismic unity of mind and body. It is a powerfully optimistic vision of human life as an unfolding of greater potentials, which contrasts sharply with Freud's dark view of existence as well as with the starkly mechanical behaviorism.

Humanistic Models of Transformation. The humanistic and existential schools add other descriptions of what is wrong. For humanistic psychology, self-actualization is the process by which the self realizes greater and greater dimensions of its potential. The failure to actualize this potential results in psychological suffering and a contracted sense of self and the world.

Actualization of our potential is the remedy in this model, by moving up the motivational hierarchy from *deficiency* needs to *being* needs, increasing satisfaction as we ascend. This growth, either through therapy or in other ways, enhances the present possibilities of the self—expanding its choices, deepening its full organismic experience, allowing the person to reach out in new ways, and expanding creative responses.

Another metaphor for describing what is wrong with the human condition comes from Wilhelm Reich's work with the body. Reich took a more organismic view of the human experience than did Freud. Reich used the vocabulary of bodily armor to describe the inhibitions and defenses against feeling that people employ. This body armor, or the chronically contracted musculature, inhibits breathing and therefore the excitement and energy that a person can feel, as well as keeps unwanted feelings unconscious.

The remedy is to soften the body armor through therapy to allow the person to experience the entire range of feelings and energies. Thus the body is able to tolerate and support the greater excitation and energetic streaming that is present in full aliveness.

The existentialists bring in yet another vocabulary to describe human experience. Fundamental to the human condition are fear, anxiety, awareness of death, lack of meaning, and fear of taking responsibility for our actions and of making choices. The avoidance of these core experiences results in an inauthentic existence, in which people do not face their experience directly and instead turn to superficial distractions, such as losing themselves in work, relationships, drugs, entertainment, et cetera, as a way to avoid confronting the existential pain and terror inherent in being alive.

The remedy in this language is to replace an inauthentic existence with an authentic one. The person is supported in facing existence head on and then grapples with the key issues of responsibility, choice, awareness of death, lack of meaning, existential anxiety, and isolation. In so doing the person is able to put aside the inauthentic distractions, face death, come to terms with existential aloneness and anxiety, take responsibility and make choices. In the process such a person can create a meaningful life that is an authentic expression of his or her values and beliefs as well as acknowledge the pain and suffering that is posited as inherent in the human condition.

THE INTEGRATING TRANSPERSONAL FRAMEWORK

But all these three forces in psychology are still within the realm of the self. Transpersonal psychology arose to place this self in a larger context. For even when the human potential movement was in its heyday, to many people it still fell short. Maslow himself longed for a psychology that went beyond the purely personal, that acknowledged the drive toward transcendence and could inspire. Many forces converged at this time of the late 1960s—the cultural fascination with psychedelics, the growing influence of Eastern religion, meditation practices—to produce the Fourth Force, transpersonal psychology. In retrospect, it can be seen how transpersonal psychology is a natural evolution of psychology, even a historical necessity, for it places the individual within the larger cosmic context—not just within intrapsychic forces, or the family, or the environmental or intersubjective field, but within the spiritual reality which manifests this whole phenomenal existence.

The idea in transpersonal psychology is to integrate the three previous forces in psychology with the perennial wisdom of the ages. None of these models are seen as wrong from a transpersonal perspective, just limited.

What is so exciting about the transpersonal enterprise is the unprecedented access to the entire range of the world's wisdom traditions. For what the world's spiritual traditions provide is the collected result of thousands of years of research (using that word in its widest sense) on the possibilities of human growth. At this time we are no longer restricted to a single system or worldview. We have the spiritual traditions, modern philosophy, and psychology to draw upon.

In the prophetic words of the mystic/philosopher Sri Aurobindo, writing over 80 years ago:

> A mass of new material is flowing into us; we have not only to assimilate the influences of the great theistic religions of India and the world and a recovered sense of the meaning of Buddhism, but to take full account of the potent though limited revelations of modern knowledge and seeking; and, beyond that, the remote and dateless past which seemed to be dead is returning upon us with an effulgence of many luminous secrets long lost to the consciousness of mankind but now breaking out again from beyond the veil. All this points to a new, a very rich, a very vast synthesis; a fresh and widely embracing harmonization of our gains is both an intellectual and a spiritual necessity of the future. (Sri Aurobindo, 1972 p.8)

TRANSPERSONAL MODELS OF TRANSFORMATION

Although the spiritual and psychological models presented above are usually seen as competing with one another, they are by no means contradictory. Rather they form a series of overlapping and complementary metaphors or images that describe the human condition and its possibilities for transformation. Each metaphor touches on different aspects of human experience, although the spiritual metaphors hold out more fundamental transformative possibilities than do the psychological metaphors.

These metaphors are summarized in the following table.

What's wrong	*Transformative possibility*
Spiritual	
Impurity	Purification
Ignorance	Consciousness of spiritual being
Psychological	
Poor conditioning	New learning over old
Wounding and defenses	Healing through lifting defenses, releasing, & working through
Lack of self structure—fragmentation	Building new self structure—developing a cohesive self
Disowned and dormant potentials	Self-actualization
Armored, constricted emotional life	Softening, openness to feelings and energetic streaming
Inauthentic living	Authenticity

With these lenses transpersonal psychology views the entire range of human functioning, from the most organically brain-damaged psychotic to the highest mystical seer. Each of these lenses provides a particular theoretical and treatment perspective. Thus the behavioral, psychoanalytic, and humanistic-existential viewpoints can be brought to bear on psychosis, borderline conditions and character disorders, "normal" neurosis or self disorders, as well as so-called "mature" personalities. Each perspective offers a unique vantage point on the entire range of functioning, from pathological to optimal.

As in the story of the blind men describing the elephant, these spiritual and psychological systems each describe essential aspects of human experience. For example, viewing the human condition as a product of learning is a superordinate way of organizing experience. Psychotics, borderlines, neurotics, all have *learned* to organize their experience in different ways. Every individual learns, via the family of origin, to stay away from (defend against) certain affects and impulses, and the severity of this staying away determines the severity of the psychopathology. All therapy is a relearning at one level.

Similarly, early wounding and the defenses against these feelings create both deficits in the structure of the self and inauthentic modes of existence, with concomitant patterns of bodily tension (armoring). The healing and working through of this wounding involves building new self structure, and discovering more authentic, meaningful ways of being in the world, with a corresponding reduction in muscular tension accompanying this.

In a transpersonal approach, however, all of this psychological work on the self is placed in a larger context of spiritual unfolding. But precisely how and in what ways this spiritual unfolding is influenced by the more psychological work on the self has yielded no clear agreement yet, as the next chapters will show. By situating the various dimensions of psychological experience that psychology has discovered within the larger spiritual context of Being, the transpersonal framework extends psychology into its ultimately spiritual source. In so doing, it opens up the range of psychology into these transitional spaces. For example, accessing the unconscious through regressive techniques may lead a person into birth experiences or possibly even intrauterine memories, which can become a gateway into the transpersonal (Grof, 1985).

One way of viewing Western psychotherapy is that it is one form or aspect of purification. Psychotherapeutic work and healing is a process of clearing away some of the most obvious levels of negative, destructive impulses, feelings, and behavior patterns while encouraging and promoting higher values such as love, truthfulness, and vulnerability. Are there other forms or levels of purification beyond the psychological blocks? Most spiritual teachers would say yes, otherwise those who completed therapy would be candidates for sainthood. But unfortunately, this does not appear to be the case. The great hope in transpersonal psychotherapy is that psychological work is one very important dimension of spiritual purification. Undoubtedly there is much beyond it which conventional psychotherapy currently does not address and which remains open for future transpersonal research.

A transpersonal orientation goes further than conventional psychotherapeutic work in that it views optimal mental health as inextricably tied to spiritual health and awareness. Only touching into a deeper level of spiritual Being can produce a profoundly transformative shift, and thus all conventional psychologies can only be palliative and partial solutions at best. Only by contacting a deeper and truer level of Being can psychological work come upon a genuine solution to the human predicament.

SOME HISTORICAL PREJUDICES

Although this is the history of the forces of psychology that is usually told, it is a very '60s version of events. A current view updates this picture considerably. While it is true that classical psychoanalysis focused mainly on pathology and that humanistic psychology arose to address much of the healthy side of human concerns that had been neglected, contemporary psychoanalysis has undergone a revolution that parallels much of humanistic psychology. Self psychology and object relations schools have distanced themselves from the drive-discharge theories of Freud and have looked at the self from a relational model of development. Self psychology examines the growth of the self and the developmental derailments that prevent its consolidation and cohesion. Its view of the self as a developing, evolving process is remarkably consistent with the humanistic growth model. Indeed, self psychology quite freely espouses humanistic ideas and has been explicitly influenced by such developments as existentialism and phenomenology. Although contemporary psychoanalysis continues to ignore the organismic, somatic emphasis in humanistic psychology, contemporary psychoanalysis and humanistic psychology are no longer quite so discrete or distinguishable these days.

Also usually omitted from discussions of the evolution of psychology is how family systems theory fits into this scheme. Actually, it is more accurate to speak of systems theories, for there are a wide variety of systemic approaches. According to the orientation of the system, they fit quite well within this current framework. Strategic family therapy, with its focus on behavior change and symptom removal, falls into the First Force category, as does narrative family therapy with its emphasis upon constructing new narratives to reframe the person or issue, as in cognitive therapy. Developmental, object relations, and family of origin approaches fall into the Second Force category. And methods such as Virginia Satir's conjoint family therapy and Carl Whitaker's existential approach fall into the Third Force category. However, given the natural affinity between family systems theories and spiritual philosophies such as Buddhism's theory of dependent origination (or "inter-being" in Thich Nhat Hahn's words), what is puzzling is the absence of such integration in either the family systems literature or the transpersonal literature. This lack is sure to be remedied within the next decades.

Behaviorism and psychoanalysis have continued to evolve during the past several decades. There has been a richness of new ideas and intellectual leadership, embodied by such things as Kohut's self psychology, intersubjectivity, and contemporary object relations. But humanistic psychology appears to have stopped growing, an ironic fate for a growth psychology. There has been little new since its heyday in the '60s and no new theorists with the intellectual stature of its founders like Maslow, Rogers, and Perls. As a movement, humanistic psychology actually did continue to evolve, as it metamorphosed into transpersonal psychology. Yet in many of its old forms it lacks the vitality and dynamism of its early years, much like the old skin sloughed off by a snake.

In one sense transpersonal psychology became heir to the humanistic agenda, extending the view of growth to encompass spirituality. However, in the process transpersonal psychology has inherited some of the humanistic prejudices as well. From its founding, humanistic psychology has had a condescending attitude toward psychoanalysis. There is a strong tendency in all new movements to play one-up by putting down the previous movement and claim superiority. "We've gone past this Freudian nonsense," was commonly heard at the time. Abraham Maslow certainly contributed to this atmosphere by saying such things as, "To oversimplify the matter somewhat, it is as if Freud supplied us with the sick half of psychology, and we must now fill it out with the healthy half" (Maslow, 1968).

While acknowledging the truth in Maslow's statement that humanistic psychology did add important dimensions to our view of human beings and human potential that had been neglected by psychoanalysis, it is a very big jump to then assume that by this addition humanistic psychology went "beyond" the discoveries of the unconscious and of motivation that psychoanalysis had made. For this led to the belief then prevalent in humanistic circles and still echoed in transpersonal circles today, which is that first a person deals with neurotic, childhood issues and then moves on to (more advanced) existential issues of growth. However, the clinical evidence does not support this. The reverse is very often the case—first a client may deal with existential issues and afterwards with childhood issues. In clinical practice I have encountered clients who had worked very deeply with their existential issues in their 20s and 30s, only to find in their late 30s, 40s, and 50s that there was still much psychodynamic work to do with their childhood wounds. This work had only been partially addressed in the existential and humanistic therapy they had done and at a certain point proved an obstacle to their continued growth.

As we look more closely, these two issues are not quite so separate as they once seemed. Issues of existential identity, authenticity, and meaning in life are intimately bound up with childhood wounds and structural deficits in the self. Authenticity is not possible if large areas of self-experience are repressed, disavowed, or otherwise unavailable. An authentic existence can only emerge by reconnecting to disowned parts of the self. Self psychology has convincingly demonstrated that self-actualization and discovering meaningful work, two key concepts of Maslow, necessitate the working through of early wounds and the remobilzation of the derailed developmental movements of the self. Filling in the self structure and eliminating defensive structures are essential to discovering the person's true ambitions, talents, and guiding ideals. Finding meaning is not only about an existential confrontation with values and philosophy but is intimately bound up with developing an integrated and cohesive self.

Psychoanalysis and humanistic psychology, it can now be seen, actually deal with similar developmental levels. Certainly psychoanalysis laid the foundation for understanding psychopathology, and it explains psychosis, narcissistic-borderline, and normal neurotic development in very sophisticated ways. It also explicates the "mature" level of development, a level of development that is rare and generally only achieved after much depth psychotherapeutic work. But humanistic psychology also works with these conditions and has done much to advance our knowledge of more severe psychopathology. The existential-humanist R. D. Laing was a pioneer in understanding psychosis through his work with a psychotic population. And there are existential-humanistic understandings and approaches to working with borderline clients as well (for example, see Schneider and May, 1994). But despite the recent professional fascination with borderlines, it is "normal neurotics" that make up the bulk of clients for both psychoanalytic and humanistic therapists. (Parenthetically, while some recent trends in psychotherapy have tried to move beyond the psychosis/neurosis vocabulary, it continues to be clinically useful and will be used throughout this book.)

It is no longer possible to say that psychoanalysis deals with pathology and humanistic psychology deals with health and existential issues. Nor is it the case that psychoanalytic and humanistic approaches are the same or do the same thing and just use different language. Rather they cover the same developmental territory but approach healing and growth in different ways.

In general, working psychoanalytically (or psychodynamically) means illuminating the wounds that led to this current constricted life position (more past-centered) and working on these ancient wounds via past memories, current outside life situations, and the transference. Thus as old wounds are healed within the therapeutic relationship, new parts of the self are reowned, new self structure is built, and greater freedom and authenticity result.

In general, working humanistically (or existentially) means a more here and now, present-centered focus, with a therapist continually inviting the person to accept responsibility for his or her current experience, and seeking to expand the available choices. Thus, a client might work toward accepting how he or she is feeling toward family, friends, career, et cetra, to own these feelings fully, and to then work on new ways of relating, such as disclosing feelings more freely, taking a stand, setting boundaries and saying no, choosing to try on new behaviors, reaching out in new ways, becoming more authentic in relationships.

Neither of these is a pure case—each approach touches on the other. Rather it is a question of emphasis in a given approach.

Sometimes a client begins working existentiallly (for some reason finding it the most accessible way of working), and after some growth (months or years) then becomes ready to work psychoanalytically to uncover the historical origins of his or her issues. Other times a client begins working psychoanalytically (for some reason this material is most accessible to him or her), and after some months or years of healing and growth then becomes ready to work existentially, to expand the choices that this greater self makes possible. Neither one of these is better, more evolved, or healthier than the other.

Both psychoanalysis and humanistic-existential approaches are concerned with retrieving and enhancing the self—by working through past wounds and expanding the present possibilities of the self—but they differ in their relative emphasis. Psychoanalysis retrieves and enhances the potentials of the self primarily by working through past wounds, lifting defenses around these, and utilizing the transference to access the deepest parts of the self. Humanistic-existential approaches retrieve and enhance the potentials of the self primarily through focusing on the present structure of the self, opening up new possibilities of freedom to express the self, and utilizing the therapeutic relationship to model new ways of being in relationship.

Both approaches explore the past and the present. Psychoanalysis goes into the past in much more detail than humanistic approaches and has a more sophisticated map of this territory. It does not ignore the present. Actually some contemporary psychoanalytic writers such as Kohut, Gill, and Stolorow come surprisingly close to humanistic and existential approaches in their focus on the present in the transference. But psychoanalytic therapists tend not to focus on expanding current possibilities so much, preferring instead to uncover the genetic roots of an issue. Hence Freud's favorite (past-centered) question, "Why?"

Humanistic-existential approaches such as gestalt therapy unfold the present experience more fully than psychoanalytic approaches and have a more detailed map of this territory. But they do not ignore the past. Completing unfinished business from the past is a key part of any humanistic-existential approach. But humanistic-existential therapists tend not to focus too much on the past, instead preferring to unfold its present structure (attitudes, chronic muscular patterns, self-limiting behaviors) and expand present possibilities. Hence the existential psychotherapist Medard Boss's favorite (present-centered) question, which challenged self-imposed limits on present action, "Why not?"

My own sense is there is a dialectical relationship between psychoanalytic and humanistic-existential therapeutic work. The humanistic-existential approach expands the available choices of whatever degree of self is present, but then a point of diminishing returns is reached, which may be after years of work. Further work then shifts to psychoanalytic work which uncovers more deeply buried wounds and brings "on line" archaic self, allowing new self structure to be built. This, too, at some point (often several years) will reach a point of diminishing returns. As the self structure expands and develops, it further opens up what can be called the existential possibilities for greater expression of this expanded self. At a later time a point of diminishing returns will again be reached and a new focus for the work opens up. The dialectic between past and present is continually shifting. A highly competent psychoanalyst will alternate between them, working through the past and present expansion, but will favor the former. A talented humanistic-existential therapist will also alternate between past wounds and expanding present self possibilities, but will favor the latter. No good therapy will do exclusively one or the other. It is mainly a question of degree.

At the very end of his life, and unfortunately mostly unknown to the larger humanistic movement, Maslow himself recanted his earlier position and became critical of the rose-colored glasses and by-passing of the dark side of the psyche that came to characterize much of humanistic psychology. Shortly before his death Maslow entered psychoanalysis and grew to value its insights into human nature. He saw how during his life he had avoided his own anger, rage, and much of his own shadow material and how he had constructed a theory of personality that bolstered his own defensive posture (Schwartz, 1995; Hoffman, 1988).

The very notion that a person gets "beyond" psychological work and "works through" neurotic, early wounding is itself a relic of an earlier era. Writers from Mahler on maintain that even the earliest object relations and separation-individuation issues reverberate throughout the life cycle. Inner psychological work helps enormously to free us from constraining, unconscious patterns and liberates whole new dimensions of the psyche, but this work may never be said to be "done." This is a conceit and illusion of the '60s. In my experience, individuals who claim to have finished their psychological work are often the most in denial about their own issues.

This said, it is also true that the psychological dimension can, after much inner work, occupy less of the foreground as a person's improved functioning permits a freer flow of psychic energy into working, loving, and living in the present. The person is not "finished," but the foreground becomes progressively more clear for other life concerns, including spirituality, though at any moment new psychological issues may come to the fore as reverberations from the past overshadow present functioning. New levels of old wounds are continually activated and become increasingly accessible with inner work. New depths of healing endlessly open up, new aspects of disowned, archaic self emerge and become structured into the evolving self. There are no known limits to the reclaiming, healing, and development of the self.

Each of these approaches to psychotherapy offer exciting and complementary dimensions to depth work. If transpersonal psychotherapy is to be truly a wider, integrative approach, this can only be achieved by letting go of those parochial prejudices which are the remnants of its beginnings in humanistic psychology and seeking for a larger, more inclusive synthesis than has yet appeared.

The hope is that transpersonal psychology can provide a multiperspectival framework and will not need to repudiate what went before to bolster itself. Transpersonal theory can encompass and welcome what behaviorism, psychoanalysis, and humanistic psychology have contributed to the depth exploration of the psyche, recognize how each of them speak to different dimensions of the human experience, and integrate them to form a rich complement for understanding the development of the self at all levels of organization.

CONCLUSION

The transpersonal view is that a complete concept of mental health must include both psychological and spiritual dimensions. It must consist of the psychological integration or cohesion of the surface self plus some degree of connection of this surface self to its deeper, unconditioned spiritual source. The greater the degree of connection with the spiritual foundation of consciousness, the greater the spiritual realization. It is important to note, however, that full connection to spirit does not guarantee perfect mental health. The spiritual literature contains many examples of highly unstable, tortured people who also had a high degree of spiritual attainment. The ideal would be both great cohesion of the conditioned part of consciousness, that is, the self, along with a free, unobstructed connection to the unconditioned, spiritual being underlying this surface self.

The difference between the theistic-relational and nondual traditions leave it unclear as to the ultimate fate of this surface self, whether it disappears entirely or is reduced to a small portion of the consciousness as a fully surrendered, willing "bride" or "servant" of the Divine. In either case, the very idea of "mental health" becomes subsumed by a greater spiritual health, unless, that is, the functions of this surface self are so poorly organized that it cannot be an adequate instrument of the deeper spiritual reality.

In this integrative framework, the expanded context of transpersonal theory changes the relative significance of aspects of human experience that were seen as primary in previous models. So, for example, it isn't that the sphere of psychic conflict which psychoanalysis has learned so much about simply disappears, but that psychic conflict is recontextualized so that it is no longer the central feature of psychological life. What is central in transpersonal psychology is the movement and growth of consciousness—its development, vicissitudes, and varied expressions in its divine unfolding.

Consciousness then becomes the proper subject matter of transpersonal psychology. Conventional psychology studies consciousness at various levels and stages of self development, that is, as consciousness is conditioned, expressed, and modified by the structures of the self. Spiritual systems study consciousness insofar as it transcends or encompasses more than the self, that is, in its unconditioned levels. Transpersonal psychology studies consciousness in all its manifestations, from its origins in the infant and the various developmental derailments and pathological manifestations that may occur in its growth to full consolidation in a mature, cohesive self, all the way through the myriad developments of spiritual realization.

Chapter Three

Consciousness

It is precisely in the area of consciousness where spirituality and psychology intersect. Both spiritual practice and psychotherapy are methods for exploring, expanding, deepening, and enhancing consciousness. And it is consciousness that constitutes both the subject matter and the methodology of transpersonal psychotherapy. However, there is much confusion as to what consciousness is.

Consciousness is one of the most elusive and difficult things to talk about, for it is not a "thing" at all in the ordinary sense of the word. Because it goes so deep, it is hard to formulate or capture. Our ideas about it always leave something out. No matter how clearly we try to define it, consciousness is not confinable to verbal maps.

With this in mind, *Webster's* defines consciousness as, "awareness; the state or fact of being conscious in regard to something." Conscious means, "Aware or sensible of an inward state or outward fact."

Psychology has investigated the nature of consciousness. In fact, one way of looking at the history of psychology is that it is an evolution of our understanding of consciousness. Each new school and force in psychology has added important dimensions to this growing understanding. Behaviorism addressed the outermost manifestation of consciousness, how it is behaviorally expressed. The second force in psychology, psychoanalysis, brought to light the inner experience of

51

thoughts, feelings, and the depth dimension of the unconscious. Initially the notions of the "conscious" and "unconscious" were considered to be mental. Cure in psychoanalysis came through "insight," which is primarily cognitive awareness. Later this became "emotional insight" which added the emotional dimension to it. Further modifications in psychoanalysis stressed the affective bond to the therapist, believing that insight was insufficient to bring about change, and an ongoing debate within psychoanalysis continues to this day over the relative primacy of cognitive vs. affective factors in producing change. The third force in psychology, humanistic psychology, largely through the influence of Reich, Selver, and Perls, added the physical dimension of the body to our understanding of consciousness. Consciousness thus became more than just cognitive-emotional but an organismic process, a mental-emotional-somatic function.

However, from a transpersonal perspective, all previous psychologies have failed to adequately grasp the nature of consciousness, for they have all been limited to a surface view. While behaviorism focused on external behavior, while psychoanalysis brought attention to the mind and feelings, and while humanistic psychology added the body or organismic level, from a transpersonal perspective the true foundation and origin of consciousness is spiritual, and it is only in including this dimension that consciousness can be fully understood.

THE METHODOLOGY OF CONSCIOUSNESS

Spiritual traditions, articulated most clearly in Hindu and Buddhist thought, go far beyond an organismic view and see consciousness as the basic nature of reality. The Hindu Divine is defined as a self-existent, blissful consciousness, *Sat, Chit, Ananda,* or Existence, Consciousness, Bliss. The Divine or God or Brahman has manifested this entire universe and all the myriad forms and persons are reflections of and coextensive with this supreme Divine consciousness.

Sri Aurobindo has put it like this:

> *Sat Chit Ananda* is the One with a triple aspect. In the Supreme the three are not three but one— existence is consciousness, consciousness is bliss, and they are thus inseparable, not only inseparable but so much each other that they are not distinct at all. . . .

Consciousness is usually identified with mind, but mental consciousness is only the human range which no more exhausts all the possible ranges of consciousness than human sight exhausts all the gradations of colour or human hearing all the gradations of sound—for there is much above or below that is to human beings invisible and inaudible. So there are ranges of consciousness above and below the human range, with which the normal human has no contact and they seem to it unconscious,—supramental or overmental and submental ranges. . . .

Consciousness is a fundamental thing, the fundamental thing in existence—it is the energy, the motion, the movement of Consciousness that creates the universe and all that is in it—not only the macrocosm but the microcosm is nothing but consciousness arranging itself. (Sri Aurobindo, 1971a pp. 234, 236, 239)

According to Smith (1976), the perennial philosophy or "primordial tradition," describes the foundation of consciousness as spiritual, and it differentiates into various frequencies—mental, emotional, physical, with matter being the most dense. Even though it is possible to refer to cognitive or emotional or somatic levels of consciousness, it must be remembered that this is really but one dimension of an entire range of spiritual awareness that is being referred to.

The domain of conventional psychology is the conditioned, surface strata of consciousness—the physical, emotional, mental levels of experience and selfhood. The domain of spiritual traditions is the more fundamental spiritual consciousness which is the foundation for the physical, emotional, mental self. Transpersonal psychology views these two domains as one indissoluble whole, although for practical purposes it is possible to speak of one or more aspects or levels of consciousness.

Much of the abuse of the word consciousness comes from its historical development. Many people say, "I'm conscious of my problem, but I still can't change it." From the viewpoint presented here, what further investigation generally uncovers is that what the person actually means is, "Intellectually/cognitively, I know about this problem." This knowing is at a distance, where there is a separation between the knower and the known. There is an image or conclusion about the problem. Indeed, in common parlance, to say, "I am conscious of such and such," generally means, "I know about such and such." But this is a very different matter from full consciousness of the issue. In complete consciousness there is full participation, at every level. It is the difference between a flashlight shining a light upon a piece of coal (cognitive knowing) and the coal glowing from within with its own light (consciousness). Consciousness is not just cognitive insight (although it also includes a cognitive dimension). Though only rarely is this ideal experienced in its fullness, consciousness is a cognitive-emotional-somatic-spiritual whole knowing.

Spiritual teachings, especially in Hindu and Buddhist traditions, speak of consciousness as the ground from which everything else emerges. Our fundamental identity is consciousness, but we identify with and cling to certain contents of consciousness. That is, we normally believe, "I am this experience of sensing . . . feeling . . . thinking." We are so identified with these outer contents of consciousness (sensation, feeling, thought) that generally only through spiritual practice is this veil penetrated to discover a spiritual essence or soul or divine consciousness which sustains these outer contents and surface self.

Transpersonal psychotherapy is the exploration of consciousness and the contents of that consciousness. Phenomenology has discovered that consciousness is "intentional." This is, in the language of phenomenology, consciousness "intends toward" the world, which is to say that consciousness is consciousness *of* something. There is a content to consciousness. Although high mystical states of consciousness include what Franklin Merrill-Wolff has called "consciousness without an object," consciousness with an object is the very definition of subject-object, egoic consciousness. For all but the most advanced mystical seers, consciousness has a content, and psychotherapy is the exploration of both consciousness and its content.

The reason most clients enter therapy is because they are stuck, not developing as fully as they sense they could. The reason they are stuck is because they are not operating with full consciousness. There are blind spots or phobic avoidances ("defenses") which prevent the awareness of essential feelings or aspects of themselves. It is as though they are living with blinders on. Hence, parts of the self which would normally develop through numerous experiences of practice, feedback, and refining fail to do so because they are "off limits."

This unitary view of consciousness resolves a major conflict in psychoanalysis as to whether cognitive or affective factors are the key to change. Lawrence Friedman (1978, quoted in Stolorow, Brandchaft, & Atwood, 1987) examined this "running battle" in psychoanalysis between proponents of the centrality of cognitive insight as conveyed by interpretation versus proponents of the therapeutic importance of affective factors (i.e., the transference) in producing structural changes within the client. From this transpersonal perspective, such a split between cognition and affect is false, an artifact of a theory which sees consciousness in dualistic, mind/body terms. Instead, a transpersonal view resolves this conflict by seeing cognition and affect as two essential but fragmentary *aspects* of consciousness. Only by including both cognition and affect together with somatic and spiritual dimensions can the mystery of therapeutic change be unraveled. The greater or more complete the consciousness, the greater the likelihood of change.

However, it behooves us to acknowledge the relational element that psychoanalysis contributes to the development of consciousness. For psychotherapy usually brings about psychological changes via the relationship. Self structure is not formed in an interpersonal void, rather it is formed in an interpersonal context. Therefore, the development and growth of the self needs to take this into account. The therapeutic relationship is a place to explore a growing consciousness of wounded, split-off, and undeveloped aspects of the self, and, particularly in psychoanalysis, how they become activated in the transference.

Thus the development of consciousness, or at least consciousness as it is modified and conditioned by the structures of the self, resumes insofar as there is a relational matrix which supports this development. The therapist serves the conventional function of facilitating the integration of affect by providing an accepting, consciousness-enhancing field or medium. New self structure is built as there is consciousness of the archaic configurations of self and other, and psychoanalysis' insight into the significance of the transference is integrated into a larger picture of consciousness expansion occurring within the context of the relationship.

However, not all transpersonal psychotherapy depends upon the therapeutic relationship. An example of psychotherapy where the relationship is not the major contributor to consciousness enhancement is in altered state work. Therapeutic use of altered states is a working with consciousness par excellence. By modifying the very stuff of consciousness itself, dimensions of consciousness are brought into high relief and can be gone into, worked with, and modified during the session and post-session work. Altered state work reminds us that not all consciousness work needs to occur within a relational matrix. Consciousness moves within its own spaces and significant development can occur in interior realms. As the meditative traditions insist, the greatest spiritual realizations come in silence and utter aloneness.

THE THERAPEUTIC POWER OF BEING WITH *WHAT IS*

The late mystic/philosopher J. Krishnamurti (1973) often spoke of seeing *what is* as the key to transformation. Along similar lines, the existential psychotherapist James Bugental (1978) has said that for insight to be effective, it needs to be inner sight. This inner sight is a total knowing, feeling, sensing, being. Similarly, a transpersonal therapist views seeing and being with *what is* as the essential ingredient in change. All the various techniques in psychotherapy are but ways of being with *what is.* Psychotherapy's many techniques allow consciousness to explore the particular issue from one side and another, dancing all around it so that consciousness may illuminate it from all different angles. It is this dancing around it, this being with it as fully as possible that frees up the stuck, frozen portions of the self. Consciousness brings movement, releases the movement inherent in the psyche.

For therapeutic purposes, consciousness = growth = freedom = movement = health. It is consciousness that frees us from our unconscious conditioning.

Transpersonal psychology can be defined as the study of consciousness. Transpersonal psychotherapy is the operationalizing of this study to explore what helps or hinders the growth, healing, unfolding, and expansion of consciousness. From a transpersonal perspective, consciousness heals.

THE THERAPIST'S CONSCIOUSNESS

The client's consciousness is, of course, the center of the therapy process. But of equal importance is the therapist's consciousness. For transpersonal psychotherapy is defined not merely by the theoretical framework but by the practitioner's own deepening spiritual journey, which gives meaning and life to this framework. It is the therapist's own actual experience of opening to the Divine (whatever form or path this may take) that provides the atmosphere to support the client's multidimensional growth. Being a depth therapist does not mean the therapist has fully healed and worked through all of his or her issues, just that the therapist is actively engaged with his or her own healing. Similarly, being a transpersonal therapist does not mean a person needs to be enlightened or a saint, just that in addition to being engaged with inner, depth work, he or she is actively committed to a spiritual path of consciousness development.

Spiritual traditions speak of the importance of spiritual seeking becoming conscious. People seek the Divine unconsciously at first, but at some point the quest becomes conscious and engages the person's intention. When being on a spiritual path becomes a conscious decision and pursuit, everything changes. Outer circumstances begin to yield to the inner spirit and the Way opens up. Consciousness becomes engaged in its own transformation.

The state of consciousness of the therapist has a far-reaching effect on the therapy process. Consciousness is seen as a field which influences, mutually interpenetrates, and provides a facilitating medium for the client's inner unfolding. This is something that most religious traditions have upheld for centuries. The traditions of guru, spiritual guide or influence, support the idea that the presence of a spiritual teacher is helpful in allowing others to contact the spiritual realm. Consciousness is contagious.

This is not to say that the therapist is in the position of guru, merely that for a transpersonal therapist to be actively pursuing a path of spiritual awakening allows him or her to be an energetic influence as well as to empathize with and recognize the terrain that is likely to be encountered by others. Therapeutic work is facilitated when the psychic field supports and enhances the client's self-exploration. It is to this truth that intersubjective approaches are pointing, although by not recognizing the spiritual or subtle energetic dimensions of being and mutual influence, intersubjectivity currently is a more partial and superficial view of consciousness and the wide field of mutual interpenetration it creates.

Transpersonal psychotherapy is realized via the consciousness of the therapist. *It is the therapist's own inner work with his or her consciousness that provides the psychic support for working transpersonally.* It is not just the cognitive mind set and theoretical orientation of the therapist, though these are important. There is here, as in any orientation, a body of knowledge, principles, and theory that need to be assimilated. But this framework is not just a theory to be believed but a felt orientation to life and therapy. *It is the therapist's intention and spiritual aspiration that count most, the active inner work of seeking to contact a deeper level of Being than just the personality level.*

Are therapists always successful in this endeavor? No. Much of the time we are struggling to center ourselves as best we can amidst a cacaphony of mental images, rushes of feeling, and physical sensations. Yet the inner movement toward a deeper level of Being, the quest for a greater spiritual reality, the dedication to a path of spiritual unfolding —these provide the living, energizing influence upon the client and the therapy process that characterizes a transpersonal approach.

Merely paying lip service to a dead set of beliefs, even beliefs that may have had much meaning at some earlier point in life, does not convey the living spirit of transpersonal psychotherapy. Transpersonal psychotherapy is a lived experience, not merely a belief system. The ongoing work with the therapist's own consciousness is what breathes life into a truly transpersonal way of working. It is this spiritual intention that infuses the work with an influence beyond the mundane. It matters less what consciousness discipline a therapist is engaged with, whether meditation practice, tai chi, shamanic journeying, or anything else, than the fact of being so engaged. With this atmosphere present the transpersonal orientation actively manifests and will facilitate whatever inner work the client is open to undertaking.

This is perhaps the clearest way in which a transpersonal orientation is clinically relevant. For although much of the transpersonal literature is very abstract, philosophical, and may seem far removed from the therapy office, the state of the therapist's consciousness has a profound effect upon the therapy process. To have ways of deepening one's contact with Being, to be more fully centered in one's Being, to be less reactive to one's personal feelings and thoughts, to be more connected to a calm presence within and a more spacious inner witness to the whole unfolding drama—there can be nothing more clinically relevant than this.

For the therapist's main instrument is his or her own consciousness. Unfortunately our English vocabulary is really very poor to describe subtle inner states. Other languages such as Sanskrit are rich in ways to express inward states of consciousness. Speeth (1982) and Epstein (1984) have thoughtfully extended psychoanalytic insights about the nature of psychotherapeutic attention into the transpersonal sphere and refer to two poles of attention, focused and panoramic, as well as two contents of attention, self and client. The therapist's attention is seen to shuttle back and forth between self and client as well as observing or monitoring this attentional flow by developing a witness consciousness or observing ego. But this makes consciousness appear to be two dimensional, that is, awareness either of self or other. What needs to be added is that there is a *depth* dimension to consciousness as well.

The depth dimension adds presence. The therapist is more fully present when he or she is more physically aware, more emotionally connected, cognitively open and alert, and, to whatever extent possible, spiritually awake. As we become more connected to ourselves in depth, our empathic potential extends. Empathy may be limited only by the therapist's self-awareness. As awareness of each level of our being deepens and extends, we become more present. The therapist's presence is a key factor in transpersonal psychotherapy.

When the therapist is engaged with a centering, meditative practice, this depth dimension opens. I notice that when this occurs in me, I become more fully connected to myself, more centered in the depths of my being. The inner space widens, opens within to a greater calm, equanimity, and loving sense of presence. Simultaneously there is an increased depth perception outwardly. I can see more deeply into my clients, empathically grasp my clients' experience more completely. Not that I become clairvoyant or a mind reader or never make mistakes. It is *very* far from that. But by contrast, when I have been very busy, overextended, with no time for myself, I become increasingly confined to a more surface consciousness. The depth dimension of Being recedes further and further. I am aware only of my superficial feelings and reactions. My view of the client loses the sense of depth and becomes more of a two-dimensional perception. My work with clients is noticeably different depending upon my state of consciousness.

Much of the work of being a therapist is about taking care of and fine tuning this instrument of consciousness. As consciousness deepens and opens, whatever tools, theories, and techniques the therapist uses automatically become more effective. To bring greater consciousness, greater light to the emerging clinical material allows those techniques or approaches the therapist is trained in to be used more creatively, intuitively, empathically. *There is nothing so clinically relevant as consciousness skills and development that deepen one's presence.*

This also requires time. Just as one or two years of psychotherapy is but a start on one's own depth work, so a few years of meditation is but preliminary practice. To experience the fullness of change offered by good psychotherapy requires that one invest time and effort over a good number of years. So with spiritual practice. Though we may all hope to be one of those rare souls who realize in a very brief period of time, in fact it takes years and decades of spiritual practice for most people to reap the benefits of consciousness work that spiritual practice can produce. Very few escape this hard fact of the inner journey. For a psychotherapist to manifest a transpersonal approach in his or her life and practice requires a patient, persistent effort over time. Even in traditions of immediate enlightenment it takes virtually all seekers many years to have a first glimpse of it and, for those rare individuals who reach that point, many more years to stabilize it. Yet a key part of what makes psychotherapy such an exciting endeavor for therapists is that our own consciousness work becomes the best investment in our professional development as well.

It is in this area of the Being dimension of therapy that transpersonal psychotherapy has great riches to offer. Certainly it has contributions to make in the Doing dimension as well, including interventions with certain kinds of clinical issues, for example, spiritual emergency, death and dying, and at the level of technique. These are not to be underestimated. Nor should this be made into a rationale for ignoring or minimizing the importance of learning both theory and technique. Simply enhancing spiritual Being is not sufficient for becoming a therapist. It is this pairing of theoretical knowledge and skills with Being, with the presence, the consciousness of the therapist, that allows transpersonal psychotherapy to happen. Both the theoretical framework and the movement of the therapist's deepening, evolving consciousness are necessary.

As important as the theoretical contributions of transpersonal psychotherapy are, it is on the Being side that transpersonal psychotherapy may have the most to offer both therapist and client. A transpersonal approach to psychotherapy suggests that it is in the deepening experience of Being that there is the greatest potential for healing. Whether spiritual Being is called the Self, essence, no self, the transpersonal self, soul, the ground of being or anything else makes little difference. For the revolutionary position of transpersonal psychotherapy is that only as we approach Being can there be the full resolution of our wounds and pain that has been the promise of psychotherapy ever since its inception.

Part 2

Specific Approaches

Chapter Four

Approaches to
Transpersonal Psychotherapy

This chapter examines the major transpersonal approaches to psychotherapy that exist today. Since the overarching theoretical and methodological framework presented in the first three chapters is so large and encompassing, a "transpersonal orientation" to psychotherapy says little about a therapist's actual clinical work. For greater definition it is necessary to incorporate a specific approach or combination of approaches such as those discussed in this chapter. Some of these approaches have evolved fairly systematically, such as Jungian therapy or the Diamond approach, while others have evolved more informally among practitioners who merged their existing orientation into a transpersonal context, such as existential-transpersonal therapy or transpersonally oriented psychoanalytic psychotherapy. Many of these theories and models are quite elaborate, having been developed over decades of work. While this chapter attempts to extract the essential points of these theories, inevitably there is a certain injustice that condensation does to the complexities and subtleties of any intricate model, for which I must apologize in advance.

The chapter begins with an overview of Ken Wilber's contributions to this field. Although he does not present a specific therapeutic approach, his writings are relevant for psychotherapy and his theory has influenced many practitioners. This is followed by three very specific transpersonal modalities that are usually thought of as unique and distinct, but which actually have a great many similarities: Jungian therapy (with Washburn's innovations), the diamond approach, and psychosynthesis. The chapter concludes by examining Grof's holotropic model and three more generic approaches that have become transpersonalized by many practitioners: existential, psychoanalytic, and body-centered approaches. Following a discussion of each approach will be an evaluation of their strengths and limitations.

KEN WILBER'S SPECTRUM MODEL

Ken Wilber is the most widely known and influential writer in the field of transpersonal psychology today. Over the past two decades he has produced a prodigious body of work from a transpersonal perspective, on topics ranging from psychology, psychopathology, and development to anthropology, physics, philosophy, and his own personal life.

Although transpersonal psychology had been around for almost a decade before Wilber first started to write, it lacked a central theoretical core to hold it together. In the late 1960s and early 1970s many people in this new field were excited by the idea the psychological and spiritual growth could go together, but there were few specific ideas about how this could happen. Then in 1977 Ken Wilber wrote his first book, *The Spectrum of Consciousness*. It was the first methodical attempt to show how the consciousness of mystical states fits with the consciousness of neurosis or psychosis. It used the analogy of the spectrum of light, where many different frequencies make up the totality of visible light. Similarly, Wilber reasoned, consciousness is composed of many different bands or levels. Different psychotherapies and different spiritual traditions speak to specific levels of this spectrum.

What is noteworthy in this model is that all psychologies and all spiritual traditions are seen as right. Rather than saying some theories are wrong, Wilber provides an integrating structure in which all competing schools and philosophies are seen as containing partial and complementary truths about human consciousness. Western psychology concerns itself with the lower and middle portion of this spectrum, with psychosis representing the most fragmented, limited consciousness.

The spectrum then moves up the levels through neurosis and existential levels, which compose the middle range of consciousness and are the limit of Western psychology. Spiritual systems comprise the upper levels of consciousness, with enlightenment representing the most unified, widest consciousness possible. Thus psychology and spirituality are married into a single spectrum of consciousness. This spectrum analogy forms the basis for Wilber's thought and is the foundation for his theories of development, psychopathology, and treatment.

When *The Spectrum of Consciousness* was first published, many people within the transpersonal community found in it the integration of psychology with spirituality they were looking for. It was a first plausible map that showed how psychotherapy laid the groundwork for spiritual development. And in a series of books over the following years, Wilber's writings served an enormously important historical function of helping to make transpersonal psychology respectable at a time when it needed a coherent vision of itself. Now that transpersonal psychology has developed a number of rigorous theories and approaches it is far stronger and dynamic than in these early years, but Wilber's historical importance should not be underestimated.

Before turning to Wilber's model, however, there is one very important idea of his that has significant therapeutic implications. This is what he calls the "pre/trans fallacy." Wilber noted a major deficiency in conventional psychology, which has been the historical tendency of Western psychology to equate transpersonal states with prepersonal states. Because there are superficial similarities between the ego loss that occurs in schizophrenia or other psychotic states and the ego loss that occurs in the highest mystical experiences of enlightenment, psychology, beginning with Freud, has assumed that they are one and the same. Even some early transpersonal psychologists have made this error by romanticizing childhood and likening the consciousness of an infant to that of a mystic. Wilber has made a very valuable distinction between prepersonal states of consciousness and transpersonal states. A state such as infancy does not have self-consciousness, but this prepersonal state, he asserts, is very different from a more developed, transpersonal state in which self-consciousness has been gone through and transcended, leaving the person still self-reflexive but not ego bound. This distinction continues to be an important one in transpersonal psychotherapy.

One remarkable aspect of Wilber's writings of the past two decades is how consistent his vision is. With only minor refinements he has held to his original theory. The one correction Wilber has made over the years to his model was realizing that he had fallen into the pre/trans trap in his first book by thinking that infancy was an unconscious state of spiritual realization, a mistake which he corrected in *The Atman Project*, and which he considered major enough to refer to his new position as Wilber II. Wilber then added on to his model by further differentiating developmental lines such as moral, ethical, object relations, conative, creativity, intimacy, self-identity, et cetera, which he calls Wilber III. Finally, in "Wilber IV" he relates this spectrum model to cultural, scientific, and social spheres. However, except for his one correction, his basic model has remained intact over the last 20 years, and he has primarily added on to it. This review will focus on those writings that are most pertinent to psychotherapy. The interested reader is referred to his other works for a more comprehensive overview (see references).

Wilber's overall map is actually quite simple, although complex in its details. In *Transformations of Consciousness* (Wilber, Engler, & Brown, 1986), Wilber links his basic spectrum of consciousness to spectra of development, psychopathology, and psychotherapy. He uses the kind of developmental model that was pioneered in psychology by Freud for ego development and by Piaget for cognitive development.

The idea in these developmental models is that at each stage there are developmental tasks that challenge the person to bring forth new abilities and levels of adaptation. As these developmental tasks are met the person's psychic organization develops to a more complex level. Each level includes and surpasses the stages that went before it. If the developmental tasks are not met at a given stage, development either stops there (arrest, fixation) or interferes with the full consolidation of the next stage.

Wilber posits three basic levels: prepersonal, personal, and transpersonal. Each of these three stages has three substages. As levels of consciousness these stages primarily combine Piaget's model of cognitive development with Wilber's nondual interpretation of the perennial philosophy although now with "Wilber III" he has added on other theorists. They are as follows:

PREPERSONAL
1. Sensoriphysical (Piaget's sensorimotor level)
2. Phantasmic-emotional (the emotional-sexual level)
3. Rep-mind (representational mind or Piaget's preoperational thinking)

PERSONAL
4. Rule/role mind (Piaget's concrete operational thinking)
5. Formal-reflexive (Piaget's formal operational thinking)
6. Vision-logic (Bruner and Arieti's hypothesized step beyond Piaget)

TRANSPERSONAL
7. Psychic (the perennial philosophy's level of mind or intermediate plane)
8. Subtle (the perennial philosophy's level of soul or celestial plane)
9. Causal (the perennial philosophy's level of spirit or infinite plane)

These are the levels of consciousness. As levels of development and pathology, they are as follows: The prepersonal level consists of what Wilber calls fulcrums 1, 2, and 3. Developmental failures at these levels manifest as the levels of psychological organization which have come to be called psychosis, borderline, and neurosis. The personal level consists of fulcrums 3, 4, and 5, and developmental failures here Wilber terms cognitive-script pathology, identity neurosis, and existential pathology. The transpersonal level consists of fulcrums 7, 8, and 9. Developmental failure here results in pathology which Wilber calls psychic disorders, subtle disorders, and causal disorders.

With this as the basic map, let's look more closely at each of these levels.

Prepersonal. Developmental failure in the first three fulcrums results in what modern depth psychology has studied the most: psychosis, narcissistic-borderline disorders, and neurosis. Wilber largely keeps his discussion limited to classical ego psychology and some object relations work, mainly Mahler, Masterson, and Kernberg, which he accepts wholeheartedly, and essentially leaves out self psychology, intersubjective approaches, and other schools of contemporary psychoanalysis.

Much of Wilber's writing in *Transformations of Consciousness* is simply laying out the psychoanalytic theory of development, which at this point has a great deal of research evidence to support it. Granted there is still much we do not know and much that can be interpreted in different ways, but this is minor. The basic psychoanalytic map is fairly well accepted today. It essentially says that the earlier and more severe the childhood wounding and trauma, the greater the psychopathology. Genetic predisposition, past karma, and the soul or spirit of the person currently play unknown roles in this process.

Wilber accepts standard psychotherapeutic practice when it comes to treating each of these three developmental positions, which is, medication is the treatment of choice for psychosis, structure building therapies are indicated for the narcissistic and borderline personality organizations, and uncovering, depth therapy is the preferred treatment for the neuroses.

Personal. The first three levels of psychic organization discussed above are a fairly straightforward adoption of common therapeutic classification. However, when it comes to the personal level, Wilber embarks upon a much more speculative view of development. He believes he has discovered, or at least articulated, three additional levels of psychopathology comparable to psychosis, borderline, and neurosis. Developmental failure at the personal level results in what Wilber terms cognitive script pathology, identity neurosis, and existential pathology.

Wilber says he derived cognitive script pathology from Eric Berne's transactional analysis and cognitive therapy, and he breaks it down into two separate classes. In role pathology the person sends multilevel messages, has hidden agendas, is involved in duplicitous transactions and confused roles. In rule pathology the person has distorted or self-limiting beliefs and rules about how to live which result in clinical symptoms. The treatment for script pathology is transactional analysis or cognitive therapy.

Identity neurosis Wilber conceives to be the many problems of identity that confront the personal self. Can the person follow his or her own conscience or is the person bound to society's rules? Can the person think for himself or herself? The person can "lie awake at night, riveted with worries or elated by anticipation over all the possibilities!"

(Wilber 1986). He notes that many object relations writers "regrettably" see these conflicts in terms of separation-individuation issues. Instead, Wilber believes that Erik Erikson's writings on identity vs. role confusion are the main psychological literature that speaks to this level of pathology. The treatment for identity neurosis is introspection and philosophizing. The therapist's task is to engage the client in a Socratic dialogue and help draw out the person's own philosophy of life.

Existential pathology is what Wilber calls the third and highest level of personal pathology. Common syndromes are existential depression, inauthenticity, existential isolation, aborted self-actualization, and existential anxiety. Here the life concerns of the individual are those articulated by the existentialists: questions of the meaning of life, coming to terms with death and finitude, finding the courage to live amidst loneliness and isolation, and the need to take responsibility for choosing a life that is a genuine expression of oneself. Existential therapy is the treatment for this pathology. Coming into a greater sense of authenticity and freely choosing one's course of life rather than fleeing into inauthentic modes of being are what the existential therapies strive for.

Transpersonal. These three levels of pathology constitute forms of spiritual pathology. Here the self has developed to its zenith. It has full self consciousness, has gone beyond its psychological wounding and the defenses against that wounding, and is actualizing its finite potentials, in short, it has gone as far as it can go. Now it emerges into the spiritual world. Pathology at this level constitutes the many "perils of the path" that spiritual traditions refer to.

Fulcrum 7 refers to psychic disorders. Wilber lists nine specific pathologies that he places at this level of development. They are:

1. Spontaneous—This is Wilber's term for spiritual emergencies. Treatment consists of either "riding it out," often under the care of someone trained in spiritual emergency, or consciously engaging the process by taking up a spiritual discipline.
2. Psychotic-like—Although the spiritual emergency literature calls this one type of spiritual emergency, Wilber lists it separately. Recommended treatment is structure- building therapy.
3. Psychic inflation—*Ego inflation* was originally Jung's term for how the infusion of spiritual energies into a person may by co-

opted by the ego, resulting in grandiosity and narcissistic inflation. Wilber recommends structure-building therapy.

4. Structural imbalance—Due to improper use of spiritual techniques, these symptoms manifest as free-floating anxiety or as a
variety of somatic complaints. Treatment is better supervision
by one's spiritual master.

5. Dark night of the soul—The period of dryness at the beginning of the spiritual path, articulated most clearly by St. John of
the Cross. Treatment consists of reading how others have
weathered this phase and petitionary prayer.

6. Split life-goals—Paralyzing confusion as to whether the person should continue to live in the world or to leave the worldly
life and pursue a life of spiritual practice. Although Wilber does
not suggest specific treatment, he says the outcome is the integration of spiritual practice with daily life. The implication is
that the person arrives at this through introspective soul-
searching.

7. Pseudo-duhkha—In certain forms of Buddhism, the investigation of the tenet that "life is suffering" itself produces greater
suffering and becomes overwhelming. Wilber suggests structure-building or uncovering therapy to work with this.

8. Pranic disorders—this is kundalini awakening in its early stages
(also a type of spiritual emergency). The treatment Wilber recommends is supervision with one's meditation teacher and a
physician if needed.

9. Yogic illness—This occurs when the development of higher
consciousness puts a strain on the body. Treatment is strength-
ening and purifying the body through exercise and diet.

Fulcrum 8 refers to subtle pathology. This is a disorder that exists
in the realm discussed by theistic-relational schools. Wilber posits three
types of subtle pathology. Integration-identification failure is, from
Wilber's nondual interpretation of the perennial philosophy, the maintaining of separation between the soul and the Divine, that is, a failure
to realize that the Divine Presence is but "an image of our own essential
nature." Pseudo-nirvana is the mistaking of subtle or archetypal forms
for "final liberation," which, Wilber notes, becomes pathology only if
one is pursuing causal or ultimate levels of consciousness. Pseudo-real-
ization is staying stuck at the realization of the inherent suffering of

existence and not transcending it. Treatment for all three of these forms of pathology involve more meditation in order to go beyond these limitations.

Fulcrum 9 refers to causal disorders. In Wilber's later works (1995, 1996), he further subdivides this stage into causal and nondual, and he discusses two forms of pathology. Failure of differentiation is the inability to accept the death of the archetypal self. "Failure to integrate," the "ultimate pathology," is a failure to integrate the manifest and unmanifest realms. Treatment again consists of further meditation so as to attain greater insight into the true nature of things and thus transcendence.

This then, in very summary form, makes up Wilber's spectrum of consciousness, development, pathology, and treatment . It is a movement from lesser consciousness to greater consciousness, from a state of more fragmentation to one of more wholeness. Psychological development proceeds along a single developmental line and leads to spiritual development. It is an elegant and logical theory of consciousness, development, and pathology.

Strengths and Limitations of This Model

Strengths. Wilber's influence on transpersonal psychology has been vast. His writings captured the imagination of a generation of transpersonal therapists and students, and they helped fuel interest in this burgeoning field in its beginning decades. As the preeminent theoretician in transpersonal psychology, his writings have helped propel the transpersonal revolution toward the cutting edge of psychological and spiritual discourse.

The great majority of writers have praised Wilber's works from the start, and it is only recently that he has begun to be subject to critical analysis from within the transpersonal field. Most of the great strengths to this model have already been amply commented upon in the transpersonal literature. As a counterbalance this discussion will focus on the limitations of this model and simply note its strengths.

1. Wilber presents an elegant picture of how psychology and spirituality fit together. By having three stages—prepersonal, personal, and transpersonal—each with three substages, he

presents a model that is logical, symmetrical, and aesthetically appealing.

2. Wilber discusses the evolution of consciousness, and this provides a larger historical and spiritual context for psychological development. He has helped make the nondual spiritual traditions more accessible to the West. In so doing he has brought new recognition to such figures as Plotinus, Eckhart, and other western figures in the nondual tradition who historically have been overlooked because of the West's theistic-relational bias.

3. Wilber rehabilitates the concept of hierarchy. Because Wilber's model is hierarchical, and because recently hierarchy has become politically incorrect and offensive to some people by becoming equated with patriarchy and oppression of women, the earth, and native peoples, Wilber has been found guilty and dismissed by some people. However, in his recent writings (Wilber, 1995, 1996) and following the lead of Riane Eisler (1987), Wilber distinguishes between good ("actualization") hierarchies and bad ("domination") hierarchies, or, in Wilber's language, "normal" and "pathological" hierarchies. By readily admitting the problems associated with hierarchies in the past and by showing how such historical problems have been misuses of hierarchy and are not intrinsic to hierarchy per se, Wilber shows how hierarchy is useful.

4. The pre/trans fallacy is a very significant theoretical construct that is also quite useful clinically. This is likely to be one of Wilber's most enduring contributions to clinical practice.

5. All psychologies are valid in Wilber's model. It is an integrative viewpoint which simply places different psychologies at different developmental levels. The model attempts to integrate all psychologies and all spiritual traditions into a unitary whole.

Limitations. 1. It has a nondual bias. Although Wilber presents his theory as the perennial philosophy, it is more accurately described as a nondual *interpretation* of the perennial philosophy, with all of the nondual biases inherent in such an interpretation, including the subtle put-down of theistic-relational traditions as merely a step on the way to the "real" goal. So even though Wilber positions himself as representing the pure truth of spiritual experience, this is not entirely accurate. A theistic-relational interpretation looks quite different. See Washburn (1990) for further discussion of this issue.

2. Wilber's three transpersonal stages of fulcrums 7, 8 and 9 do not accurately reflect spiritual unfolding. Although some mystics experience psychic phenomena (fulcrum 7), many others do not. Both theistic-relational and nondual traditions generally hold that psychic experience may or may not come to the seeker. It is not a stage that all must or do pass through. And it may come before *or after* the realization of soul or spirit. Similarly, the experience of the soul and the subtle level (fulcrum 8) does not necessarily precede the nondual experience (fulcrum 9). Ramana Maharshi, whom Wilber holds out as an exemplar of nondual realization, emerged directly into the nondual experience without "passing through" either the psychic or subtle "stages." The Buddhist literature is full of many, many examples of people directly realizing the impersonal emptiness of the nondual. Additionally, in one school of interpretation of the *Bhagavad Gita*, the path that the *Gita* seems to prefer out of the several it teaches has the nondual *atman* realized first and then afterward the level of soul is realized; Sri Aurobindo would be an exemplar of this tradition.

   Spiritual realization can begin with any one of these three realms and proceed in any order to one or both of the other two. In the spiritual domain a single invariant sequence of development does not appear to exist. Thus, these three spiritual realms cannot properly be called "stages."

3. As Grof & Grof (1986) have pointed out, Wilber is not a clinician but instead comes to psychology as a theoretician. Hence, although his model is strongly organized at the level of mind, it is not experientially grounded. His division of pathology into prepersonal, personal, and transpersonal is symmetrical and theoretically neat. But it does not make sense clinically. The middle third of the spectrum is, I believe, a purely imaginary, nonexistent structure. Chapter 2 goes into more detail about why the humanistic-existential school is an approach to psychotherapy for all developmental levels and is not just for a particular developmental level. That Wilber's creation of the "personal" level pathologies has not found support in the clini-

cal literature is evidence (although certainly not proof) that it lacks clinical validity.

To be more specific let us consider fulcrum 4, role self and cognitive-script pathology. What Wilber describes as "role pathology" ("hidden agendas, crossed messages, confused roles, duplicitous transactions") is seen by most experienced clinicians as simply the *form* that neurotic communication takes. While Wilber says this comes from Eric Berne's transactional analysis (TA), in retrospect it is clear that TA's impact on psychology was very minor in the mid-1970s and has all but disappeared today. It was simply one way of describing neurosis at the level of communication patterns. So-called "rule pathology" is similar. This type of pathology deals with the cognitive manifestations of neurotic styles rather than their depth, dynamic dimension. Cognitive therapy differs from depth psychotherapy as an approach to these neurotic disturbances, but it does not deal with a different kind of disturbance.

Let's move on to fulcrum 5, identity neurosis. Although Erikson's term "identity crisis" originally applied to adolescence, it has come to refer to any developmental level, not any one in particular. Mostly what Wilber describes here is a classic self disorder, the kind of fragmenting self that Kohut's theories describe so well. This also is generally conceptualized within the domain of neurosis (or self disorder), and it is not a new pathology.

Lastly, let's consider fulcrum 6, existential pathology. This again is built upon the myth (see chapter 2) that the existential level is beyond or different from the neurotic level rather than simply an explication of life issues at *any* level (although primarily the neurotic level, for this is the level most existentialists have worked with). The existentialist Rollo May, for example (whom Wilber uses in support of his case), brought an existential perspective to his therapy work, mostly with "normal neurotics."

"Existential pathology" is also a level of disturbance that is quite well studied and explored by psychoanalysis and is generally conceptualized within the domain of neurosis (or self disorder), not a "new" pathology.

Thus, fulcrums 3, 4, 5, and 6 are all simply differing descriptions of neurosis. Fulcrum 3 describes neurosis from the depth, psychoanalytic perspective, fulcrum 4 describes it from the perspective of communication patterns and cognitive structures, fulcrum 5 uses Erikson's language, and fulcrum 6 uses the existential vocabulary to describe it. It is the same elephant that is being described, not four different animals.

The overwhelming majority of people (probably over 99%) develop into either psychotic, narcissistic-borderline, or neurotic ego structures, with so-called "normal neurosis" the level of ego structure reached by the vast majority of people in societies throughout the world. The spectrum model, then, in essence declares 99% of the world's population to be prepersonal. But this is to miss what the self-reflexive, self-conscious ego is, or else to give very idiosyncratic definitions to the terms personal and prepersonal.

The developmental pie can be sliced in many different ways. What Wilber is probably trying to get at with his middle three stages is something all depth therapies aim for, which is a movement of healing and growth beyond neurosis. Psychoanalysis speaks of a "mature" stage beyond neurosis, Maslow spoke of self-actualization, gestalt calls it "organismic self-regulation", the existentialists refer to an "authentic existence", Rogers wrote of operating from "organismically felt values", and so on. Most all depth therapists agree that this post-neurotic stage takes years of psychotherapy to reach, for the unconscious defenses are too strong to be overcome spontaneously or in isolation. But how much can this stage be further subdivided? I believe a three way division of the "mature" stage stretches it far beyond its actual significance.

If fulcrums 3, 4, 5, and 6 were condensed into a single fulcrum, and the "mature" stage was assigned its more likely value of a single stage, and fulcrums 7, 8, and 9 were also condensed into a single tripartite fulcrum, although altering Wilber's model significantly, it would not challenge the fundamental idea on which it stands. That is the claim that only fully healed and integrated post-neurotics or "mature" individuals are eligible for and capable of true spiritual development and realization.

4. However, this claim is highly problematic. In *The Eye of Spirit* (1997) Wilber confronts this issue head on. He states that he can agree that psychological and spiritual growth can be viewed as separate only when spirituality is defined as the line of ultimate concern, which in the prepersonal and personal stages ranges from the desire for food and security to such things as belonging and meaningful work. But when spirituality is defined, as it generally is in the transpersonal literature and as I also use it in this discussion, as emergence into the intermediate, celestial, and infinite realms (or psychic, subtle, and causal stages in Wilber's language), then Wilber is clear in answering the question, do people need to first pass through the 3 prepersonal and 3 personal psychological stages "in order to make genuine spiritual progress?" Wilber states, "the answer is yes, definitely." (p. 225) This is the fundamental assumption on which the spectrum model stands. There are, however, a number of anomalies which undercut this assumption.

The first is that, contrary to this model, spirituality can emerge anywhere along the spectrum, not just at the top of it. Although Wilber acknowledges that spiritual *experience* may occur at any developmental step, his model claims that truly transpersonal growth and spiritual realization can occur only after neurotic and existential issues are worked through.

Since contemporary psychoanalysis has convincingly shown how deeply neurotic structures are embedded in family systems and human culture, moving beyond neurosis into the "mature" level of psychic organization tends to occur only with a good deal of psychotherapeutic working through and inner work. Though the specific neurotic configurations predominant in a culture vary, there do not seem to be any human cultures where "normal neurosis" is not the norm. Psychoanalytically-informed cross-cultural research shows that many eastern cultures, for example, tend to produce neurotic configurations related to family enmeshment and a difficulty in the self differentiating and individuating from the family system, whereas western cultures tend toward neurotic configurations related to disengagement and an isolated, fragmentation-prone self with low or fragile self-esteem. Wilber's model is tantamount to saying that the only people on earth who can be spiritual are those middle- and upper-class Americans and Europeans who have the access to therapy, and the time and financial resources to allow them to spend years working through their wounds and neurotic difficulties. Individuals in all other cultures, classes, and periods of history are doomed to be unspiritual.

The spectrum model in effect puts psychotics at the bottom of the human evolutionary scale. Is it really conceivable that an entire class of people can be relegated to the bottom of the evolutionary ladder? Although to some it may seem an improvement over putting women or native peoples on the bottom, does it not merely substitute one marginalized group for another and so amount to no change at all? Among the wide variety of people who are in the grip of psychosis, some clearly exceptional souls shine forth. Most compassionate psychotherapists who have actually worked with some of these extraordinary beings would find the belief that they are on the bottom of the human evolutionary scale nonsensical.

If psychotics are really at the bottom of the human evolutionary scale, and if, as depth psychotherapy teaches us, getting stuck in our development toward adulthood is virtually a universal phenomenon, whether at a psychotic, narcissistic-borderline, or neurotic level, then one logical conclusion of the spectrum model might be, when put into the paradigm of reincarnation, that during people's first few lives they are born into situations where by adulthood they become psychotic. As they evolve spiritually they gradually get born into family systems where they will develop narcissistic and borderline ego structures. As they progress still higher up the spiritual ladder they then incarnate as neurotics. Then, after much spiritual evolution they advance to incarnating as existentialists, and finally they get enlightened. The implausibility of this is clear.

To believe spiritual attainment is the right only of the psychologically "well adjusted" does not square with the facts. There are a number of very disturbed or crazy, borderline, and highly neurotic saints and spiritually advanced or enlightened beings. There is a whole tradition, certainly within Hinduism and Christianity, of "holy fools," or divine madness, where saints of genuine spiritual realization had ego structures that were very shaky. The suggestion that all shamans, psychics, clairvoyants, saints, and sages have worked through their childhood wounds and neurotic distortions is not supported by historical or clinical evidence. Some descriptions of the greatest saints and most illumined beings paint a very pathological picture.

Chogyam Trungpa, someone who has had great influence on Wilber, was at one level a very clear being who produced high-level teachings, while simultaneously he was a hopeless alcoholic who drank himself to death. Even a towering spiritual figure like Ramakrishna can hardly be called a paragon of mental health. His intense sexual inhibition and repression, his major depression, and his psychotic episodes illustrate that spiritual realization can occur at any level of personality organization. It may even be the case, as Kakar (1991) has suggested, that Ramakrishna's psychological wounding served to fuel and to channel his spiritual energies in ways that made his great spiritual attainments possible—psychological dysfunction in the service of spiritual development. Such examples abound in the spiritual literature. Saints and sages come in all sizes, shapes, and diagnostic categories. According to Wilber's model, these things should not be.

If psychological and spiritual growth do indeed form simply one continuous line of development, then Wilber's model may well be one valid map (taking into account the first three critiques above). If, on the other hand, psychological and spiritual development are separate and distinct processes, then this points to a fundamental flaw in the spectrum model.

Spiritual traditions speak of the importance of not confusing the surface appearance (ego) with the deeper spiritual reality (soul or spirit). While the inner spiritual identity has some outer manifestation, the two are not identical. Wilber's model confuses two different orders of psychic experience. Curiously, Wilber himself is cognizant of this distinction, for in his numerous volumes detailing different spiritual traditions he does make reference to it (1997 p. 328). Indeed, in Wilber's encyclopedic chronicles of various spiritual traditions and experiences there are very few phenomena that are not noted somewhere in his writings. (This has been a source of frustration for Wilber's critics who, when pointing out gaps in his model, find Wilber replying that he actually does refer to this area at some point in one of his books.) However, it is one thing to enumerate the details of various spiritual systems and quite another to adequately account for those details when constructing a theoretical model. The spectrum model does not do this. Essentially it makes the two one rather than keeping them distinct. His model clearly and necessarily ties spiritual development to egoic, frontal development, fusing the two into one line of psycho-spiritual development, and in effect erasing this difference. This is essential in order to maintain a single spectrum model of consciousness. But as transpersonal psychology advances, as we examine consciousness more closely and refine our perceptions, we see more differentiations, distinctions, and phenomena than a single monolithic structure can explain.

To continue in the reincarnation paradigm, Wilber's model amounts to mistaking the psychological development of the self that occurs *over a single lifetime* with the emerging spiritual development of the deeper soul or spirit that occurs *across numerous lifetimes*. There may be highly developed spiritual natures with poorly integrated egoic vehicles and very young, undeveloped souls with very well integrated egoic vehicles.

Human development is a complex affair. Physical development occurs along many different pathways. There are predictable and distinct sequences for gross and fine motor coordination, for the process of physical growth in the nervous system, the hormonal system, and each of the various other systems, as well as for the organs of the body. Cognitive development has numerous different lines. Mathematical and verbal development, musical ability, visual-spatial skills, and logical and intuitive modes of processing information all develop along different lines and at different rates. Emotional development also is a many-sided affair and is described in a number of different ways by different systems such as self psychology, object relations, et cetera. There is no reason to believe that spiritual development is any less unique and complexly varied than each of these other capacities. The spectrum model claims that first a person does psychotherapeutic work, and then, when that is done, he or she is able to truly undertake spiritual work. But since psychological development and spiritual development do not necessarily coincide, the spectrum model amounts to commingling two different orders or dimensions of development. To say that spiritual development and psychological development are but one continuous process no longer seems tenable.

Clinical practice reveals other anomalies. I have worked with clients who spent decades as part of a religious community and whose spiritual development is clearly at a highly advanced level, yet who function at quite primitive levels psychologically and interpersonally. With other clients psychological and spiritual development are more balanced. With still others, psychological development far exceeds spiritual development. Spiritual growth can lead a person to the highest levels of realization while the self remains in basic psychological conflict, and, conversely, a very self-actualized person who is very effective in the business world or with interpersonal relations may have no spiritual experience or interest. Even though the psychological and spiritual pathways of development may intersect at times and so *appear* to be a single line, Wilber's model does not adequately account for the clinical data. While sometimes there may be a correlation between the psychological and spiritual lines of development, they do not seem to be identical, as Wilber proposes.

Wilber's recent writings (1996, 1997) show him attempting to explain some of these anomalies to keep his single spectrum model intact. He has begun to stress a looser interpretation of development by saying that although there is a "center of gravity" to development, it can spill over a bit, with some parts being above or below the current rung of the ladder on on which a person is stationed. While there is obviously a truth in this, this particular way of explaining it begins to sound like trying to have it both ways. The problem with a "single spectrum model" is that it cannot be two things at once. Either psychological and spiritual development occur in a single line (Wilber's position), or they form two separate, discrete developmental pathways (which is not Wilber's position). It seems to me that these are two mutually exclusive possibilities and that the data are better explained by the second view.

Trying to maintain mutually contradictory assumptions eventually disrupts the integrity of a theoretical model. Wilber's grafting spiritual evolution onto psychological growth conflates two dimensions of development. His theory rests on the basic assumption that psychological and spiritual develop-ment form one continuous line or spectrum. When this basic assumption is challenged by viewing these as two separate developmental processes, the foundation of the spectrum model collapses. (See chapter entitled "Principles of Transpersonal Practice" for a further discussion of this issue.)

As critical thought is increasingly directed toward Wilber's model, it is important to remember that Wilber's work has served to focus much of the theoretical discourse in this field for some time. He has organized a great amount of material. His model has provided a bold and provoca-tive first formulation of how psychology and spirituality might be inte-grated and has produced a structure for theorists to respond to, in the process setting the standard for a comprehensive transpersonal theory. His historical influence and theoretical support for transpersonal psy-chology in its early years have been enormous. For these contributions, no matter what the ultimate fate of Wilber's theories in the coming decades, the transpersonal movement will always be in Wilber's debt.

CARL JUNG'S ANALYTICAL PSYCHOLOGY AND MICHAEL WASHBURN'S RECENT INNOVATIONS

All of Western psychotherapy can be seen as an exploration into what causes the ego, the self, to be in pain. What is the source of psychologi-cal distress? Ever since Freud, Western depth psychology has looked past the ego to the unconscious for the answer. The ego, the limited sur-face self, cuts itself off from its own deeper sources, and the result is psy-chic pain, inauthentic existence, defensive, contracted consciousness, false self—however the language of the system describes it.

Healing, wholeness, integration, cohesion, or health depends upon reconnecting the ego to its deeper source. Regardless of the lan-guage, all systems seek to ground the ego in its larger native base of the unconscious, which, due to wounding, repression, faulty self structure, learned defensive avoidance of pain and anxiety, the ego keeps down and separates from itself. These are the common themes in all depth approaches to psychotherapy.

Western psychotherapeutic approaches stay within the realm of the personal, limited, finite self. Historically, psychology very much wanted to be respectable and "scientific," and so scrupulously stayed away from the spiritual world and language. But Carl Jung, on the other hand, did not. Jung kept his psychology and his spirituality together, melded them into one.

Jung's model was the first transpersonal psychology. In seeking to explain what is wrong with the human condition, he, too, located the self's pain and anguish in its separation from the unconscious, but for Jung this was a *transpersonal and spiritual* unconscious. This was an unconscious that contained mythic, archetypal, and spiritual energies as well as the id's "seething cauldron of desire" of Freud.

Jung, who was accused by the Freudians of romanticizing the unconscious, viewed the unconscious as a redeeming power of intelligence, creativity, and spiritual transcendence. He believed everyone had both a personal unconscious and a *collective unconscious*, which is shared by all humans. This collective unconscious has within it the archetypes, or the universal forms that shape the psyche and organize psychological experience. Examples of the archetypes include the divine child, the great mother, the maiden, the witch, the warrior, the trickster, the fool, the wounded healer, the king, the queen, the wise old man or woman, et cetera. Psychological health is the capacity to allow these archetypes to move through us, to give shape to our psychological experience by organizing our thoughts, feelings, actions. Psychological pain and distress result from only being able to identify with a few archetypes and thus having a constricted sense of identity and feelings.

For example, if a man's sense of identity is wedded to playing the stern boss at work and he can't let into his experience the other archetypes even when he goes home, such as the *puer* or eternal child, the lover, the fool—if he can only play the stern boss even when playing with his kids or making love with his wife—then his life is greatly limited. The full richness of life's feelings and creativity and spontaneity cannot flow through him.

The idea is to open to the other archetypes or universal energies and to allow these energies to infuse our experience. It is a similar process to other psychological systems of reowning the disowned parts of the self rather than operating in fragmentation and repression, but the Jungian model uses a different language and different metaphors.

The central archetype of the psyche is the Self. This is represented by mandalas and quadrated circles, which are images of the Self, the archetype of the center. Jung believed that we could not directly experience the Self, but it had to be known indirectly. We get its guidance and direction through symbols, dreams, and images. The images that represent the Self change as the person moves in new directions. The Self remains the same, but the images that represent the Self change and need periodic renewal. As the individuating psyche is in movement, new symbolic or mythic images emerge to the ego that express this movement. The conscious ego then needs to reorganize along the lines shown by the Self. Reorganization then happens on both these levels, the conscious ego and the archetypal depths.

According to Jung, the ego develops in the first half of life and is focused on the world and action—doing things, accomplishing, forging an independent ego and achieving a certain mastery in the world. But at about 35 to 45 or older, at mid-life, the adult ego starts to suffer a sense of alienation and lack of meaning, and it begins to turn within. The second half of life is characterized by focusing on the inner life and on bringing forth what had not been developed in the first half of life. For example, if the masculine "doing," active side of the psyche was dominant in the first half, the feminine, "being" side will become more dominant in the second half of life. If the person does not listen to this inner movement, he or she will experience increasing psychic pain, emptiness, and alienation.

Jung saw the ego as important in psychic life, but as something inferior to the source or ground from which it comes. Since the ego is ignorant of this source, it becomes committed to a false stance of independence. The task for the ego is to learn its proper place and come into proper relationship with the superior, supporting bases of its being. The mid-life crisis, for Jung, represents the emergence of the Self. As the ego feels increasingly depressed, inauthentic, and gives way to the unconscious energies emerging from the Self, it experiences a kind of death of this inauthentic self only to be reborn to a higher, spiritual form of Selfhood.

Jung and Jungians tend to focus more on the transcendent aspects of the unconscious, although they acknowledge the id or prepersonal content also. Psychoanalysis, by contrast, sees only the id or prepersonal unconscious.

There are certainly many other aspects to Jung's psychology: He divided people into introverts or extroverts, depending upon their orientation to the world. He thought people developed dominant and inferior modes of experiencing the world that were either mental, feeling, sensational, or intuitive. He had his own vocabulary for discussing the repressed contents of the unconscious, which he called the shadow. He believed that everyone had both masculine and feminine aspects to their psyche; the anima is the female component of the male psyche and the animus is the male component of the female psyche. And his main therapeutic techniques involved dreams, art, and imagination, for he believed that the wisdom of the Self is contacted through images and by entering into the imaginal realm. But for the purposes of showing the essential features of Jung's transpersonal model, this brief synopsis will suffice.

Jungian psychology, of course, is a highly elaborated system with its own literature and various institutes of training throughout the world. But until the 1960s it was a relatively small and isolated stream of thought which had little influence on the rest of mainstream psychology. Jungians tended to keep to themselves and were viewed as a far-out fringe by the rest of scientific, professional psychology. But as the culture changed in the '60s and '70s and transpersonal psychology started to gain momentum, Jungian psychology suddenly became respectable within a larger professional context. Jung was "discovered" by psychotherapists. As more of the field has turned its attention to issues such as spirituality and psychology, issues that the Jungians had been dealing with all along, Jung has now become popular.

Michael Washburn's Recent Innovations

As Jungian thinking enters mainstream cultural dialogue, there is one theorist who is seeking to connect Jungian thought specifically to the wider transpersonal field. His name is Michael Washburn, and he has written two important books *The Ego and the Dynamic Ground* (1988) and *Transpersonal Psychology in Psychoanalytic Perspective* (1994) that position Jungian thought in contradistinction to Wilber's model, heretofore the dominant model in the transpersonal field. Washburn takes the Jungian model, revises it somewhat, and presents it in the language of transpersonal psychology.

As Washburn is a philosopher by training, he explicates the underlying philosophical assumptions of Jungian thought and locates this model in a Western, theistic-relational interpretation of the perennial philosophy rather than the Eastern, nondual tradition of Wilber. This difference is a crucial one, for it raises a key question in transpersonal psychology: What is transcendence? And the psychologies that derive from the answers to this question look very different.

Although Washburn frames his model as a sharp contrast to Wilber on a number of issues (e.g., dynamic-dialectical vs. structural-hierarchical, regression to origins vs. straight ascent to find transcendence, spiral vs. ladder model), many of these images or metaphors are peripheral to both schemes and it is possible to apply each of these images to elements of either. Rather the central differentiating perspective between these two models lies in their different approaches to transcendence, to what transcendence looks like, and their differing interpretations of the perennial philosophy.

Is transcendence no self, or is it a self united with its transcendent ground, a kind of two selves in one? Wilber is in the Eastern, nondual tradition of Buddhism and Advaita Vedanta and places the ultimate goal of transcendence as the dissolution of the separate self into identity with Brahman or Buddha-nature. Washburn, on the other hand, is very much in the Western, theistic-relational tradition. In his view, transcendence does not eliminate the self, it transforms it into a higher unity. The self still exists as part of the psychic structure, but since it is united with its transcendent source (the dynamic ground), it is no longer independent. It has become the lesser side of an integrated duality or, to use Margaret Mahler's famous phrase in a new context, it becomes part of a *dual unity*. The path to this transcendent state of ego/Self integration involves what Washburn terms "regression in the service of transcendence." That is, the ego returns (regresses) to its pre-egoic origins in the unconscious (the dynamic ground) so that it may become integrated with its source and become trans-egoic.

Washburn takes issue with Wilber's view of the pre/trans fallacy. Wilber accuses Jung of committing the classic pre-trans mistake, and he criticizes Jung for such things as confusing infantile narcissism (pre) with altruistic selflessness (trans), or primary process (pre) with visionary cognition (trans). But Washburn believes the issue is more complex than a simple either/or dichotomy, that these two are intimately related. He acknowledges that Jung did not make the pre-trans discrimination in his thinking, but he refines Jung's theory to show how prepersonal and transpersonal reflect the very same potentials at two different levels of expression. Washburn proposes that the nonegoic potentials (the dynamic ground) when expressed through an ego that is immature or weak look prepersonal. Whereas these very same nonegoic potentials when expressed through a mature, strong ego appear transpersonal. So, for example, impulsiveness is a prepersonal expression of the dynamic ground which becomes creative spontaneity when expressed after ego development, a transpersonal form of these very same energies. The dynamic ground remains the same. What changes or develops is the ego that experiences and express these potentials. Thus the nonegoic resources (the dynamic ground) can be expressed before ego develop-ment and look pre-egoic, or they can be expressed after ego develop-ment and look transegoic.

Washburn takes the mid-life crisis as the exemplar of this move-ment of the ego's return to origins in its movement toward transcen-dence. During the first half of life the ego emerges from the collective unconscious, or what Washburn terms the dynamic ground, and engages the outer world. Driven by the outward flow of libido and ori-ented toward external accomplishment, the ego is generally out of touch with its own inner archetypes, complexes, and subjectivity. But at mid-life the outward flow of libido ebbs. The libido recedes from its external focus and starts to flow back toward its source in the dynamic ground. The ego, following this course of the libido, turns inward also. As the libidinal cathexis to the outer world withdraws, the ego loses interest in the world and becomes drawn toward its own subjectivity and unconscious. This mid-life reversal is the return to origins which brings the ego back to its original source in the dynamic ground. The ego begins the individuation process by which it is brought back and reunited with the archetypal Self. Whereas the original unity was unde-veloped and pre-egoic, this new unity will be fully developed and transegoic.

For an illustration of how the mid-life crisis is a "regression in the service of transcendence," Washburn turns to the sixteenthth-century mystic St. John of the Cross in his spiritual masterpiece, *The Dark Night*. The early phase St. John calls the dark night of the senses, and it is experienced as arid, dry, and desert-like, the first phase of purgative withdrawal from the world. Washburn relates this to the libido withdrawing from outside as it de-cathects the world. There is a loss of meaning and pleasure in life and relationships. Old satisfactions no longer are gratifying. St. John speaks of gaining self-knowledge, of being confronted with one's own wretchedness and dark impulses. Washburn sees this as encountering the shadow as the person is drawn down into the underworld of the unconscious and begins to contact forbidden thoughts and feelings.

As the aridity develops and the ego, having been divested of its defenses, is pulled away from the world, at a certain point in this process there is a joyous, ecstatic breakthrough into positive spiritual experiences. This breakthrough is an encounter with the spiritual energies of the dynamic ground, which now begin to act on the ego more directly. At first the person may believe that the goal is attained, an experience of initial awakening in Buddhism referred to as pseudo-nirvana. But it is simply an oasis in the desert and heralds the second phase, the much darker night of the spirit, where there is a direct spiritual action of the nonegoic ground to purge and purify the psyche.

As the derepression continues the person feels like he or she is sinking into a black hole, as if being swallowed up in the dark belly of a beast (like Jonah, says St. John), pulled further down into darkness. The person feels lost, alone, abandoned by God and friends. As this occurs the negative side of the person's early object relations are activated. The experience of other people is colored by the angry, wrathful, judging/condemning oedipal father and the engulfing/abandoning pre-oedipal mother (bad mother). The self feels exposed to the world. Its badness, worthlessness, and wickedness are there for everyone to see. The ego's vulnerability and the belief that others can see through it is a natural outgrowth of its lack of defenses and the derepression that is occurring. One feels naked before God. There are both intra-psychic and interpersonal or object relations dimensions to this experience. Washburn is careful to note that it is not that the dark night of spirit can be reduced to childhood wounds and neurotic fixations but that this process of spiritual purification is experienced *through* this early conditioning. This is the meaning of "regression in the service of transcendence." The ego goes back over the old ground of the psyche and childhood for healing and regeneration, though these are yet to come.

How long this process continues depends upon how the person relates to it and upon the higher spiritual power that is active, but St. John says this process of purification goes on for years. As it continues there comes the discovery that this is not simply an external ordeal one is undergoing but an internal process. When this occurs the person can more consciously turn to face what is happening and surrender to the process. This is a decisive moment as the person turns within rather than trying to escape. There is the beginning of regeneration in spirit.

As the ego begins to welcome and surrender to its interior depths, this marks the start of integration between the ego and nonegoic, dynamic ground of the psyche. Increasingly positive feelings and spiritual experiences emerge. There is a healing of childhood wounds as the positive side of childhood object relations are reawakened. The person experiences the world through the lenses of the good mother and father as well as a feeling of intrinsic goodness within the self. Negative experiences subside, positive spiritual experiences increase and become stabilized. Regression has been in the service of progression.

The ego, rather than being dissolved, becomes harmoniously wedded to its nonegoic sources, which it now experiences as its own higher life. There is a state of ego/Self integration, for this is a unity that contains duality rather than pure unity. It is a state of two-in-one rather than just one. In Washburn's language, the ego and the dynamic ground are fused. In Jung's language, the ego is now open to the archetypal, spiritual energies of the unconscious.

For Jung and Washburn, this is the goal of life. Jung himself believed that this integration was approximated but never fully achieved. Washburn differs but concedes such an integrated life is extremely rare, such as we see in exceptional spiritual personalities such as St. John of the Cross or St. Teresa of Avila.

Washburn believes that there are fundamental differences between Eastern and Western perspectives on the nature of the self and transcendence, that these are logical differences rather than differences of degree or emphasis, and that therefore a unifying paradigm of Eastern and Western approaches in transpersonal psychology is a poor prospect.

Strengths and Limitations of This Model

Strengths. 1. It clearly articulates at least one known pattern of transpersonal growth and transcendence, the mid-life crisis.

This exploration of the themes of mid-life has a great deal of clinical applicability. The language and metaphors used to describe the dark night of mid-life speak very powerfully to many people.

2. It stakes out a Western, theistic-relational approach to the transpersonal issue of transcendence. It provides a direct challenge to the Eastern, nondual bias that had dominated the transpersonal field from its inception.

3. It provides a model in which psychology and spirituality are fused into one unified perspective as against the step ladder model of Wilber's in which psychology is a discrete first step, then followed by the discrete step of spiritual transcendence.

4. It provides a vastly expanded, transpersonal view of the unconscious, which is a source of spiritual illumination as well as instinctual desires. A higher view of dreams derives from this, which may come from the higher, mythic, spiritual realms or the lower, instinctive realms of the unconscious.

5. Archetypes and the collective unconscious (or dynamic ground) are significant psychological notions that now permeate the entire psychotherapeutic field.

6. Jung's work pioneered the use of imagination, fantasy, and art in psychotherapy, techniques which work extremely well for some people.

7. The concept of "regression in the service of transcendence" is an important process to identify. This appears to be a process that is common to all depth psychotherapeutic approaches and is not exclusive to Jungian therapy. Insofar as transcendence involves a psychotherapeutic component, this process of regression in the service of transcendence will probably be present to some degree as the person uncovers and works through old wounds and archaic structures of the self to new and higher levels of integration. On the other hand, where growth involves more of a purely spiritual process without much of a psychological component, it is possible that this may be seen more in terms of a straight ascent.

Limitations. 1. By its focus upon mid-life and older it ignores half of human existence. Is there no hope until a person is 35 to 45 or older for spirituality or psychological awareness? But in fact numerous people do experience spiritual awakening and engage in deep inner work on themselves much earlier than mid-life. It is a model of development that simply does not fit many people nor accord with clinical observation. There are many 25 year olds who are far more self-aware than most 60 year olds.

2. It is a theistic-relational and Western interpretation of the perennial philosophy. How it deals with nondualism is unclear.

3. At the level of technique Jungian work focuses upon working with the imaginal realm, chiefly through fantasy, dreams, and the creative imagination. While these techniques can be powerful for some people, many others find these approaches "heady" and lacking grounding in the body and feelings.

4. The relationship of the psyche to spirit is not clearly spelled out. What relationship does the Self have to soul or spirit? How does the dynamic ground or archetypal realm actually act on the self? What conditions allow this to happen?

5. This model, being based on clinical work with clients, is not the kind of two-step model that Wilber proposes (first step—psychological work; second step—spiritual work). Indeed, Jung pioneered the view that spiritual, archetypal depths can be accessed from the first and may even guide the entire therapy. This is a clinical discovery of immense importance.

However, this model may tend toward a weaker version of Wilber's theory and to see spiritual work as only occurring through psychological work or even culminating only as psychological work concludes. To the extent that this position is asserted, this model is also subject to the same critique as was raised about Wilber's model which amalgamates psychological and spiritual development.

While the tendency to see the two as one may be especially strong for psychologically-minded theorists, it is possible to work transpersonally and yet be open to non-psychological approaches to spiritual development and experience. Spiritual development does not necessarily follow from nor is it identical with psychological work.

HAMEED ALI'S DIAMOND APPROACH

Hameed Ali, who writes under the pen name of A. H. Almaas (*almaas* is Arabic for *diamond*), has created perhaps the fastest growing transpersonal approach on the scene today (Almaas, 1986, 1988, 1995, 1996). Ali's diamond approach is a particular way of putting object relations and body sensing together with Sufism. Although he considers his work to be spiritual work rather than psychotherapy, it nevertheless has come to be incorporated by a growing number of therapists into a transpersonal way of working.

Interestingly, although Hameed Ali has said that he was never drawn to the Jungian approach, he has created a system which in many respects is quite similar to Jung's, though it uses a very different vocabulary. Instead of the Self, Ali uses the term *essence*; instead of Jung's archetypal energies, Ali uses *essential qualities*; and both systems come upon a person's deeper spiritual identity through delving into psychological conflicts, unconscious wounds, and defenses. To be sure there are important differences between the two systems: Ali focuses on the body, whereas Jung does not; Ali gives little importance to images whereas Jung values images highly; Ali believes that the essence can be directly experienced whereas Jung believed the Self cannot be. But the parallels strikingly overshadow the differences.

As with any spiritual system the diamond approach seeks to shift a person's sense of identity from ego to spirit, or as it is termed in this system, to shift a person's identification from the self-image to presence or essence. This involves experiencing ourselves more subtly, having a more refined perception of ourselves, for essence is already present within. Ali uses the word soul in the way it was used long ago, as synonymous with self, that which experiences, hears, learns, understands, et cetera. Essence is who we intrinsically are, a presence, a sensitivity, our spiritual identity which reincarnates. The experience of essence is not always the same. It can be experienced across a spectrum from extreme subtlety as a mere fragrance to a palpable substantiality. Essence can be sensed with our physical senses and is not just an abstraction. It can also be experienced as very personal as well as impersonal. Essence has certain qualities or differentiations of it, such as will, strength, guidance, truth, awakeness, compassion, and value. As in Sufism, Ali's path is not monastic but very much in the world so that essence can experience itself in many different ways.

The ego according to Ali is a defense and a denial of essence. Babies are born in touch with essence. But because the parents are not in touch with essence, when early wounding occurs, there is a lack of mirroring and support for experiencing essence and for identifying with it as who we are. It wilts for lack of reflection. This creates a void or hole or lack of essence. To compensate for this loss of essence, a self and object relations matrix is created. Slowly, with many repetitions of this process, a psychological sense of ego evolves which is more and more cut off from the underlying essence. After awhile the person loses touch altogether with essence and lives in a world of images, the world which psychoanalysis, particularly object relations, describes so well. Thus the ego is a compensation for the loss of essence. Reversing this is a process of working through the early object relations in order to experience essence once again.

One of Ali's most original contributions is his theory of holes. He believes that for our personalities to be "essentialized," that is, for the person to have access to real capacities, strength, wisdom, love, et cetera, it is necessary that all the early wounds be deeply explored and worked through so the holes can be filled with the essential aspects that are missing. *Holes* in Ali's terminology are those places where people experience themselves as missing something, as deficient, not enough, or inadequate. The hole is the experience of the absence of the essential quality. As a person goes into this experience, for instance, of defi-ciency, he or she discovers the hole or gap, the absence of essence. In working with this and experientially entering into this hole, the person begins to explore the substance and texture of the hole. Often this uncovers difficult and unpleasant issues. The person needs to uncover what this gap means psychologically in terms of early object relations and trauma. In working this way over time, the structure that covers this hole then dissolves, which leads to energetic contact with an essential quality. Essence then allows the person to meet the situation as is appro-priate rather than experiencing deficiency and then defensively fleeing and covering over this hole. For example, a person can experience strength where he or she once experienced fear or weakness.

Ali has created a unique synthesis of object relations work and body-work. Although most diamond practitioners do little if any "hands on" body-work, many do utilize breathwork derived from the tradition of Reich. Although this aspect of working has been less and less used as Ali's teaching evolves, when it is done it consists of deep breathing in order to increase energy in the body and facilitate the experiencing of feelings. As always, the focus is upon the meaning of these feelings as they relate to early object relations, how they serve to compensate for a loss of essence, and to get to what is just beyond the feelings—the energetic context.

There are three main parts to the diamond approach's method of practice:

1. Individual one-on-one work, which looks very much like focusing and body sensing-oriented psychotherapy within an object relations framework. It attempts to shift the student's identification from object relations to presence. It is akin to existential psychotherapy in that it is present-centered and experiential. The orienting question is, "How do you experience yourself now?"

2. Small groups that are personal process groups in which individual practices such as meditation and chanting are emphasized.

3. Large groups in which the teachings of the diamond approach are taught theoretically and then elucidated by exercises in dyads and triads to allow the student to understand them experientially.

Strengths and Limitations of This Model

Strengths. 1. It is the most sophisticated synthesis of contemporary object relations with somatic work and spiritual development that has emerged on the scene today. It includes the body, which is ignored by psychoanalysis and Jung.

2. Although Hameed Ali does not claim to be a fully realized being, he nonetheless does hold himself out to be someone of genuine spiritual attainment. This gives him a special authority in speaking of some transpersonal states of being.

3. It is a contemporary spiritual path. Although all spiritual paths implicitly contain some kind of psychology, most religious traditions date from hundreds or thousands of years ago and their respective psychologies are so outdated as to be mostly irrelevant. Ali takes full advantage of modern psychoanalytic theory and somatic work, yet does not assert that this is the only way to spiritual growth.

Limitations. 1. There is some lack of clarity about what essence is in relationship to other spiritual systems. Although Ali says that essence is how humans experience spiritual Being he uses this to mean different things at different times. He positions himself in the nondual tradition with its accompanying biases and accepts the Buddhist notion of no self, yet speaks of essence as something that mediates between the individual and the Absolute. Sometimes he seems to equate essence with *atman* or Buddha-nature while at other times he attributes qualities and feelings to essence that do not appear in any classical descriptions of *atman* or Buddha-nature. Essence does not appear to be the soul, for Ali defines soul differently than the perennial tradition does and does not refer to a Personal Divine.

2. He downplays the importance of images. Given that Ali's goal is to free people from the trap of identifying with their conceptual minds this is understandable. But by neglecting the power that images and symbols may have for inner deepening and therapy, it leaves an important door of inward experience shut.

3. The focus on inner states neglects the reality of interpersonal relationships, which are seen in this system through the lens of how early object relations condition interpersonal relating. Keeping an intra-psychic focus downplays the importance of the intersubjective field.

4. As with any system that uses breathwork or any kind of altered state of consciousness, it is subject to the limitations of this work, namely that whatever is worked through in an altered state must also be explored in normal consciousness for a complete working through.

5. Given that staying with and exploring deep, early wounds and conflicts in depth therapy can at certain moments open into a more integrated, coherent state of being—a common and widely recognized fact of clinical experience among therapists of all orientations—how does this differ from what Ali is describing? It is reminiscent of Fritz Perls speaking of the movement from a sterile, dead void into the creative void through awareness. It is not entirely clear how this experience which Perls and the gestaltists strive for, or which the existentialists focus on in the experience of being, differs from essence or how essence is spiritual rather than organismic.

There is the sense in Ali's writing that a sufficiently deep therapy is the purification necessary for spiritual realization.

But traditional spiritual practices aim at more than this. In Ali's model the obstacles to spiritual realization are the person's psychological wounding and the concomitant residue of internalized early object relations as opposed to these obstacles being experienced through this object relations matrix. It is a subtle yet crucial distinction, for if, on the other hand, as Washburn maintains in his model, moving beyond the obstacles to spiritual transformation is *experienced through* the lens of the early object relations matrix but cannot be *reduced to* these internalized representations, this then implies that more is involved in spiritual realization (perhaps much more) than psychotherapeutic working through.

6. As a new spiritual path, it is a bold yet still unproven experiment. Most spiritual paths have been established by founders who had attained the goal, reached liberation or union with the Divine. Ali explicitly says he has not. Although Ali may have the capacity to experience certain inward states and believes that his path will eventually reach the goal, it is still unknown where it will lead. And it is not clear to what extent his unique abilities and spiritual capacity have produced a system that works for him personally and to what extent it can be generalized to work effectively for other people.

ROBERTO ASSAGIOLI'S PSYCHOSYNTHESIS

At least a brief mention should be made of the other historically important transpersonal psychotherapy that was formed at the same time Jung was working, the Italian psychiatrist Roberto Assagioli's psychosynthesis. Like Jung, Roberto Assagioli was an early adherent of Freud's who became disenchanted with Freud's materialistic bias. Working independently in Florence, Italy, during the first decades of the 1900s he created the other original transpersonal approach that has many parallels to Jung's model. Psychosynthesis became popular in the '70s when transpersonal psychology first started. But it quickly made its contribution to the field and has now faded away with no more than a handful of training centers left in America.

The basic theory is very simple. Assagioli believed that there should be a "height" psychology as well as a depth psychology and tried to devise techniques to contact the superconscious or Transpersonal

Self, which the "I" was then to align itself with. This occurs first by identification with the contents of the lower unconscious and its various
"subpersonalities," a helpful term that has now entered the larger therapy field and is equivalent to what other systems call complexes or disowned aspects of the self. This is then followed by a process of
disidentificating from these lower contents and contacting the higher
unconscious or Transpersonal Self. Psychosynthesis was a pioneer in
the field in the use of guided imagery, its major technique, and its image
of the "inner child" is now part of mainstream culture. Current psychosynthesis therapists also make use of other techniques such as
gestalt empty chair work, interpretation, et cetera.

Strengths and Limitations of This Model

> *Strengths.* 1. It is historically important in bringing spiritual con-
> cerns to psychotherapy. Both Jung and Assagioli used imaginal
> techniques, Jung pioneering active imagination, Assagioli lead-
> ing the way in the use of guided imagery.
>
> 2. It is a very similar map to Jung's that originated independently.
> Instead of Jung's Self, there is the Transpersonal Self to which
> the I or ego is to subordinate itself; instead of the collective
> unconscious and archetypal energies there is the higher uncon-
> scious and the transpersonal will; and in both systems the path
> to transcendence lies through the personal wounds, complexes,
> and subpersonalities of the unconscious.
>
> *Limitations.* 1. Like Jungian therapy, psychosynthesis ignores the
> body in its focus upon the imagination and visualization. For
> some people visualization can be powerful, but for many others
> such techniques keep the person in the realm of the mind.
> Similarly, the process of moving from identification to disiden-
> tification is merely an intellectual exercise for most people.
> Although psychosynthesis presents this as but another step in
> the therapeutic process, to be able to disidentify from the
> "lower self" and to live from the transpersonal self is a lifetime
> work (at least).
>
> 2. Like many movements that were started by a brilliant and
> charismatic personality, such as Rankian therapy, Adlerian
> therapy, gestalt and transactional analysis, once the founder

dies the system stagnates. As with these other systems, psychosynthesis has remained basically where it was when Assagioli died. Although it still has followers, it lacks the vitality of its earlier years. Also its literature is so small that it can be read in its entirety within weeks. Such a meager literature leaves so many gaps and unanswered questions about the vast scope of the human condition that it can have only limited impact upon the larger field of psychology.

STANISLAV GROF'S HOLOTROPIC MODEL

A distinctive transpersonal psychotherapy that uses altered states of consciousness to achieve therapeutic goals comes from psychiatrist and LSD researcher Stanislav Grof. Using what he calls holotropic breathwork, Grof has now conducted sessions for tens of thousands of people, and although many people do not respond to this method, it has attracted a number of adherents and practitioners.

Grof spent decades studying the effects of LSD, first in his native Czechoslovakia and later in the United States, and out of his studies he developed a map of consciousness that went beyond Western psychology into transpersonal, spiritual realms. Essentially, Grof takes the map of consciousness derived from his LSD work and utilizes deep breathing and loud music to produce an altered state of consciousness in an attempt to mimic the effects of LSD.

Grof began his work in psychiatric hospitals in Czechoslovakia in the 1950s, giving LSD to mental patients of all diagnostic categories. As his research developed he worked with less disturbed populations, including alcoholics and drug addicts, trauma survivors, normal neurotics, et cetera. He found that people went through similar realms of consciousness in their LSD psychotherapeutic work, and this became the basis the map of consciousness he developed from his observations.

The basic map involves three broad territories—the realm of the sensory barrier and the personal unconscious, the perinatal or birth-related realm, and the transpersonal realm. As the sensory barrier is broken with LSD, there is revealed a vastly expanded sensory consciousness (see the chapter "Altered States of Consciousness" for greater detail). This realm also leads into the personal unconscious, a realm that Grof believes is well described by Freud and classical psychoanalysis.

The second realm discloses what Grof calls the Basic Perinatal Matrices, or the birth-related experiences, which serve as central organizing principles of the psyche. Grof identifies four Basic Perinatal Matrices corresponding to the four stages of birth—the undisturbed intrauterine state, the onset of the birth process, movement down the birth canal, and birth itself. Grof finds that these four organizing matrices contain within them related psychological material or complexes, which he calls COEX systems (which stands for systems of condensed experience).

Basic Perinatal Matrix I (BPM I) corresponds to the prenatal period in the womb when the fetus is floating in the uterus before contractions have begun. While this can be associated with positive, unitive experiences, there can also be a variety of physical, chemical, or psychological interferences ranging from abortion attempts to the parents not wanting the child. Related positive psychological themes, or "COEX systems," include such material as feelings of bliss, safety, warmth, heavenly paradise, and unity. Negative images, feelings, and COEX systems include underwater dangers, polluted streams, schizophrenia (especially with paranoid symptoms), psychotic loss of boundaries, hypochondriasis, and nausea.

BPM II corresponds to the beginning of the birth process. Contractions have begun, but as yet there is no movement down the birth canal. The person may feel crushed by overwhelming, cosmic forces, with no possibility for escape. Related psychological material includes a sense of cosmic engulfment, memories of being a helpless victim or being trapped with no chance of escape, being swallowed by a monster, great feelings of loneliness, existential anxiety and despair. Sartre's play *No Exit* captures this psychological state.

BPM III is the process of moving down the birth canal. Although there is a sense of movement, the baby is still subject to immense pressure as the birth contractions propel the baby toward birth. The COEX systems pertaining to this phase of birth contain such themes as struggles for survival, crushing physical or emotional pressures, sadomasochism, rape, sexual and physical abuse, and death-rebirth struggles.

BPM IV is the process of birth itself, emerging from the birth canal into the freedom of the outer world. There is a release into a new existence, a transcendence of previous problems, and a joyful sense of fresh beginning. The COEX systems that correspond to this phase include such psychological themes as recovery from serious illnesses, surviving dangerous situations or accidents, merging into the light, feelings of redemption, liberation, and rebirth.

Grof emphasizes that people do not necessarily work through their psychological and birth material in a linear way. Various aspects of each of these four matrices may emerge at any time. But as they are worked through psychologically, they tend not to reappear. So the general trend over time is toward resolving the issues and moving toward the fourth matrix of birth.

The third realm moves into the transpersonal, where the individual may experience a variety of spiritual states or themes. Grof has documented experiences that correspond to themes from all the world's major spiritual traditions, including the Universal Mind or Big Mind, the cosmic void, kundalini experiences, and a rich number of psychic experiences such as out of body experiences, recall of previous lifetimes, identification with different animals or even organs and parts of the body, and telepathy.

Grof sees his system as integrative in that it includes several different psychologies. Specifically he believes that clients move from a Freudian stage to a Rankian-Reichian-existentialist stage and finally then to a Jungian stage.

Grof's belief is that as a person works through the first two realms and emerges into the third, the person's psychopathology will be worked through in the process. Although Grof has said that he would prefer to use LSD in therapy, since LSD is now illegal he has come up with a substitute—deep breathing accompanied by loud music. Holotropic breathwork can be done with from one to several hundred people in a room. Typically done in groups, the group is instructed to divide into pairs. One member of the pair lies down and is instructed to simply breathe deeply while the other member of the pair sits beside the person to facilitate if necessary. The idea is that the oxygen increases the energy in the person's system, similar to what LSD does, and this increased energy activates the parts of the psyche that need healing.

Over the next two hours or so, very loud music is played, beginning with stimulating music, leading into very moving, stirring selections, and ending with very peaceful, quiet music. If the person needs help during this time, the sitter may assist or enlist the help of one of the trained facilitators in the room. In the next session the breather and sitter reverse positions. At the end of a session Grof encourages people to draw mandalas of their experience as a way to help integration, as well as allowing time for verbal sharing in the group.

Strengths and Limitations of This Model

Strengths. Stanislav Grof has been a major force in the development of transpersonal psychology. His has contributed as a researcher, a clinician, and as an activist for the transpersonal movement as president of the International Transpersonal Association. There are four main areas where Grof's influence has been significantly felt.

1. Grof is an outstanding researcher of the first order. He developed the field's most far-reaching and influential map of LSD states and their clinical significance. In his pioneering work with LSD he has given scientific respectability to the use of psychedelic compounds in psychotherapy. His well-documented research represents transpersonal science and research at its best. He is certainly the world's most influential writer in the field of psychotherapy with psychedelic drugs.

2. Grof's holotropic breathwork is a uniquely transpersonal way of using altered states of consciousness psychotherapeutically. It is an experiential therapy that is very powerful and helpful for some people. It seems to be especially helpful for some people to access trauma and birth-related material. Because deep breathing is not LSD, some people feel safer and less threatened in trying it. Consequently, it has allowed certain people to experience spiritual openings of various kinds.

3. Grof's eminence as a pioneer in giving new prominence to the importance of the birth experience for the psyche is enormous. This has helped give respectability to such things as rebirthing and the pre- and perinatal psychology movement, and it extends the range of psychotherapy into new regions. His map of the four stages of birth has become a standard way of organizing birth-related trauma.

4. Grof has also been a major thinker and clinician in the emerging field of spiritual emergency.

Limitations. 1. Grof's view of psychoanalysis is considerably outdated. The psychoanalysis he refers to is the psychoanalysis of Eastern Europe in the 1940s and '50s, a relic of the drive-discharge theories from almost half a century ago. Psychoanalysis has changed dramatically since then. Grof's failure to come to terms with contemporary psychoanalysis, which is still the most widely influential, dynamic psychological approach today, represents a serious gap in a theory that attempts to provide a complete map of consciousness.

2. A problem with Grof's map of consciousness is that he applies something derived from LSD work and applies it in toto to ordinary reality. State-specific learning is explored in greater detail in another chapter (see "Altered States of Consciousness"), but one problem that arises in taking a map of consciousness from LSD research is that it produces a *state-specific map* of consciousness.

Grof appears to subscribe to a belief that was prevalent in the '60s that psychedelics are analogous in psychology to a microscope in biology or a telescope in astronomy. This belief is less tenable today, for it is clear that unlike a microscope or telescope, LSD substantially *changes* the consciousness it is seeking to explore. Because LSD alters consciousness and the relationships between the various contents of consciousness, it is therefore questionable how applicable the LSD insights are to ordinary reality. While his map of consciousness may fit the LSD experience extremely well, it has not gained wide support as particularly relevant to normal consciousness.

Also, the limitations of any technique that involves altered states apply here. *State-specific working through* is one result, leaving much in normal consciousness untouched, because much of the ego and the ego defenses are by-passed. Also, the absence of a longer term, ongoing therapeutic relationship prevents the building of new self structure, which contemporary psychoanalytic theory sees as crucial for long-term results. The implication in holotropic breathwork is that you can simply breathe your way to mental health, and the internal resistances, wounds, and traumas will come tumbling out on their own. Alas, if only it were so simple.

3. It has limited applicability. Only a select few are interested in this kind of experience, which can involve a certain aerobic effort. Of those who try it, many never move beyond feelings of tetany (muscle contraction) and some vague feelings that may have little content. Most people tend not to continue. That breathwork is not LSD is both a strength (as noted above) and a limitation. People who have tried both generally find that deep breathing is a poor substitute for LSD.

EXISTENTIAL TRANSPERSONAL PSYCHOTHERAPY

The existential approach to transpersonal therapy is perhaps the easiest and most natural synthesis of spiritual practice and psychotherapy because of the great similarity in language, values, and concepts. Granted there is a very large gulf between the completely materialist existentialist on the one hand and a spiritual outlook on the other, but when this philosophical difference is removed there is much in common. In both spiritual practice and existential therapy there is a great distrust of theories and a strong emphasis upon actual *experiencing*, upon *present-centeredness*, upon *awareness*, upon *being*, and upon facing basic life issues such as death, loneliness, and the meaning of life.

From its origins in European philosophy, existentialism and its sister movement, phenomenology, had a major impact upon the field of psychotherapy. The founder of existential philosophy, Sören Kierkegaard, began his inquiry into the basics of existence, which he viewed as a conversation between life and death. Confronted with the inevitability of death, the human response is dread, angst. For Kierkegaard, the response to this angst and dread was a very spiritual (and transpersonal) one, faith. Kierkegaard was a devout Christian, and his existential inquiry led him into spirituality even more deeply. However, with the exceptions of Buber and Tillich, most of the prominent existential thinkers who followed did not share this spiritual perspective. Nietzsche, Sartre, Camus, and others all shared a disbelief in any spiritual reality and saw no meaning outside of what human beings create.

Hence existentialism began to attend to the actual "lived experience" of being human, apart from any theological or theoretical constructs.

A bias against theorizing and heady philosophical discourse brought existentialism to a focus upon experiencing. Phenomenology, a particular application of existential philosophy which also emerged during the first decades of this century, provided a methodology for the study of lived experience. Phenomenology tries to uncover experience just as it is. To do this, phenomenology employs a method called *bracketing*, which is the acknowledgment and then suspension of all beliefs, theories, and metaphysical preconceptions in order to inquire into human experience. In so doing it becomes possible to attend to the thing itself, as it is actually lived in all of its sensory and embodied fullness.

Bringing these existential and phenomenological approaches to human experience to psychology in the 1940s, '50s, and '60s, Medard Boss (1958, 1979), Ludwig Binswanger (1956), Rollo May (1958, 1969, 1977), Irvin Yalom (1957), James Bugental (1976, 1978, 1987), and others brought an existential *way of working* to psychotherapy. With a suspicion of theories, the existential therapists made a sweeping critique of Freud and psychoanalysis as too intellectual, too removed from fundamental life issues and experience, and trapped in a Procrustean bed of theory into which they forced their clients. By contrast, early existential therapists attempted to get clients into their lived experience, not just "talking about" their problems or trying to analyze them or figure them out. As currently practiced, this experiential focus brings clients back to the basic existential issues of death, anxiety, fear of responsibility and making choices, lack of meaning, and the temptation to flee all these concerns by creating an inauthentic life. The existential approach aims at bringing a client into a deeper experience of being and to confront these basic life issues. Out of this exploration with the various defenses and escapes that had been employed to avoid these difficult human issues, a more authentic existence emerges, one that has been freely chosen and which reflects the inner values and choices of the person.

It is interesting that both spiritual traditions and existential psychotherapy involve a strong emphasis on *being*. Existential psychotherapy believes that the actual experience of being has therapeutic effect and that it is essential for a client to feel at home in his or her beingness. However, it should be noted that in traditional existential approaches, the awareness of being is as a finite being. It is akin to our basic existence, and as such is characterized by finitude and limitation, even though it is a much more expanded state of being than people normally live in.

An existential transpersonal psychotherapy takes this one step further. From a transpersonal perspective, being is the border to spirit, the gateway to the transpersonal. In connecting to being, the transformative possibilities of Being can be glimpsed. It is but a small conceptual jump (although a much larger experiential jump) from the finite being of existence to the infinite Being of spirit. And it is into this larger awareness of Being that existential transpersonal psychotherapy seeks to invite us.

Although the existential approach can be used with any orientation, one school that became an exemplar of an existential approach is gestalt therapy. Although gestalt originated in a strict existential, materialistic framework, when freed from its materialistic origins and placed into a transpersonal context, there are five key areas that have remarkable similarity to spiritual approaches. These are a focus upon:

1. Present-centeredness
2. Awareness
3. Full sensory and bodily involvement
4. I and Thou
5. Morality

Present-centeredness. Viewing the present as the only reality is a common feature of existential approaches, which have a vertical rather than a horizontal time frame. That is, all forces are seen to be acting now, in this immediate moment. This is in contrast to the horizontal time frame of psychoanalysis, in which the present is only a point on the line extending into the past and forward into the future. In an existential view, the present is this very second right NOW, which is disappearing faster than we can hold onto it. The past exists here and now as memory, history, regret, et cetera, but when we remember, we remember now. The future exists here and now as anticipation, hope, rehearsing, dread, et cetera, but when we imagine the future we do so now. Rather than excavating the past, gestalt looks to see how the past is alive in the present in the form of unfinished business and still festering wounds.

The temporal focus on the here and now also exists in spiritual approaches and has its greatest expression in the Buddhist literature. Indeed, sometimes gestalt has been viewed as a kind of Zen therapy and co-founder Fritz Perls as a modern-day therapeutic Zen master. The exquisite attention to this present moment is a hallmark of Buddhist meditative traditions, which are full of injunctions to stop daydreaming and fantasizing and be here, right now. Fritz Perls believed gestalt therapy provided a methodology for doing just this, for what prevents people from being in the now is the endless fantasies which arise from old wounds and the defensive compensations for these wounds. As the wounds heal, gestalt teaches, the person opens to the immediacy of the present moment.

Awareness. In all existential approaches to psychotherapy a central goal is to liberate the person into his or her experience. Gestalt therapy does this by placing awareness at the center of its approach and as the key to actual experiencing. The gestalt awareness continuum, wherein the person verbalizes his or her awareness of the present moment (e.g., "Here and now I'm aware of . . . ") can be viewed as a kind of verbalized meditation, highlighting what is in awareness and making it more vivid by attending to it.

Central to this approach is the view that a person is whole now. There is no need to work at it. Health comes from experiencing Being directly, when a person stops covering it up. What prevents this is living in fantasy (our wounds and defenses), but gestalt counsels engaging the wounds and defenses directly, to become fully one's experience without dissociating, to be fully with whatever is in experience. Even when "nothing" appears to be the experience, fully entering this can be powerfully transformative, moving as Fritz Perls (1969) said, from "the sterile void to the fertile void," a particularly Buddhist image.

It is much like the Buddhist notion of "intrinsic health," in which wholeness is here already and can be contacted immediately. A transpersonal gestalt approach views this intrinsic capacity for wholeness and healing as how spiritual Being is reflected in the wisdom of organismic self-regulation.

Full sensory and bodily involvement. The organismic approach of gestalt places a great premium upon fully inhabiting the physical and sensory realm of bodily existence. Through the influence of Reich and

Charlotte Selver's sensory awareness, Fritz and Laura Perls paid special attention to the sensorimotor system. In gestalt, to be present and open to the immediacy of present experience means to be grounded in the body, not dissociated in a mental world of fantasy. This led Fritz Perls to say his oft quoted, "Lose your mind and come to your senses."

Again the similarities to Buddhism and Zen in particular are striking. Charlotte Selver, who pioneered the field of sensory awareness, has had her work described as "the essence of Zen." The Zen literature pays exquisite attention to the sensory feast available in the moment and is full of rich perceptual details. Coming alive to the senses is highly prized in both gestalt and spiritual traditions.

I and Thou. Gestalt was very influenced by one of the few existential thinkers who had a spiritual orientation, Martin Buber. Buber contrasted I-It relating with I-Thou relating. I-It relating was normal, secular relating in which the other is seen as an object, a thing to be used, a means to an end. I-Thou relating, on the other hand, brought a person into a sacred relationship in which the other is viewed as an end in itself. I-Thou establishes a relation of equality. Gestalt criticized psychoanalysis for its traditional doctor-patient roles, its distancing of the therapist from the client, and its cold, I-It mode of relating. In the 1950s psychoanalysis was under attack by existentialists of all persuasions making this same critique. Gestalt sought to humanize the process by establishing a more reciprocal, mutual, person to person relating that the Perls' characterized as I-Thou. Interestingly, psychoanalysis has now, almost half a century later, come around to this same position, which is currently termed the *intersubjective* approach. The I-Thou approach translates into the demand for greater therapeutic presence on the part of the therapist and has a correlate in wanting the client to also be present and engaged in the therapy process. Bugental (1978, 1987) has written with special insight about this.

From Christ's teaching of the Golden Rule, to Buddha's focus upon compassion, and Krishnamurti's statement that the fundamental spiritual issue is that of "right relationship," spiritual traditions throughout the world have emphasized the necessity to sacralize relationship. While intersubjectivity and the existential focus on authentic relationship parallel this value on relationship in a secular way, it reaches its highest culmination in a transpersonal perspective which truly embraces the sacredness of relationship.

Morality. Naranjo (1993) has pointed out that gestalt views conventional morality as an imposed set of shoulds that constrict the person's impulses and feelings and help cause neurotic disturbance. It has a deeper trust in the intrinsic morality of the organism, which it seeks to liberate. Spiritual traditions are marked by a seemingly opposite view. They begin the process of spiritual purification with sets of rules around morality and view the resulting constriction of impulses and feelings as good and helpful to quieting the mind and passions. However, once spiritual liberation is attained, all spiritual traditions say such a saint or sage is beyond conventional morality and is free to the do the will of the Divine. Hence in both approaches there is a trust in a deeper source of morality beyond the conventional rules of conduct. In gestalt the moral rules are challenged and thrown out as soon as possible, and in spiritual practice they are dispensed with only after reaching the goal. The goal is similar but the means differ.

Strengths and Limitations of This Model

 Strengths. 1. There is a natural match between existentialism and spirituality in the vocabulary of human experience and concerns.

 2. Existentialism and Buddhism are very close and have been a point of entry from psychology into spirituality for many people. Both approaches seek to uncover experience as it is, apart from theoretical categories and systems, and so value experiencing over theories, present-centeredness over flights into the past or future, deepening inquiry into the nature of mind over speculation, sacred relationship over utilitarian relationship, and grounding in full organismic, sensory awareness rather than mental fantasy.

 Limitations. 1. Existential psychotherapy is not a systematic and thorough, content-rich model. It is more a way of working, an openness to a dimension of human experience. Even a more developed approach such as gestalt has a comparatively meager literature and leaves many psychological issues unaddressed. Gestalt's heyday was in the '60s and '70s but it has declined rapidly since then. And like psychosynthesis, its theory has barely changed since its founders died.

2. Existentialism and Buddhism are a particularly good fit, but what about other traditions? Deepening a person's actual spiritual experience is the goal of all spiritual traditions. There is much still to be done in linking other spiritual traditions to existential approaches.

TRANSPERSONAL PSYCHOANALYTIC PSYCHOTHERAPY

Psychoanalysis is the psychotherapeutic approach that is perhaps farthest from the realm of spirit. Beginning with Freud's anti-religious bias (see, for example, *The Future of an Illusion*), psychoanalysis started out disdainful of religion and has maintained, at best, a skeptical attitude toward it ever since. And whereas existential psychotherapy has a great overlap of vocabulary and concerns with spiritual work, psychoanalysis has a language and focus that seem very far from such things. But with the rise of transpersonal psychology, many current psychoanalytic therapists are attempting to bring their psychotherapy and spirituality together and are discovering that a spiritual perspective considerably expands the view from psychoanalysis. Indeed, in putting the two together it appears that there are some similar trends in each, and both may be able to profit from such an integration.

So far there has been no methodical and comprehensive attempt to reconcile these two heretofore separate streams of inquiry. What has been written consists mostly of comparisons between Buddhism or Taoism and psychoanalysis, and it exists primarily at the level of theory rather than practice. The most notable contributions thus far are by Engler (1986), Epstein (1984, 1986, 1988, 1989, 1990, 1995), and Suler (1993).

There are six main areas of convergence that this discussion will center on:

1. Value of becoming conscious
2. Self - No self/higher self
3. Refining perception
4. Facing whatever arises
5. Temporal orientation
6. Compassion

Value of becoming conscious. Freud stated early on that the goal of psychoanalysis was "to make the unconscious conscious." To this end psychoanalysis was developed. While considerable debate has raged (and continues to rage today) over what constitutes making something conscious, nevertheless there is general agreement on the goal. All approaches to depth psychotherapy share this goal in some form, but it was Freud who first articulated it.

This is also the goal of all spiritual practices, to wake up, to become conscious of our true identity—spirit. While both psychoanalysis and spiritual traditions share the general goal of becoming conscious, the endpoints are very different, as are the techniques for getting there. Heretofore psychoanalysis has never considered becoming conscious past the realm of the self and its unconscious, whereas spiritual traditions point to a soul or spiritual reality beyond the finite self. A more contemporary restatement of Freud's goal comes from Robert Stolorow (1992 p. 159), who states it as, "the unfolding, illumination, and transformation of the patient's subjective world." This is fully compatible with the spiritual search, even if the "ultimate" realms of this subjectivity differ. Similarly, as Suler (1993) has noted, both psychoanalysis and spiritual systems believe that self-knowledge leads to transformation, although again, what transformation looks like is very different in the two approaches.

All psychologies, but psychoanalysis first and foremost, strive for an integrated, cohesive self. Such a self is paradoxically both strong and stable and at the same time more fluid, flexible, and capable of navigating inner spaces, such as are encountered in spiritual practice. A poorly integrated, fragmentation-prone self is tied in to more rigid, inflexible defenses and unconscious avoidances. Such a self makes spiritual practice more challenging because so much of the self is operating outside of consciousness.

Self – No self/higher self. Where the self has been the entire focus of psychoanalysis, spiritual systems open the prospect of transcending the self. As we have seen in the differences between Wilber and Washburn, transcending the self means different things depending upon the spiritual frame of reference. Nevertheless, the view that there is so much beyond what is conventionally termed the self is a profoundly humbling one for psychoanalysis, for until the transpersonal movement came along, psychoanalysis saw all experiences of no self in purely pathological or regressive terms. A transpersonal perspective in psychoanalysis forces a reevaluation of this position and the admission of higher, post-egoic, transcendent states that are developmentally beyond the conventional self.

There are some remarkable similarities between psychoanalysis and spiritual systems in their views of what the self is. Engler (1986) has written insightfully about this. Object relations and Buddhism both see the self as a series of representations, a continually constructed, rapidly moving series of discrete images. These fixed images move through the mind so quickly that there is the appearance of a stable, continuous self, but both systems believe that this self sense is an illusion, a kind of mirage created by the rapidity with which the images flicker by.

A theistic-relational view of the self may find more of a correspondence with Kohut's self psychology. Kohut sees the self as continuous in time and space, as an integrating center of initiative. As a person's self develops, the "nuclear program" moves the person in the direction of self-actualization and the realization of his or her destiny. In Kohut's moving from drive theory to self theory, the urge toward wholeness becomes central rather than the instincts. Development can be seen as an evolutionary movement of consciousness as it is organized by the self. In putting these views of the self into the spiritual framework of the theistic-relational traditions, here the self is not seen as an illusion to be dissolved but a link between the soul and the world. As the self reestablishes its link with the Divine and becomes surrendered to this higher power, the person's spiritual destiny can be realized. There is potentially a great concordance between these two views of the self, and Jones (1991) has ventured tentatively into this area, but a full integration of them has yet to be undertaken.

Refining perception. Both psychoanalysis and spiritual practice proceed by a gradual refining of perception. For example, working with the transference, particularly as described by Merton Gill, Heinz Kohut, and the intersubjective schools, involves an increasing attention to the subtle nuances of feelings, images, and perceptions of the relationship between client and therapist. It is a process of coming into the here and now to pay exquisite attention to the present relationship, of refining perception and articulating the client's experience of the relationship in order that he or she may reexperience the pathogenic feelings and experiences of childhood so that they may be healed. This refining of perception is precisely what meditation attempts to do, to bring exquisite attention to the here and now experience of thoughts, feelings, and perceptions in order to ultimately go beyond. The goals are of course different, healing versus transcendence, but the process of refining perception of inner states is similar.

Opening to the richness of inner experience reveals new vistas of the psyche, vistas which can be either pathological or spiritual, or perhaps contain elements of both. For example, Epstein (1989) has written on the inner experience of the void from psychoanalytic and Buddhist perspectives, and he has concluded that where the psychoanalytic investigations have focused on deficiency states of the self, Buddhist literature of the void has focused on transcendent states which take a reasonably developed self as the starting point. The enhancing of perception, the articulation and differentiation of subtle inner states, is a hallmark of both psychoanalysis and spiritual practice. The domains of inquiry, the self and its pathological states for psychoanalysis and transpersonal states for spiritual practice, have up until now been separate. But a transpersonal orientation allows us to integrate these two domains and to begin to explore possible relationships between them, how a state of inner deficiency and emptiness may at times even be a gateway to transcendent states of great fullness, depth, and beauty instead of only having pathological significance as traditional analysis maintains.

Psychoanalysis is also catching up to existential approaches in becoming increasingly distrustful of theories and cognitive maps, and in this it shares much with spiritual practice. Psychoanalysis has long been criticized for its fixation on elaborate theories and for attempting to fit clinical data into the Procrustean bed of its theoretical framework. Kohut's emphasis upon becoming experience-near in clinical practice rather than maintaining a more theoretical, experience-distant stance helped pave the way for intersubjective theories to bring existential and phenomenological values into psychoanalysis. This coming into immediate contact with one's actual inner experience is also what spirituality seeks to promote.

Facing whatever arises. Many meditation practices stress the importance of becoming aware of whatever arises in consciousness, neither condemning nor justifying the thoughts, feelings, and images. This finds an extraordinary parallel in psychoanalytic free association, where the client is asked to report every relevant feeling or thought without censorship. Psychoanalysis has developed a keen study of the many obstructions and defenses that prevent this free flow from occurring. This stance is further developed in becoming a psychoanalyst, which involves adopting the analytic attitude of non-defensiveness and a readiness to explore anything that comes up. Both meditative and psychoanalytic approaches are actually technologies for opening to inner experience without suppressing or avoiding so that inner experience begins to reveal itself more and more fully.

There has been very little written that attempts to directly apply spiritual practice to clinical practice in psychoanalysis. Epstein (1995) is one writer who has made such an attempt from a Buddhist perspective. Although in bringing Buddhism into psychoanalysis he often sounds more like a gestalt therapist than an analyst, he nevertheless offers an original and intriguing contribution in this area of exploring whatever arises. After the defenses have been worked through and the central childhood wounds come into view, Epstein proposes to shift into a meditative mode. He suggests that rather than focusing upon feelings, at this point the focus of therapy should shift to the sense of the "I" and its insubstantiality. This redirects attention from emotional pain that Epstein believes will never go away toward the spiritual search for emptiness and egolessness that Buddha taught are the only cure for suffering.

Epstein's contribution is very much in line with the other transpersonal approaches to psychotherapy presented in this chapter in that it seeks to use the pathways developed in psychotherapy to make the next leap into Being, expressed in Buddhist language as seeing the insubstantiality of the self on the way to no self or Buddha mind. However, by stating that these early wounds and feelings should not remain the object of therapeutic focus, Epstein does not show great faith in the healing power of the self and its capacities for arising from the ashes of childhood wounds with spontaneous new vitality and creativity. Teaching Buddhist meditation toward the end of therapy is an innovative suggestion. But if done prematurely it can become a subtle kind of spiritual by-passing which still leaves important psychological work undone. Nevertheless, it is an innovative step toward a synthesis of psychotherapy with spiritual practice. And while it is unclear what portion of therapy clients could make use of this strategy, it is very much in harmony with the transpersonal focus upon the necessity of connecting with Being for real transformation.

Temporal orientation. Psychoanalysis has long been criticized for its focus on the past. Freud was a puzzle solver, and he spent his life trying to figure out how the present was determined by the past. This temporal focus upon the past led him to conclude that there were far more reasons from the past than necessary in order to account for the present, hence his belief that the present was "overdetermined" by the past. Even Freud's concept of the present was overshadowed by the past, for to Freud the present meant the last few days. This may seem humorous in retrospect, as we now see the present as this precise moment in time, RIGHT NOW. The analytic insight that our present behavior is largely determined by our past experiences is by now taken for granted by all depth therapies, but the detailed examination of the past remains a defining element of psychoanalysis.

Meditative approaches, on the other hand, are a way of waking up from our preoccupation with the past and coming into the present moment. The detailed exploration of the here and now is the province of meditative practices. There would appear to be a rather severe contradiction between these two views, except that contemporary psychoanalysis has undergone considerable change with regard to time. Self psychology, contemporary object relations, the influence of Merton Gill in working with the transference, and current intersubjective approaches all have a much more present-centered focus. The transference, which even from the beginning of psychoanalysis had been one place where the here and now was explored, has currently assumed an even more central role in psychoanalysis. And working with the transference has become a process of paying extraordinary attention to the details of the here and now communications between therapist and client. It can almost be seen as a kind of interpersonal meditation. A transpersonal orientation supports this movement into the present moment and highlights the many ways in which both therapist and client are tempted to flee the immediacy and power of the present by going into the past.

Compassion. Psychoanalysts have never been accused of being an especially warm-hearted group. Traditionally, the usual expectation of walking into an analysts' office is that the temperature will drop about 10 degrees. Ever since Freud's initial admonitions to psychoanalysts that they should model themselves after a surgeon, psychoanalysts have been roundly criticized for being cold and detached. But recently there has been a warming trend in psychoanalysis. Led by Kohut, who criticized analysts from inside the psychoanalytic establishment for doing to patients exactly what led to their problems in the first place, a kinder, gentler approach to psychoanalysis has been gaining ground. Here again, Gill and the intersubjective schools further contributed to freeing the analyst to express more human warmth and spontaneity.

Spirituality brings an atmosphere of compassion and warmth to our relationships. A transpersonal orientation brings the perspective that more is going on for both therapist and patient. Both are seekers, co-journeyers on the spiritual path. In viewing the patient as not so entirely "other," a more heart-centered, compassionate atmosphere emerges naturally and spontaneously.

Strengths and Limitations of This Model

Strengths. 1. Bringing a transpersonal orientation to psychoanalysis moves it closer to existential and humanistic approaches to therapy. Psychoanalysis leaves out the body, but a transpersonal approach involves greater embodiment and thus entails more of a here and now, sensory and organismic perspective.

2. The synthesis of psychoanalysis and spirituality vastly expands the domains of each. Psychoanalysis has a detailed map of the self and its unconscious, and spirituality places this self in an immensely enlarged context. The framework for examining the wounds to the self, as well as the healing, growth, and transcendence of the self, increases.

Limitations. 1. Psychoanalysis is the most developed, elaborated, and sophisticated model of the self that Western psychology has produced. To bring a spiritual and transpersonal perspective to this orientation holds great promise for illuminating the human condition. However, as yet there has been no methodical attempt to do so. There are intriguing parallels and areas of convergence between psychoanalysis and spirituality, numerous similar conceptualizations about the nature of the self, but these are still two worlds that seem to exist in parallel universes. The systematic, careful integration of these two approaches to consciousness promises to be one of the most fascinating areas of development in the next decades.

2. The similarities between psychoanalysis and spirituality explored in this section are not the exclusive property of psychoanalysis. All depth therapies share the concerns listed above, although psychoanalysis has paved the way in certain instances.

BODY-CENTERED TRANSPERSONAL APPROACHES

The multiple body-centered approaches to working transpersonally share one thing in common: using the body as the doorway to the transpersonal. Here again there is as yet no formal, systematic integration of the various body approaches. Instead there are a variety of body-oriented approaches to transpersonal psychotherapy. All of them use a similar strategy shared by the other clinical orientations discussed in this chapter, although the somatic approaches use very different techniques and methods to accomplish this strategy. The strategy employed by the various transpersonal psychotherapies is to access the transpersonal through the psychological work with the self. Each orientation uses different methods to do this. In somatic approaches entering deeply into the bodily consciousness is the pathway into a wider spiritual consciousness.

All somatic approaches trace their lineage to Wilhelm Reich, who laid the foundation for viewing the body as central to freeing up a person's emotional life. While Reich and many of the original offshoots were not particularly transpersonal, by now there are a number of body-centered approaches that integrate spirituality into bodywork. Some of these approaches include Hakomi, John Pierrakos' Core Energetics, Bodynamics, the Lomi school, Eva Reich's work, Jack Rosenburg's work, rebirthing, and, important to mention because of its great influence even though it is not a psychotherapy, Charlotte Selver's sensory awareness.

Each of these body-centered therapies have different ways of working, but they have a number of things in common. They all share the assumption that becoming present in the body is the key to becoming present both emotionally and spiritually. Since feeling is rooted in bodily life, bringing awareness to the body will awaken the sensations and the emotional energy of the person. Greater physical-emotional awareness results in greater presence, for as awareness of the body and feelings expands, so does awareness of the whole self, including the mind and mental images. Awakening bodily life thus becomes the road into the larger domain of consciousness. There are three major strategies employed to bring this about: bodywork, the use of breath, and sensory awareness or mindfulness.

Bodywork. Reich's enduring legacy to psychotherapy was the twin insight that feeling is embedded in the body and that the repression of feeling is a *psycho-physical* phenomenon, not just a psychological process as Freud believed. To deal with the emotional pain of early childhood wounding, and in the absence of being able to experience it in an atmosphere of empathic support, children originally manage this pain by deadening it through holding their breath and tightening their musculature. This at least provides temporary relief. After years of this, these muscular patterns of contraction become chronic, habitual, and unconscious. These holding patterns also determine how development occurs and how experience is organized somatically. The result is a deep-rooted deadening of feeling, a stifling of breathing patterns, and a diminishing of the person's life energy.

Bodywork, from Reich onwards, aims at working through the chronic patterns of muscular tension that Reich called the body armor. By loosening the ingrained contracted musculature, the person's feeling capacities and vital energy are restored, splits are healed, and the sense of self is enlarged. More recent approaches, however, look at restoring the arrested developmental pathways and bringing about a more natural organization of experience. Approaches differ on how to best do this. Some involve direct manipulation of the muscles, some do it through stress exercises, others rely on breath or simply attention. But they all share a focus on bodily aliveness and feeling. As the feeling life is restored in the body, greater aliveness and presence result. Ego dissolution involves release from body contraction.

Breathwork. Working with the breath is a main focus in body approaches. The breath is seen as a key connector between the conscious and the unconscious, so attention to both voluntary and involuntary breathing is important. Times when the person is holding the breath show that feeling is being inhibited. And deep breathing for extended periods of time is one way to increase the energy in the person's system. It is interesting that both somatic approaches and many spiritual traditions make use of the breath. *Modifying the breathing pattern* and *breath awareness* are two methods both traditions employ.

While *modifying the breathing pattern* is something both traditions share, they tend to move in opposite directions with it. In almost all yogic *pranayama* techniques, for instance, the breath is slowed down, made very even and steady. This is to quiet the mind and heart, to enhance stillness and a deepening consciousness within. Somatic therapies, on the other hand, tend to increase the breathing, to speed up the breath in order to arouse and bring to the surface buried feelings and impulses. This can result in unconscious feelings emerging into awareness or simply an enhanced sense of what is currently being felt, which assists the working-through process. In approaches such as rebirthing or holotropic breathwork, the emergence of highly charged emotional material may catapult the person into transpersonal and altered states of consciousness. The goals are different—stilling and bringing peace to the mind and heart versus stimulating and activating mind and heart. The methods are different—slowing the breath versus increasing the breath. But both use breathing as a way to deepen internal experience and as an avenue to the transpersonal.

Breath awareness is simply bringing attention to the process of breathing. Increasingly in somatic approaches, creating basic awareness of the breath, without modifying the breath, is employed to enhance a client's self-awareness. Similarly, meditation on the breath is a practice that occurs in Buddhist, Hindu, Sufi, Christian, and Jewish traditions (Kornfield, 1993b). There are even meditative traditions, explicated in Buddhist texts such as the *Satipatana*, that view breathing and body awareness as a path to liberation. Meditation upon the breath is designed not to increase or change the breathing pattern but to refine perception of it as it moves in and out the body. The nature of the breath and the body's sensations is impermanence. The awareness of the rising and passing away of the myriad body sensations dissolves the illusion of solidity and permanence, leading to wisdom (Kahn, 1985). Here again the goals are different, but the methods are similar.

Sensory awareness/mindfulness. The area of awareness and mindfulness is certainly a major overlap into the transpersonal. The pioneer in this approach is Charlotte Selver, who for most of this century has been exploring how to open the senses as a path to greater aliveness and spiritual awareness. Her work, which was so influential in the development of gestalt therapy and the human potential movement, has been described as "the essence of Zen" by Alan Watts. Hakomi is another somatic therapy that makes use of mindfulness as one of its central tenets, directly borrowing this from Buddhist meditation practice and applying it to bringing greater attention to the client's lived bodily experience.

Another approach to body awareness is focusing. Developed by Eugene Gendlin (1981, 1996), focusing brings awareness of the bodily felt sense into sharp relief. Very much in the tradition of Reich's and the existentialists' distrust of the mind and verbal approaches that may stay intellectual, focusing uses the awareness of the bodily felt sense to access the body's wisdom of emotional life. It is noteworthy that it has been adapted by transpersonal therapists working both in theistic-relational traditions (e.g., Campbell & McMahon [1985], two Catholic priests) and in non-dual traditions (e.g., Welwood [1980], from the Buddhist tradition). Both traditions insist that one obstacle to spiritual development is the mind, and one way of getting out of the head is by tuning in to the body. Focusing can be a powerful way of accessing feelings by tuning directly into the "edge" of emotional-somatic experience.

The body-centered approaches collectively ask the question: how can we go beyond what we don't engage in? Bringing awareness or mindfulness to bodily experience is the first step in becoming present, in grounding the person in his or her somatic reality. The body is the entry point to presence. As presence deepens and the sensitivity to perception refines, there is an opening into the transpersonal, a movement beyond the self into the immensities of sensory wonder and spiritual awe.

Strengths and Limitations of This Model

Strengths. 1. The movement into spirit can easily leave the body behind. Transcendence is often equated with transcending the body. What the body-centered approaches remind us of is the importance of grounding spiritual life in its material base. An embodied spirituality is the goal here, not a disembodied transcendence. Body-centered approaches use bodily experience as the entry into emotional healing. Consciousness may then expand into the spiritual realm while retaining its connection with the earth and physical life.

2. Awakening the senses leads into a greater appreciation of here and now experience, and as the senses open more fully, awareness of feeling ensues spontaneously.

3. The body can be seen as a tangible expression of personality structure and may offer a reliable litmus test for a client's state of mind.

4. Insight must be "translated" by the body for a full working through. As humanistic psychology has pointed out, the greater the organismic involvement (the greater the consciousness), the greater the working through.

Limitations. 1. Interesting parallels can be drawn between the evolution of somatic approaches and the thinking in psychoanalysis. Just as contemporary psychoanalysis has moved beyond Freud's drive-discharge models of the psyche to focus more on how the self and object world (interpersonal world) are organized by the self or psyche, so somatic psychotherapy has moved from Reich's embodied drive-discharge, cathartic approaches to seeing how experience is organized somatically. However, it does not appear that the focus in contemporary psychoanalysis on the depth and complexy of the intersubjective field can be adequately captured purely in terms of somatic processes or muscular patterns.

2. Body-based models have been criticized for being reductionistic, equating emotional life, the self, and its defenses to muscular patterns and somatic processes. The human being, the self, cannot be fully explained by or reduced to animal or biological functions. This is in the very opposite direction to which spiritual experience points.

CONCLUSION

With the exception of Wilber's theoretical model, all of the clinical approaches presented in this chapter represent different psychotherapeutically based *strategies for accessing spiritual Being*. The great leap forward in healing and growth that transpersonal psychotherapy represents can be typified by this underlying commonality. Accessing the transformative power of Being is the key to full resolution of the psychological difficulties which perplex and confound human existence.

Clearly there is a great deal of healing and growth that is possible within the purely psychological context of the self. But as long as we remain tied in to the psychological structures of the self, identified only with this surface manifestation of identity, there is no end to psychological pain, healing, and finite, egoic existence. Only in going beyond the structures of egoic existence can there be an opening into greater Being and a transformation of the nature and structure of psychic life, the awakening to a greater identity.

Each person can enter the interior depths of Being more easily in some ways than others. Each of these therapeutic models uses specific pathways, pathways which will work for some people but not others. Jungian therapy and psychosynthesis enter Being via the imaginal realm, which is good for some people but not others (or perhaps even most). Body-centered approaches use the body for entering deep within to contact Being, which is good for some people but not others (or perhaps even most). The diamond approach enters via the person's object relations and a deepening experiencing of presence; psychoanalytic approaches enter through the archaic configurations of self and other, and existential approaches enter through organismic experiencing, all of which are good for some people but not others (or perhaps even most). Grof's work uses altered states of consciousness to access Being, which also is right for some people but not others (or perhaps even most).

These are the pioneering approaches that have been developed thus far. Transpersonal psychotherapy may make use of any of these more systematized approaches or may be a more eclectic blend. Although much has been discovered, it is clear that there is still very much to do and that the field of transpersonal psychotherapy is still in its beginnings.

Part 3

Clinical Issues

Chapter Five

Meditation and Psychotherapy

What is the relationship between meditation and psychotherapy? In what ways can meditation practice help or hinder psychological growth? Are some meditation practices especially indicated or contraindicated for certain personality structures? How can psychology illuminate why some meditation practices are less effective than others? What are the essential actions of meditation on consciousness? Can a combination of meditation and psychotherapy make either or both more effective?

Although the initial enthusiasm and hope that meditation could become an effective psychotherapeutic approach in itself, maybe even replacing the various approaches of Western psychotherapy, have by now largely dissipated (Russell, 1986), the convergences and divergences of meditation and psychotherapy are areas that continue to generate much excitement. Any discussion on these topics, however, must be prefaced with the acknowledgment that we are still at the very beginning of even formulating our questions, let alone answering them, in this quest to understand how these two approaches to human consciousness, the psychological and spiritual, are similar, complementary, and/or entirely separate.

While there have been many approaches to this area, it is possible to discern two major thrusts of investigation, both of which have contributed much to our understanding of meditation and the psyche. The first approach has seen meditation as a self-regulation strategy to produce relaxation; the second has viewed all meditation practice through the lens of Buddhism. A brief review of each is in order before moving on to a discussion from the perspective of the perennial philosophy.

The view that meditation is in essence a kind of "relaxation response," virtually identical with other kinds of relaxation techniques, such as autogenic training, hypnosis, or progressive relaxation, was a perspective that was in vogue in the 1970s, generated a good deal of research efforts (for example, see Wallace, 1970; Allison, 1971; Banquet, 1973; Glueck, 1975; Michaels, Huber, McCann, 1976), and achieved its most popular articulation in Benson's book *The Relaxation Response* (Benson, 1975).

It is understandable that Western science's first research into meditation would be at the most outward, visible, and measurable level of body and behavior. That marked physiological changes could indeed occur as a result of "just sitting" was in itself quite surprising to many Western scientists, although it was simply a confirmation of what has been claimed for thousands of years by meditation teachers from many traditions.

To summarize this research, some of the verified physical changes include: reduced muscular tension; slowed metabolic and heart rate; lowered blood pressure (over time); changes in blood chemistry and hormone levels; and EEG patterns consistent with relaxation. The therapeutic benefits attributed to this relaxation response are both psychological and physical. Psychological changes range from lowered stress and anxiety, to improvements in post-traumatic stress, mild depression, phobias, and insomnia. Physical health improvements include help with cancer treatment, reduced blood pressure and cholesterol levels; and lessened severity of asthma, migraine, and chronic pain (Walsh, in Walsh & Vaughn 1993; Murphy and Donovan, 1985).

However, most of this research has used only one particular type of meditation, TM or transcendental meditation, a form of *mantra* meditation. While this research has served to demystify and make more accessible to a wide public this one particular kind of meditation, there are a number of problems with this research, only two of which will be discussed here.

One problem is that it lumps all meditation practices together. But it is clear by now that *mantra* meditation is only one form of meditation among many. Although physiological relaxation very often accompanies *mantra* and other forms of meditation practice, there are some meditation practices that can evoke highly stimulating responses involving states of physiological arousal, and still others that are more neutral with regard to physical responsiveness. Lumping all meditation practices together into a single homogenous phenomenon was an overgeneralization—a mistake that was easy to make 20 years ago, but is no longer tenable today. Meditation practices come in many forms with widely differing effects on consciousness and on the body.

A second problem with this research is that focusing on physical relaxation ignores the subjective state of consciousness the person is experiencing, which varies greatly. Any outer, physiological measure of the body can offer only very limited implications about the inner experience of consciousness. As Walsh (1993 p. 66) has wryly observed, "More attention has been given to heart rate than heart opening." For a fuller critique of this research, see Bogart (1991).

The other major approach to meditation inquiry comes from perceiving all meditation practice through the lens of Buddhism. Goleman (1988), Kornfield (1993a), and others have espoused this position, and it has received widespread, though uncritical, acceptance within the field. To summarize this position, all meditation practices are viewed either as a form of concentration (awareness narrowing) or as a form of awareness expansion (mindfulness or insight).

This is an extremely valuable and powerful viewpoint that simplifies a very complex field in which there are hundreds of diverse meditation practices. In Buddhist thought the ground of the psyche is awareness. With its focus on mind, it sees all meditation practices as either opening up or closing down awareness. It also fits in nicely with a psychoanalytic way of viewing psychotherapeutic interventions as either "covering" or "uncovering" the emergence of unconscious material (Blanck and Blanck, 1974), and thus forms a good bridge between meditation and psychotherapy.

However, as important as this perspective has been as a way of organizing this field, it also has its limitations. The two greatest limitations are, first, trying to explain more phenomena by the word "concentration" than can be covered by this word, and second, because of its nondual worldview, ignoring all other aspects of consciousness which other spiritual teachings describe. Each of these require further unpacking.

To begin with, it is unclear which are concentration practices and which are awareness practices. Goleman (1988) places *bhakti* (devotion) practices and prayer in the category of concentration, whereas Kornfield (1993a) places bhakti in the category of awareness practices, and Washburn (1988) believes that while some prayer should be classified as concentration practice, other kinds should not be. This confusion arises because the word "concentration" is being stretched to describe far more psychological phenomena than can be accommodated by this term.

In the Buddhist view the inward effects of concentrating on the breath, or the serenity that comes from the repetition of a *mantra*, or the God-intoxicated ecstasy of divine love experienced by the *bhakta*, or opening to new depths of inner consciousness of the soul with its power, joy, peace are all seen as simply varieties of concentration. The vast phenomenological differences of these states are ignored, and they are lumped together into a single category. However, from the perspective of the perennial philosophy, the term concentration is wholly inadequate to describe the wide variety of consciousness changes that result from these practices, which raises the second major limitation to this approach.

Buddhism explicates the nondual world of the Impersonal Divine superlatively well, but it entirely ignores the theistic-relational dimension of the Personal Divine. Although both Personal and Impersonal aspects can be found in most religious traditions, Buddhism is an exception to this. Buddhism firmly maintains that there is no soul and that reality is impersonal and nondual in nature.

From the perspective of the perennial philosophy, the Buddhist perspective of meditation practice, though a useful one, is nevertheless limited. In its preoccupation with mindfulness, it misses the various soul aspects and manifestations of spiritual consciousness and *being* which most of the world's other spiritual disciplines have explored. But since from a Buddhist perspective there is only mindfulness, this issue can only be raised from a position outside of the Buddhist worldview.

It is necessary to have a way of organizing this field that honors all dimensions of spiritual experience that the world's perennial traditions have discovered and that does not try to fit experiences into categories that are too narrow to hold them. In this it is important to consider the goals of the meditation practice, the common factors underlying the techniques used, and the effects on consciousness that are produced. And in keeping with a phenomenological approach, it is desirable to keep any categories as "experience-near" as possible, rather than "experience-distant" and at too high a level of abstraction, a problem with some classification models (e.g., Naranjo [1990] or Rowan [1993]).

It is possible to distill five major psycho-spiritual practices that are utilized in both spirit and soul paths.

Meditation Practices

SPIRIT PATHS
  Mindfulness techniques

SOUL PATHS
  Devotion - *Bhakti* - Surrender - Prayer practices

SPIRIT PATHS AND SOUL PATHS
  Evocative practices
  Suppressive practices
  Concentration-building practices

It is also important to keep in mind that in any classificatory scheme, the differences are more clear verbally and conceptually than actually. Even with the mindfulness/concentration distinction, both functions interpenetrate. As Suler (1993 p. 122) notes, "The attempt to dichotomize into categories will eventually uncover an intertwining of the dichotomies that confuses the categories." All aspects of consciousness imply one another as they interact, combine, and fuse together to create the whole. Thus any way of classifying is necessarily suggestive rather than definitive. The holographic nature of consciousness makes any sharply delineated distinctions more apparent than real.

SPIRIT PATHS—IMPERSONAL DIVINE

Mindfulness Practices

Although the term "mindfulness" is specifically Buddhist, I am using it here to cover a broad class of very similar meditation practices that have received their greatest refinement from the nondual spiritual traditions. This practice appears throughout the many strands of the Buddhist tradition—in Tibetan Buddhism (mindfulness), in Theravada Buddhism (bare attention or *vipassana*), in Zen Buddhism (*zazen*). Although a different vocabulary is used in the Hindu traditions to describe this process, and these meditation practices are therefore usually misclassified as concentration techniques, there is an essential similarity between them and Buddhist mindfulness practices. In the Samkya tradition it appears as the process of separating the witness *purusha* from the nature *prakriti*. It is taken up in this form in Sri Aurobindo's integral yoga as the witnessing or detached observer meditation. In the Advaita tradition it is discriminative awareness, wherein the *atman* (the eternal) is discriminated from all that is not *atman* (not eternal.) Nisargadatta Maharaj's looking for who seeks and Ramana Maharshi's self-inquiry meditation of progressive disidentifiication and searching for the source can be seen as variants of this process. Gurdjieff refers to this as self-remembering. Krishnamurti popularized this approach in the West with his "non-method" of choiceless awareness. This also appears in Christian practice (Washburn, 1994) but is not so fully developed in the theistic-relational traditions.

In all of these traditions a similar practice has evolved: attending to awareness itself, to whatever the contents of awareness are, not clutching at or judging what we see, feel, think, sense, but simply witnessing it all as it emerges into consciousness and then passes away. Like observing a cloud pass in the sky, the seeker is directed to observe in a detached way everything that comes up, without identifying with it or holding onto it. The idea throughout is to detach from our normal complete identification with the contents of awareness and to discriminate or have insight into the process of awareness itself.

The result of this practice is a much greater present-centeredness, a coming into the *now* as consciousness begins to open up. Another result is greater clarity and greater equanimity. We begin to settle down into ourselves. The mind becomes less noisy, more quiet. We feel more awake. And a certain spaciousness begins to open up, a certain depth. As we stay with this, perception becomes more and more acute, more and more in the present, more and more refined. Ultimately, this refinement in awareness leads to the perception that the self itself is something that is put together moment to moment through a series of very rapid images that seem to flicker by so quickly that there is the experience of a continuous self, just as the rapid flickering of still pictures in a movie gives us the experience of continuous movement. The goal is to pierce through that illusion, to see that there are spaces between those images, and that in reality there is no stable enduring self. It is this deeply experienced insight that liberates.

There has been a good deal of interest in this meditation practice in transpersonal psychology over the past 20 years because it seemed initially that enhancing awareness was exactly what psychotherapy tried to do (in Freud's words, "to make the unconscious conscious"). For awhile, there were many who believed that this meditation practice would obviate the need for psychotherapy, since it went deeper and seemed to accomplish more efficiently what psychotherapy attempted. However, in recent years there has been a growing consensus that although meditation and psychotherapy both work with awareness, they work with awareness in different ways. Not mutually exclusive ways, for some of the ways they work with awareness overlap, but ways that are different enough that there are increasingly few people who still believe that meditation alone can allow a person to dispense with psychotherapeutic work or vice versa.

The similarities between these forms of meditation and psychotherapy are readily apparent. These meditation practices and psychotherapy both result in a greater feeling of being centered into one's depths, a sense of generally being more peaceful and less agitated, and most centrally, a fuller awakening to the here and now. This opening up into the present moment is one of the key areas of intersection between psychotherapy and meditation. It may be expressed in the humanistic-existential language of completing unfinished business, growing up, trying on new behaviors, and relinquishing the outmoded, habitual patterns from the past. Or it may be expressed in the language of self psychology and object relations of resuming thwarted developmental strivings so that the archaic configurations of the self and object may develop into more mature forms. These amount to the same thing: less preoccupation with the past (old wounds, developmental deficits) and a greater vitality and openness to the present on every level—mental, emotional, and physical/sensory. Psychotherapy does this by working with the content of awareness (i. e., the self); meditation does this by being less concerned with the particular content and by attending to awareness itself.

The differences between the approaches of meditation and psychotherapy to awareness center on the quality of engagement with the contents of consciousness. More specifically, meditation and psychotherapy each involve a different degree of identification with psychological content. For example, in these mindfulness practices, the person does not hold onto any particular content that emerges. The observer learns to disidentify with whatever content comes up. We observe it arising and passing away. And the more we observe, the more it begins to slow down, the more deeply we can see into that process (Bowman, 1987). Psychotherapy, on the other hand, is a process of actively identifying with, holding onto, and engaging the emerging material in an attempt to understand its meaning. Whatever comes up is the fertilizer for psychological growth, as we work it into the soil of our psyche, turning it over and over, working it from this side and that, as the working through process unfolds. By grappling with it (whether "it" is feelings, old wounds, images) and identifying with it fully, feeling and experiencing what it is about and connected to within us, we work through and heal a disowned aspect of ourselves on a journey toward increasing wholeness.

It is clear that we engage the material very differently in these two approaches. In psychotherapy we identify with it fully, grasp it firmly and dig into it. Whereas in meditation we try to hold it more loosely, to disidentify with it, and let it pass away.

Another difference is that in meditation, feelings are seen as nothing special (Welwood, 1980), simply part of the "stuff" of consciousness, like thoughts, images, and sensory data. In psychotherapy, however, feelings are the coin of the realm. Indeed, psychology is moving more and more into the explicit acknowledgment that affects and affect regulation are at the heart of psychological life and therefore at the center of psychotherapy (Basch, 1988; Stolorow, et al., 1987; Tomkins, 1962, 1963, 1991; Nathanson, 1992). Meditation and psychotherapy place very different value on the particular contents of consciousness, particularly with reference to feelings.

Three other areas are significant in exploring differences in these two approaches. One pertains to the interpersonal situation in which they occur. Meditation, although it is often learned in a class or from a teacher, is in essence something done alone. It is only in journeying to the depths of one's aloneness that the illusion of being a separate self is pierced. Psychotherapy, in contrast, occurs in an interpersonal field or system, that is, a dyad or group (Bowman, 1987). Most current therapeutic approaches acknowledge that the very self which is attempting to heal and grow does so only in relationship to others. Family systems, self psychology, object relations, gestalt—every depth therapy stresses the importance of the early relational matrix in which the self developed (or failed to develop) and notes the special significance of the intersubjective field of the therapy relationship itself for psychotherapy's effectiveness (by stressing either the transference or the "new" aspects of this relationship). Meditation occurs alone; psychotherapy occurs in relationship.

The second difference relates to language. Meditation is ultimately a nonverbal experience, even though there is usually a protracted encounter with one's verbal, thinking mind. Depending on the school, psychotherapy places differing emphases on the importance of nonverbal experience but consistently places a high value on verbal expression and speaking one's truth. Articulation of internal experience is seen as an essential ingredient in integrating and structuralizing our progressively unfolding self experience (Stolorow, et al., 1987). Meditation is nonverbal; psychotherapy is verbal.

The third difference relates to the goal of meditation and psychotherapy. In psychotherapy, life enhancement occurs through the growth, development, and healing of the self. But in these meditation practices, life enhancement occurs through the elimination of the self. At first glance they appear to head in opposite directions, but much of transpersonal psychology can be seen as an attempt to realign these seemingly irreconcilable directions. a common belief in transpersonal psychology is that as the self is integrated, firmed, strengthened, made more resilient, new vistas of transpersonal development become more accessible. However, along the way, psychotherapy and meditation give very different values to the self and its experience in light of their different goals.

From this discussion, the following Venn diagram can be generated illustrating the similarities and differences in how mindfulness
meditation and psychotherapy work with awareness.

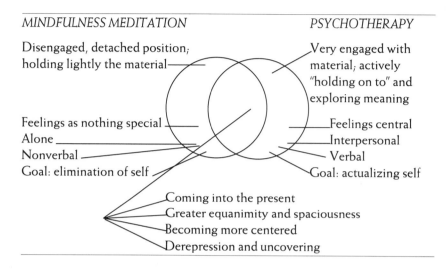

MINDFULNESS MEDITATION   *PSYCHOTHERAPY*

Disengaged, detached position;   Very engaged with
holding lightly the material   material; actively
                                                  "holding on to" and
                                                  exploring meaning

Feelings as nothing special   Feelings central
Alone   Interpersonal
Nonverbal   Verbal
Goal: elimination of self   Goal: actualizing self

Coming into the present
Greater equanimity and spaciousness
Becoming more centered
Derepression and uncovering

The psychotherapeutic effects of these mindfulness meditation
practices include very clear advantages and potential (though in practice probably universal) disadvantages. The benefits are several. The
most obvious convergence between meditation and psychotherapy lies
in the expansion of awareness as a major goal. As Blanck and Blanck
(1974) have written, therapy techniques can be classified into "covering" techniques (those that bolster defenses) or "uncovering" techniques
(those that lower defenses). Mindfulness meditation practices can be
viewed as a form of "uncovering" techniques as well (Engler, 1986). This
"uncovering" is clearly an important help to the therapeutic enterprise.

Additionally, as we sit and mindfully observe whatever arises in
our consciousness, our ability to be with our inner experience increases.
There is an expansion of our capacity to attend to our inner world, to
take the inner journey and identify thoughts, feelings, images, sensations, and felt senses that previously would have escaped our attention.
Indeed, I have noticed with many of my clients who have been long-
term Buddhist practitioners that they bring a highly developed ability
to observe, identify, and verbalize their inner experience. They have
well-developed attentional skills that allow them to stay with their

material to a degree that is unusual in beginning clients. The importance of this capacity for depth psychotherapy can hardly be overestimated.

However, this capacity also brings with it some dangers, dangers which are theoretically avoidable, but which in practice few seem to escape. Engler (1986) has suggested that until the self has attained a certain degree of development and integration, uncovering techniques such as mindfulness meditation can be destabilizing, for example with borderlines. For this reason he believes these meditation practices are contraindicated with such clients.

For the vast majority of normal neurotics, however, the possible negative consequences tend to be less dramatic. For many people I have worked with, mindfulness meditation practices appear to encourage a mental detachment, contrary to their intention. Mindfulness practices, although designed to bring awareness to the inner world, can paradoxically be a subtle way to avoid emotional and psychological issues. The result is a disavowal or dissociation rather than true detachment. Part of this may stem from the differing goals of psychotherapy and meditation. Meditation tries not to engage the emotional/psychological level in order to pierce the very illusion of selfhood, whereas for psychotherapy, this emotional/psychological self is precisely where the action is. The overall consequence is that there can be a tendency for the meditation practitioner to be clear but cool, a bit too "mind-y."

Related to this is the second major risk of mindfulness meditation, which is that in actual practice there is a very thin line between pure witnessing and superego judging. Again, contrary to all the meditation instructions to not judge or condemn, the seemingly irresistible tendency of the normal neurotic meditator is for the superego critic to blend unnoticeably into the pure witness. As a result, after years of practicing meditation without therapy, many meditators have created a whole new set of spiritual or "mindfulness shoulds" that result in repression, denial, suppression, and internal criticism every bit as harsh as when meditation practice was begun. I have seen this in every long-term meditator I have worked with, including myself. This downside effect of meditation needs much further attention (perhaps even its own clinical subspecialty).

The third major limitation is that even when a person does reach a very advanced level of perception—a state of great clarity, equanimity, present-centeredness, and awareness where there is a good deal of freedom from the normal, narrow grooves of fettered perception—it is incredibly difficult to live at this level of mind subtlety. Pretty soon most meditators come back down into their everyday personality and "ego stuff," and they find themselves as angry, as frustrated, and as unevolved as ever. The ability to "transcend" the egoic realm and live continuously in the pure air of spirit is not a statistically likely outcome. The psychological problems of life, for the majority of people, must also be dealt with at the psychological level.

Spiritual practice does not have the theoretically developed map or the therapeutic tools for working with the psychological level that psychotherapy has. Many a client of mine has complained that even after a two-year meditation retreat, while they were able to observe with exquisite attention their childhood wounds, their early traumas, et cetera, none of it ever went anywhere. They kept watching it repeat over and over again. The meditation teacher did not know how to work with this material except to say observe it or occasionally to suggest reading a particular psychology book. Only in psychotherapy were these individuals able to work through and transform these early wounds, and doing so ultimately proved to be a great aid to them, not only in their life and relationships but in their meditation practice as well.

This is an area that is fertile for further investigation. Most writing has stressed how meditation can help psychotherapy, but psychotherapy's help to meditation practice may prove to be one of the most significant contributions that Western psychology has to make to spiritual practice in the future.

SOUL PATHS—PERSONAL DIVINE

Bhakti, Devotion, Surrender, Prayer Practices

In the soul path tradition of the Personal Divine, God is seen not only as a vast impersonal consciousness pervading all existence, but as a supreme Divine Being or Presence as well. The goal in this tradition is to develop an inner, personal relationship with this Divine Presence. As mentioned in chapter 2, this Divine Presence can be experienced either without form or it may be conceived of or imaged in any of a great number of forms (e.g., the Divine Mother, the Divine Father, Christ, Krishna, Tara, etc.). This Divine Presence may be seen as within the aspirant (where the individual soul is a portion or spark of the Divine), or there may be the perception of the total otherness of the Divine without (as in Judaism), or both of these perceptions may be held simultaneously.

The goal is to connect more deeply to the inner soul and to the Divine. An inward focus on prayer, call, surrender, aspiration, faith, opening to the Divine, devotion, *bhakti*, love—these are the godward movements that bring the seeker into deeper connection with the inner soul and which call on the Divine to manifest in a communion with the soul.

The phenomenological experience of the soul path traditions contains enormous variations, but it is marked by an increasing relationship with and connection to the Divine and to one's soul, experienced variously as a descent, deepening, opening, or ascent into love, consciousness, love, power or force, purity, peace, and joy. As the opening or deepening occurs, it is generally experienced as connecting to one's true identity. Any or all of these soul qualities may manifest. The infusion of these qualities into oneself has a transforming effect on one's outer, surface being, an effect which has cognitive, emotional, and physical results, often characterized by a reorientation toward life and toward the Divine. Christian, Islamic, and Jewish prayer, and Hindu practices such as *Krishna-bhakti*, are all designed to connect the person to the Divine, to the soul level, and to bring these soul qualities increasingly into the outer, surface being.

It is important to note that although *bhakti* or devotion meditation practices are the major practices in theistic-relational traditions, they also occur in nondual traditions, where they are considered preliminary or purificatory practices. Dzogchen in the Tibetan contains devotional, heart-centered practices, as does Mahayana Buddhism. Advaita Vedanta also includes these practices as part of a sequence of development and purification. Just as mindfulness practices achieve their highest expression in the nondual traditions, even though they exist in the theistic-relational paths, so *bhakti* practices achieve their highest expression in the theistic-relational traditions, even though they are also present in nondual paths.

How then are these meditation practices relevant to psychotherapy? That is, how does the development of consciousness from the soul path traditions interface with the development of consciousness from a psychological direction? Although the phenomenological effects of "soul emergence" are often experienced as a global process, the primary psychological effects may be broken down into the development of presence, love, joy, peace, and empathy, and the diminishing of fear. Each of these deserve further elaboration.

The increasing connection to one's soul is often experienced as a deepening or a widening of one's identity not into an insubstantial void but into a powerful, very substantial sense of presence. This sense of presence is felt as supporting one, indeed being the very core of oneself, yet at the same time encompassing and vastly surpassing one's outer, surface self, which by contrast is experienced as shaky, flimsy, almost empty. Whatever sense of substantiality or presence one has is seen to derive from this deeper, spiritual source. To feel grounded in this sense of solidity becomes a source of psychological well-being and a source of strength in the face of life's circumstances. Although the means differ, feeling more present, more "there" and grounded in the depths of one's being, is also a goal of psychotherapy. In psychotherapy, it is accomplished through working with and integrating the psychological fragments; in the soul path practices, it is accomplished by looking deep within to connect with the ultimately spiritual source of psychological experience, of which most people are at present unconscious.

Opening to an inner source of love and compassion is a second major consequence of the soul path practices. In some traditions, the soul itself is seated in the heart (consider, for example, the many pictures of Christ pointing to his own open heart). To take the spatial metaphor a step further, the discovery of the soul is preceded by the opening of the heart chakra (fourth chakra), which opens the person to an infinite source of love, compassion, *bhakti*, devotion. Coming upon an inner source of love and compassion is also self-evidently helpful in growth and personal development. If we take seriously Freud's famous dictum of mental health as "the ability to work and to love," then increasing our capacity to experience love within us will be of great help in enhancing psychological health.

However, how fully and with what completeness this inner opening manifests in the outer personality varies a great deal. For while the person may initially feel transformed by this experience, most often the outer self remains in its habitual patterns or is only partially touched by this opening. It is from this partial surface mixture that there can come one of the many possible drawbacks to this practice, which will be considered shortly.

A third effect of soul meditation practices is connecting to a source of inner joy and happiness. The sense of joy is a quality that is self-existent, independent of outer circumstances. This joy also brings with it a deep sense of peace (in the Biblical phrase, "the peace that passeth all understanding"). Along with the obviously psychotherapeutic effects of joy and peace comes the by-product of the reduction of fear and anxiety. There are few qualities that are more desirable in mental health than these. To be liberated, even a little bit, from the constricting effects of fear and anxiety is a great boon to anyone. Phenomenologically, it is not that fear disappears, but that as a deep sense of peace emerges from within and the person's inner being opens, fear becomes more a surface movement, less powerful and constraining. Since fear and anxiety are behind most of our psychological resistances and defensive maneuvers, reducing fear can open up the potentials of the self. Self-actualizing is optimized in freedom, and fear is the negation of freedom.

Empathy enhancement is the other major psychotherapeutic by-product of this type of meditation practice. By connecting to the depths of our own being, we can feel an intuitive connection to all other beings and nature. There is a spontaneous empathy for others, an ability to grasp the experience of those around us more deeply. As the current focus on the importance of empathy and empathic values in fields as diverse as child development, therapy, and ecological awareness shows, this is a quality that is much needed at this time to heal the fragmentation of our culture and planet.

The practices in this tradition have an effect on consciousness which descriptions such as refinement, connecting to Divine essence, emergence of soul force, purification, and spiritual transformation begin to suggest. Derepression happens in soul path meditation practices also. Viewing devotion/surrender practices as merely forms of concentration or as "covering" techniques is inaccurate and misses the dynamic action these practices have on the psyche.

From this discussion another Venn diagram can be generated, illustrating the similarities between and differences in how devotion/surrender meditation practices and psychotherapy affect consciousness.

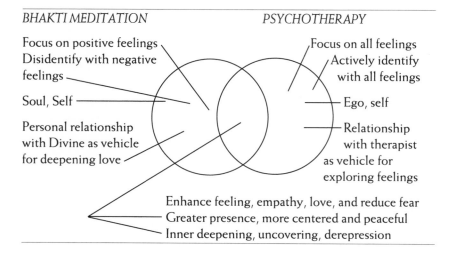

BHAKTI MEDITATION

Focus on positive feelings
Disidentify with negative
feelings

Soul, Self

Personal relationship
with Divine as vehicle
for deepening love

PSYCHOTHERAPY

Focus on all feelings
Actively identify
with all feelings

Ego, self

Relationship
with therapist
as vehicle for
exploring feelings

Enhance feeling, empathy, love, and reduce fear
Greater presence, more centered and peaceful
Inner deepening, uncovering, derepression

The soul path traditions have their psychotherapeutic pitfalls as well. The first is the danger of the person's movement of aspiration being captured by the superego. Just as witnessing can easily get turned into superego judging, so aspiration for the Divine, for love, or for peace can easily (and almost inevitable does somewhere along the line) get turned into desire, demand, new spiritual "shoulds" that the superego uses in the service of repression in the attempt to live up to an ideal image. For example, the aspiration for love, in itself a pure aspiration of the soul, can subtly and easily turn into a meditatively enforced focus on positive feelings and an inner demand to be an all good, loving person, characterized by the stereotype of a Christian pastor—the image of a very nice, sweet person who seems to have little or no shadow side and often lacks passion. The superego creates spiritual shoulds that fortify the old repressive aspects of the psyche, keeping down the "negative" affects and only allowing the positive emotions expression, suppressing emotional vitality and authenticity in the process.

Given the psychological structure of most of us in Western culture (and perhaps the world), this inner conflict between our ego and superego organizes how we relate to everything in our life, including how we relate to our spiritual path. There is probably no psychological pitfall so pervasive or so pernicious as this, and there appear to be very few individuals who are so clear as to avoid this altogether. It seems practically inevitable that our psychological conflicts and distortions will wrap themselves around our spiritual aspirations and twist them into a new version of our old patterns. Indeed, any practice in which there is an aspiration for a "higher," "clearer," or in some sense "better" state of consciousness (and is not all spiritual practice founded on some such aspiration?) leads to an almost automatic creation of an ideal and thus a new should. Except for a few rare spiritual geniuses who seem to escape this, it generally feeds straight into the basic neurotic structure of the personality and reinforces it. It isn't that the practices are bad, rather it's how they are interpreted by the psychological character of the person.

Without working with this inner split, any meditative or spiritual practice will necessarily have limited effectiveness. Purely spiritual approaches such as meditation appear to have *some* effect on our neurotic twists, but they are usually insufficient to eradicate them. Psychotherapy provides a way of seeing and working with these distortions that can free up the potential spiritual growth that is now getting detoured into our psychological quagmires, otherwise known as "spiritual by-passing."

Another common pitfall of experiencing a deep heart opening is that this inner opening of heart energy may get translated by the person into either a syrupy, sentimental, overly mushy "loving," or else it becomes a merging, codependent way of relating in which the person loses appropriate boundaries in being carried away by the ecstasy of love (becoming "drunk on love"). These hazards have probably been witnessed by people who frequent New Age gatherings. They are also hazards that psychotherapy is in an excellent position to help remedy. Working with heart energy and with how it interacts with the psychological material of the person, how the person forms an image of a "loving person" and acts from that image, how the by-passing of self integration can predispose a person to a blurring or loss of boundaries and create confusion between spiritual union and interpersonal merger—these are issues that are both within the scope of transpersonal psychotherapy and frontier areas in this field that need more exploration.

Another potential risk in these practices comes when an inner source of energy, love, joy, or expansiveness is contacted and the self is flooded with these energies. There can be an exultation and ego-inflation, leading to the emergence of split-off grandiosity and an interpretation of these energies as proof of one's superior or "chosen"—even messianic—status. The eruption of repressed psychological material when the floodgates of the psyche are opened is a well-known phenomenon and accounts for much of the difficulty in spiritual emergence (Grof, 1989). It requires a certain degree of psychological balance and discernment to integrate these energies rather than have them captured and distorted by the surface self. Here again, psychotherapy can be helpful in effecting this integration.

Another possible difficulty is that connecting to a source of inner consciousness can provide an escape from outer life to an inner plane of self-absorption. That is, this meditative practice can work either (a) to open the person to an inner consciousness, a greater vulnerability which allows greater attention to psychological issues, psychic discrimination, an ability to be with inner experience, et cetera, or (b) to cause the person to avoid the psychological level by retreating to an inner consciousness, bolstering defenses, and fostering an inner fantasy life so that the person lives in an inner world which is part real, part imagination, dissociated from the psychological level. This is one difficulty which pastoral counseling and spiritual direction try to deal with and prevent (May, 1982).

PRACTICES SHARED BY SPIRIT AND SOUL PATHS

An area of meditation that spirit paths and soul paths share lies in the use of three major practices: evocative practices, suppressive practices, and concentration-building practices.

Evocative Practices

In these practices the idea is to evoke or awaken new states through the one-pointed absorption of consciousness in a particular direction. In a wide sense, all meditation practices are evocative in that they are designed to bring forth our spiritual nature, for example, mindfulness practices evoke spirit through awareness and *bhakti* practices evoke the soul through devotion and love. But in a narrower sense, which we will consider here, evocative practices have a more specific objective, namely to activate certain aspects of consciousness or to purify the consciousness so that it will be more receptive to soul or spirit. In these practices attention is absorbed by a spiritually significant object (e.g., nature), center of consciousness (e.g., a particular chakra), or symbol (e.g., a flower) in order to shift consciousness in the direction of the object. Thus absorption in nature may open consciousness to spiritual calm and beauty. Absorption in a particular chakra stimulates this center to create psychic functioning corresponding to this center for example, focusing upon the sixth *chakra* may awaken the occult mind and psychic abilities. Absorption in a flower may open consciousness to purity or to some other quality symbolized by this flower.

In psychology, evocative practices are similar to guided imagery where an image activates a psychological or physical state, for example, using imagery to help the immune response in cancer. But in evocative meditations the realm to be identified with is far beyond the normal limits of the self. In concentrating on, for example, the fourth chakra, feelings of love and compassion may be evoked. The absorption in silent rapture in the midst of a spectacular natural setting may evoke depths of beauty and clarity from within. The vast space around one may allow an inner spaciousness to emerge. What the self is enlarges as the outer is viewed as a kind of mirror of the self, or even as identical with the self, one's true nature, which is revealed as the absorption deepens.

One variant of evocative practices is contemplation. Contemplation is the focusing of the mind on a single theme, idea, or abstraction, for example, contemplation on a spiritual concept such as *ahimsa*, or the nature of pure space and time. Through contemplation the object of focus gradually reveals its inner meanings to the mind of the meditator. Sri Aurobindo (1973b p. 304) writes, "By concentration on anything whatsoever we are able to know that thing, to make it deliver up its concealed secrets."

From a psychological perspective, contemplation is similar to the technique of free association. In psychotherapy, which has the self as the focus, free association leads the person deeper and deeper within, to reveal progressively greater significances and meanings, that is, it leads to unfolding the self. Contemplation expands the use of this concentrative and associative flow to learn about things that are not usually defined as "self." When unfocused, both contemplation and free association can easily spin off into fantasy and ungrounded mental constructions to become a kind of "free dissociation."

More questions arise than our present knowledge can adequately address. What are the limits of what the mind can know? What implications are there for mind if one can tap into larger, universal pools of knowledge? Where does this intuition come from? As with most all spiritual experience, these questions take us into realms far beyond what psychology conventionally studies.

Suppressive Practices

These practices seek to suppress an impure or undesirable state of consciousness. In these the focused imposition of a symbol or phrase creates a particular quality in the seeker and the opposite state is suppressed.

The idea is to replace ordinary, unhealthy, impure states of mind with more pure, wholesome, healthy states of mind. The action of suppressive practices can be explained by the reciprocal-inhibition model. Indeed, Goleman (1976, 1988) goes so far as to identify the principle of reciprocal-inhibition as central to the efficacy of Buddhist meditation. "The key principle in the Abhidharma program for achieving mental health is the reciprocal inhibition of unhealthy factors by healthy ones," (quoted in Bogart, 1991, p. 389). While some practices emphasize the cultivation of positive mind states, others emphasize the suppression of negative mind states, but both involve imposition and suppression.

In considering this set of practices, it seems useful to make a distinction between practices that suppress affect and practices that suppress thought. As an example of a well-known Tibetan and Christian practice that is designed to eliminate obstacles to purity by suppressing sexual feelings, a seeker struggling with lustful feelings and images may be directed to concentrate on the image of a decaying corpse, on how badly it smells and looks, to imagine worms crawling through the dead flesh, and to concentrate on how temporary the beauty of the body is and the dust into which it will turn. This practice is essentially the use of a counter-conditioning technique to suppress desire.

The problem psychologically with such a suppressive technique is perhaps obvious. Anyone who seriously believes that lustful feelings and thoughts will be eliminated by thinking of a rotting corpse is in for a big surprise. As Freud discovered long ago, suppression is not a solution. Suppression that becomes habitual eventuates in repression. What is suppressed comes back again and again. Our real feelings do not just go away because we want them to, rather they continue to assert themselves and press for awareness and expression (the "return of the repressed"). Any suppression technique is temporary at best, and invariably produces a certain degree of psychological tension in the process. Suppressive practices are a form of "covering" techniques (Blanck and Blanck, 1974). As such they have their appropriate role in psychotherapy, though this role is a limited one, confined mostly to clients requiring supportive psychotherapy or for borderline or psychotic conditions. However, despite our psychological knowledge of the process of emotional suppression, it would be rash to judge it as *always* unhealthy. There may be circumstances in which the judicious, time-limited use of this suppressive technique is helpful not only for a person's spiritual or but even psychological growth. However, recommendations for its use must acknowledge its hazards as well.

An example of a practice designed to suppress thought or cognition is the use of *koans*. In the Zen tradition, a *koan* serves to suppress the discursive mind via one-pointed absorption in the koan (e.g., "Mu!"). Through this total absorption or mental "overload," thought ceases its habitual wanderings and there is then the possibility of awakening to a wider perception of being than the ordinary mind allows (*satori*). The parallels to "thought-stopping" in cognitive therapy are striking, although the goals of the two are very different, as is the intensity of the absorption in the two practices. Exploring the effectiveness of *koan* meditation would be a fascinating research project if research into spiritual development ever evolves to the point of discovering which practices are most effective (with which kinds of people and for what kinds of spiritual realization).

The Gray Area between Evoking and Suppressing

Sometimes it is not clear whether it is evoking or suppressing which is occurring, or if both are occurring together. Consider, for example, the use of Buddhist *metta* (loving kindness) meditation or the use of affirmations. These practices present an interesting set of dilemmas from a psychological point of view. On the one hand, it is certainly psychologically desirable to be able to connect to a deep source of peace or loving kindness within ourselves, or, as in the case of affirmation, to be able to feel love for ourselves or to affirm our worth as a person. On the other hand, these same practices may serve defensive purposes, by masking surface feelings, imposing another feeling over the original one. For example, if someone feels like a bad person, the affirmation may be given, "I love myself. I'm good, and I'm getting better every day." Rather than simply awakening an inner feeling of self-love and acceptance, such affirmations may also (if not only) tend to talk the meditator out of his or her feelings. Obviously, the deep narcissistic wounds that result in a pervasive feeling of "I'm bad" cannot be healed or eradicated by such surface manipulations or change in self-talk. Most dynamic therapists would agree that a much deeper working through process is required.

Another psychological question is whether the effects of this are simply short term or whether they are effective in bringing about long-lasting psychological or spiritual shifts. Most anecdotal evidence I have collected would indicate that the effects tend to be ephemeral. It is easy to see why this would be so. For example, if an angry person diligently practices a meditation on love, this person may indeed succeed in evoking a loving feeling from within, and, while practicing this technique, even feel great waves of love and compassion. But when this person is once again confronted with the narcissistic slights and disappointments that are the stuff of daily life, the anger and hostility tends to come back as forcefully as before.

To put this in the language of self psychology, rage proneness is a product of specific developmental failures and consequent deficits in the structure of the self (Kohut, 1977). *Trying to be loving or trying to focus on loving feelings will not change this.* Only when the early pain and wounding is worked through and the corresponding structural defects in the self filled in will the person be able to perceive and respond to the world in a more balanced, mature way. The unconscious, archaic grandiosity and entitlement must be integrated, modified, and structured into the self before the person will cease to be enraged over minor insults and setbacks.

Western psychology thus becomes a far more efficient technique for certain kinds of spiritual purification than purely meditative, suppressive techniques. It is not that these techniques do not work at all. That they have a purifying effect is attested to by centuries of spiritual practice. For some people affirmations can be a kind of cognitive-behavioral intervention, which may be fine in situations where a deeper working through is not needed or desired. And when the inner conditions are right they may provide the outer touch that can release strong forces within the psyche. However, in most people they work so slowly that their effects may be difficult to notice and can take decades to become evident, and it may be that their action in some people is negligible. If this were not the case, using affirmations or meditations on love would long ago have ameliorated all psychological difficulties and replaced the need for long-term psychotherapy.

Concentration-Building Practices

It is worth noting that while the ability to concentrate is essential in *all* meditation practices and hence remains a constant regardless of the method, there are a number of practices designed solely to increase the capacity for concentration. In these practices the ability to concentrate is exercised and strengthened, much like a muscle. A specific object is chosen (e.g., the breath) and the seeker is directed to do such things as count the breaths or to simply notice the effects of the inhalation and exhalation. Naturally, the mind wanders, and one then simply returns to the object of concentration. The rationale for this technique is that as one increases the ability to concentrate and consciousness is no longer dispersed in many directions, whatever other meditative practice one is pursuing becomes all the easier and more powerful. Buddhism especially makes use of these practices, although they are also present in Christian traditions (Meadow & Culligan, 1987).

One important question is: to what extent does a person's personal psychodynamics help or hinder the ability to concentrate? From one perspective concentration can be viewed as simply a skill or capacity which can be increased through practice, much as a muscle gets stronger through exercise. From another perspective the ability to concentrate is also a by-product of a person's psychological integration. That is, having much "unfinished emotional business" draws a person's attention away from the task at hand toward the deeper emotional issues that are clamoring for attention. Psychotherapy works to reduce this unfinished business so that a person can be more fully present. Here again Western psychotherapy may offer another approach for enhancing concentration rather than through trying to override the "distractions" of important emotional needs via a concentration practice.

Another question relates to how generalizable concentration is. The late John Lilly contended that going to graduate school for an advanced degree was really a Western equivalent of this kind of concentration practice, and that graduate school brought about the development of one-pointedness so that many westerners could dispense with this discipline. However, what many graduates discover when they attempt to meditate is that the ability to concentrate on an external object is very different from the ability to maintain an inner focus for concentration. Subtle inner states and feelings may require a sensitivity that is not necessarily correlated with the ability to be absorbed, for example, in a course of academic study, a football game, or a surgical operation. Exactly how concentration develops, and how an inner or an outer focus of concentration alters overall attentional capacity are areas that are ripe for more extensive research.

The Question of Mantra Meditation

Another type of meditation practice is the repetition of a *mantra* or phrase or a name of God (*japa*). The most well-known form of *mantra* meditation in the West is transcendental meditation, but this is a form of meditation that occurs in almost every spiritual tradition. In *mantra* meditation the seeker repeats a name of God (e.g., Krishna, Shayam, Om) or a word or a phrase (e.g., "Aing," a sound of the Divine Mother; "Ma," a name of the divine mother; "Om mane padme hum," a Tibetan mantra; "Jesus Christ, Son of God, have mercy on me," the Christian prayer of the heart; "Hail Mary, Mother of God," the Rosary). This repetition, made silently to oneself throughout the day, is designed to have a number of effects, depending upon the spiritual tradition explaining it. It is used to evoke states of consciousness such as peace or devotion, to invoke the presence of the Divine in various forms, to stimulate and raise kundalini, and to activate different spiritual energies within the person.

There are at least three different views on how a *mantra* works. In spirit path traditions, repetition of the *mantra* is said to bring silence to the mind, to disengage it from its ordinary activity and turn it to more subtle levels and, ultimately, to the source of the mind itself—atman, the Self, or Buddha nature.

In soul path traditions, *mantra* meditation is said to invoke the spiritual energy, quality, or state that is being named, or it invites the presence of a form of the Divine. As that spiritual energy (e.g., Christ or the Divine Mother) flows into the seeker, a progressive purification takes place. The word, sound, or *mantra* has a force or power within it which, as it is repeated by the person, awakens this power or force within consciousness.

A third, more critical view comes from Krishnamurti (1973), who held that the repetition of a word or a phrase over and over again dulls the brain into quiescence. It does produce a sort of silence, he held, but a silence that is deadened and dulled—not alive, awake, and alert in its silence. Krishnamurti maintained that the word or phrase itself was irrelevant, and that Coca Cola was as good a *mantra* as any.

The psychotherapeutic benefits of *mantra* meditation appear to be twofold. First, the state of calm and relaxation that it produces has been amply commented upon in the literature already. In the stressful environment of today's world, the healthy effects of a relaxed, calm body and mind can hardly be overstated. Second, for many people it may produce a sense of being more centered, connecting to a place deeper within themselves from which to relate to their outer, daily life. This also seems self-evidently good for psychological health.

The dangers of this practice lie in the possibility of psychic numbing and the flat affect that can result from this. As Krishnamurti points out, the danger of running the mind into a habitual groove is that it loses its resilience and fluidity, producing a tranquilized calm rather than true peace. *Mantra* meditation can then be used as a kind of psychic Valium to deaden or soothe unpleasant affect states that the person has difficulty integrating.

Mantra meditation can be viewed as either (1) a suppressive practice, (2) an evocative practice, or (3) a form of prayer—devotion practice. Clearly Krishnamurti's view is that *mantra* meditation is a suppressive practice. His position is that pounding a word or phrase into one's consciousness imposes a kind of peace, albeit a dull and deadened peace, and it effectively suppresses the normal mental functioning. The TM community would say that *mantra* meditation is an evocative practice. When the seeker is fully absorbed in the repetition of the phrase, consciousness is allowed to unhook from its ordinary activity and the deeper peace of the Self can be evoked. And the soul path traditions view *mantra* as a form of prayer or devotional practice. Although the outer technique may look like *mantra*, inwardly the person's focus may be on an increasing opening to the Divine, or on an ever-deepening feeling of devotion, *bhakti*, love.

Even though there has been more investigation of this practice than any other, it is an area that has just begun to be researched. What is the essential process at work—evocative, suppressive, devotion/prayer, some or all of these? It seems likely that there is no one way *mantra* meditation works. Rather it can be used in different ways, depending on the consciousness of the person.

From the perspective of modern physics, everything can be viewed as a form of vibration. The sound of the *mantra* contains a certain power or vibration. When this *mantra* holds great meaning for the person, this sense of meaning also is a frequency of vibration. Similarly, *bhakti* or devotion is an energetic waveform that vibrates to a certain frequency. The power of *mantra* may lie in the way these vibratory waveforms resonate together and interact. A mechanical repetition of the *mantra* would have an effect, but the combined resonances of a *mantra* that had great meaning and feeling would probably have a much different effect. Psychotherapy has a role to play through making the self more integrated and cohesive, thereby creating a more coherent and focused vibrating energy pattern which the person would practice from. An unintegrated self would result in a more chaotic, fragmented energy pattern which could make it harder for a *mantra's* power to manifest.

CONCLUSIONS AND DISCUSSION

Is meditation helpful to psychotherapy? Is psychotherapy helpful to meditation? In general the evidence points to a strong yes to these questions. The psychotherapeutically relevant consciousness functions that emerge from the spirit paths of awakening lie in the development of awareness and attentional skills, whereas soul paths of awakening are geared to the development of love, joy, peace, and the receding of fear.

These developments in consciousness have profound implications for psychotherapy. The expansion of awareness and the emergence of love, joy, and peace into a person's psychological life are noble goals for psychotherapy and may even be the sine qua non of mental health. Conversely, the psychological dangers of meditation practice are equally worth noting as the defensive structures of the self are also usually engaged in meditation practice as a person's characterological distortions continue unhindered (e.g., harsh superego condemnation or withdrawing from interpersonal relatedness).

This contribution is potentially very great for clients. It may be even greater for therapists. A meditation practice helps the therapist to be more centered in his or her depths, to be less reactive, more focused, and more present for client work. And as empathy enhancement is a documented effect of meditation practice, there are few therapists whose therapy would not be enriched.

What has received less attention in the transpersonal literature is how psychotherapy can enhance spiritual practice. Only as psychotherapy is reaching new levels of sophistication are we able to see why many methods of spiritual practice are much less effective than they could be. This area raises new possibilities for matching meditation practice with individual differences. For example, do *bhakti* (devotion) meditation practices work best with certain character structures? Is it a bad idea to use them with hysterical or borderline character structures, since these people have a hard time containing feelings? Or is it a good idea to work with the strengths of the person and to build on them? Are *bhakti* practices better for schizoid types that have difficulty with feeling? Or is this going against the grain? Are there some schizoids for whom *bhakti* practices would be helpful and others for whom it would not be, and if so, how could the differences be discerned? How does the "maturity of the soul" figure into this rather than just considering the surface characterological structure of the person?

Similarly, given Engler's often quoted warning against borderlines using mindfulness techniques, an opposite position can reasonably be advanced. The use of mindfulness techniques may actually allow some borderlines to strengthen their observing ego, to become better at containing and neutralizing affect. With the meditation teacher acting as an idealized selfobject and the other meditators acting as alter ego selfobjects, for some borderlines the entire context may provide a container for both structure building and uncovering. Since borderlines who have benefited from this do not attract clinical attention the way those who become destabilized do, such helpful effects are less likely to be noticed clinically. The question then becomes how to discern which borderlines this would be helpful for and which ones it would be destabilizing and contraindicated for.

Transpersonal psychology allows us to start formulating some of the questions involved in matching spiritual practice to personal psychodynamics. But we are a long way off from being able to answer them with any degree of certainty. For transpersonal psychology reminds us that there is much more at work than *just* personal psychodynamics. How the spiritual dimension supports and interacts with personal psychodynamics is an area that has not yet begun to be really explored.

What role does meditation have in psychotherapy? Here again we are really at the very beginning of trying to answer this question. At present, my own sense is that for long-term therapy the powerful effects of meditation practice are most helpful when used in combination with psychotherapy, that is as an adjunct, rather than as a therapeutic technique in itself. However, in the case of symptom-focused therapy, then specific meditations or visualizations may be a central part of the therapy (e.g., stress reduction or healing work with visualizations, etc.). With some clients experiencing great anxiety or difficulty containing strong feeling states I have successfully used a breathing meditation (eyes closed, focusing on the effects of the breath in the body on both inhale and exhale). Some clients have sat daily and breathed their way through very intense affect states for months at a time and emerged feeling very relieved and more confident in their capacity to contain and tolerate strong anxiety and otherwise overwhelming feelings.

Meditation practice and psychotherapy are designed to do two different things. Neither is a substitute for the other. However, each can enhance the other. I believe it is this combination of meditation and psychotherapy that is the most promising contribution transpersonal psychotherapy has to make to psycho-spiritual growth.

What is the action of meditation? Since meditation is not a single entity, more accurately the question should be how do different types of meditation work? There are five ways of understanding meditation which emerge from this discussion.

1. Meditation as relaxation and self-regulation strategy
2. Meditation as uncovering repressed unconscious contents
3. Meditation as revealing higher states
4. Meditation as reciprocal inhibition
5. Meditation as growth of new consciousness and transformation

The first of these, meditation as a self-regulation strategy and relaxation response, is by now fairly well documented, especially using *mantra* meditation or using some concentration techniques such as focusing on the breath. Although not every single type of meditation has this effect, most types do. It seems clear from the preponderance of the research evidence that over time, most meditation practices bring about both physical relaxation and a greater sense of inner peace and calmness. If a person's meditation practice is not doing at least this, something is probably wrong and more instruction is indicated. But this is still the most outward and superficial view of meditation's action.

The second view, meditation as uncovering, attempts to go deeper in understanding what occurs. Here also it is clear that both mindfulness and *bhakti* practices bring the person to a more interior, awake consciousness. The attention to whatever arises in mindfulness practices and to the affective dimension of experience in *bhakti* practices serves to lift the defensive structures and bring about derepression. Engler (1986) has articulated this view most cogently and noted its dangers for borderlines in particular. While this view has enormous appeal, especially to therapists, it also has limited usefulness and fails to explain important phenomena. For one, there are many borderlines who do not experience the psychic disruption this should bring about, and second, most neurotics, even after many years of intensive meditation practice, do not experience any major lifting of their defensive barriers. Indeed, most people's defenses and neuroses are relatively intact after sustained meditation practice. While most people experience some mild derepression and a very few people even experience major regressive episodes, in general mindfulness and *bhakti* meditation practices do not appear to have a significant effect upon the psychological defenses of the self.

This observation leads to the third view of meditation's action and has led Russell (1986 p. 69) to declare that meditation opens up higher unconscious states but is fairly neutral in its effect upon lower unconscious states, that is, those brought about by repression and other defenses. He concludes that, "the higher states and the unconscious content are thus conceived to be largely unrelated." In this view meditation may help to sensitize a person to inner states but has little or no therapeutic benefit. While Russell may be overstating the case, his argument is a logical explanation of why meditation has not replaced psychotherapy as a method of psychological growth.

The fourth view, viewing meditation as a process of reciprocal-inhibition, comes from behavioral psychology and has been advanced by Goleman (1976, 1988). Reciprocal-inhibition was originated by Wolpe (1958), who hypothesized that a fearful, phobic reaction would be extinguished if it could occur at the same time as an incompatible response such as relaxation. Repeated pairing of voluntary relaxation with the feared stimulus soon allows the body to learn a new, non-fearful response to the stimulus. Goleman takes this simple behavioral strategy and applies it to states of consciousness to explain how meditation works. Healthy, more desirable states of consciousness cancel out unhealthy, undesirable states of consciousness.

The difficulty with this fourth view is apparent by discussing how the fifth view sees the action of meditation, which is as a way that inner states of consciousness are awakened or evoked from within the person. That is, certain states of consciousness lie dormant, and meditation serves to activate these inner states (much like the third view so far.) As these states become awakened, however, in this view (unlike the third view) they act in ways that reorganize and purify the surface consciousness. According to many traditions, as the inner consciousness awakens, it refines, transforms, and uplifts the old consciousness. Much of this initially occurs behind the veil, so that the action on the surface consciousness is oftentimes not evident without sustained practice. The purifying, subtlizing effects of meditation do not act in strictly psychotherapeutic, derepressive ways, which is why it is not a substitute for psychotherapy, nor can its action be considered strictly uncovering.

When a higher or more expanded state of consciousness is activated, what happens to the problems and issues of normal consciousness? They may no longer be seen as problems or their significance may change. The old, normal consciousness is absorbed into and transformed by the expanded state. The consciousness functions of the old consciousness are not "cancelled out," they are subsumed into the new one.

Reciprocal-inhibition is an inadequate paradigm to explain this growth of consciousness. It operates as a simple, digital, on-off process—either one or the other. But in consciousness evolution, old forms are not simply turned off but transformed by emerging new configurations.

Reciprocal-inhibition works well to explain the dominance of one affect over another, how one affect cancels out another, incompatible affect. Here the digital, either/or logic works well. But old "undesirable" mind states are not just eliminated but are taken up, reorganized, filled with a greater consciousness.

These two models are not totally incompatible, but they do point in different directions in seeking to uncover the action of meditation. Is it a suppressive action that awakens or an awakening action that transforms? Is it some combination of each? Even where it *appears* that one of them is occurring, such as, suppression (reciprocal-inhibition), perhaps an evoking or awakening, say from the power of the *mantra*, is actually working on the consciousness.

The reciprocal-inhibition model does have specific, limited usefulness when discussing suppressive meditation practices. But for other practices, such as mindfulness or *bhakti* practices, reciprocal-inhibition is entirely inadequate. Similarly, this fifth view can incorporate the observations of both the second and third views of meditation (the uncovering view and the revealing of higher states), as well as the first view of meditation as relaxation, for as inner states of peace and equanimity are experienced during meditation, these states then flow out to influence and penetrate the surface consciousness, including the body. I would suggest that an evoking, awakening, unfolding model of consciousness development is the most appropriate for beginning to understand the meditative process.

In all of this it is clear that meditation has a much more subtle action on consciousness than language can capture or that we are in a position to yet understand. What does it mean to awaken a new state of consciousness? How exactly does a more desirable state of consciousness transform a less desirable state? What is occurring at the deeper levels of consciousness in meditation even when it may appear that nothing is occurring on the surface? What is the process of purification? What consciousness is purifying and what consciousness is purified? What, then, is spiritual growth or transformation? While these tentative questions encourage us to look in certain directions, they lead us even further into the profound mystery of psyche and spirit.

Chapter Six

Spiritual Emergency

People generally think of the spiritual path as safe—if not easy, then at least a protective haven from the existential insecurity of life, a soothing balm from the inevitable anxieties, fears, and pain of living. But like any great endeavor, the spiritual journey also has its risks and dangers. Spiritual traditions throughout the world speak of these dangers and over centuries of spiritual practice have evolved ways of dealing with them.

There are numerous perils that spiritual customs speak of, from getting sidetracked into the more subtle phenomenal worlds of inner visions and senses, to becoming enamored with various powers or *siddhis* that may come. Warnings against a "fall from the path" occur in most traditions, many times caused by grandiosity being stimulated in the rush of exhilarating experiences.

Besides the danger of ego-inflation, there is the danger of the self, the vehicle, getting battered or shattered by the uncontrolled inflow of spiritual energies. Kundalini awakening or other forms of spiritual energy can rapidly stream throughout the person's body and consciousness, disorienting the person and disrupting the normal structures of the self. Beyond the physical symptoms of *kriyas*, or uncontrolled shaking, early wounds and other neurotic contractions within the person can be dramatically lit up and activated as part of this purificatory process.

155

Without proper support the person can be engulfed not only by spiritual energy but by unconscious forces of the psyche that are unleashed in this process, leaving the person adrift in a sea of energies that he or she is not equipped to deal with.

"Evil spirits" is something nearly every culture is familiar with and which even children refer to. There are dangers of subtle beings attacking or trying to take possession of those who open to inner planes. In Christianity they are described as demons. In Hinduism these beings are known as *asuras, rakshasas,* and *pichacas,* depending upon their plane of origin. Such beings are also well known in shamanic traditions, and Buddhist temples have statues at their gates to provide protection from such beings. The danger of influence or attack by demonic or anti-Divine forces is a universally recognized spiritual hazard. Leaving aside for the moment the philosophical and epistemological issues raised by such phrases as "demonic forces" and concentrating solely on phenomenological experience, how the psychological structures of the self respond to such an attack or to a powerful influx of energy is one of the most fascinating areas of inquiry in the transpersonal field.

Transpersonal psychotherapy alerts us to the limitations and dangers of purely psychological approaches to inner states, cut off from spiritual traditions. For the spiritual traditions caution that everything a person opens inwardly to is not just strictly psychological. Besides inward spiritual states of consciousness, light, and knowledge, there are many intermediate zones or grades of experience in which seekers can become lost on the inward journey.

Until recently Western psychology has lumped all such experiences under the common rubric of psychopathology and rather summarily dismissed them. People entering these realms of experience have been treated identically to a typical schizophrenic by the mental health establishment, that is, given large doses of anti-psychotic medication and generally hospitalized. However, transpersonal psychology has brought such experiences into a new light and has coined the term *spiritual emergency* to describe them. Spiritual emergency, which is one of the best examples of how transpersonal psychotherapy is a synthesis of psychology and spirituality, refers to how the self becomes disorganized and overwhelmed by an infusion of spiritual energies or new realms of experience which it is not yet able to integrate.

What transpersonal research has discovered, and many spiritual traditions affirm, is that although spiritual emergency appears disorganized and uncontrolled, there is a deeper order that is seeking to be born through this seeming disorder. Spiritual emergency heralds a new development of consciousness in which the breaking up of old structures gives way to fresh growth and a more spiritual orientation to life. This "breaking up" of old structures can be very frightening and destabilizing for the unprepared. Attempting to hold on to the known or trying to stay in control of the process may push the person beyond his or her limits. However, when a person in the midst of a spiritual emergency can be facilitated to let go into the process and be born anew, the end result can be a higher level of integration for the person, both psychologically and spiritually.

It is important to acknowledge that having a transpersonal orientation does not imply "buying in" to any particular belief system or philosophical worldview. Transpersonal therapists are on a continuum, ranging from those who hold very empirically centered, Zen or Christian worldviews, for example, on one end, through those who hold increasingly complex views of occult worlds and subtle planes of existence, all the way through those who have beliefs about such things as UFO abductions. The transpersonal field has not yet come to the point of trying to establish a consensual view of "reality."

The concept of spiritual emergency is important for three main reasons. For one it brings into view a range of human experience that was formerly unseen or misinterpreted by traditional psychology. Second, it is clinically useful in proposing a diagnosis and treatment for a set of psychological symptoms. Third, and perhaps most important although least commented upon, it poses a major challenge to the dominant, biologically-based psychiatric paradigm. Let's consider each of these in turn.

A NEW VIEW OF SPIRITUAL EXPERIENCE

With few exceptions, psychology has not treated religion or spiritual experience very well. Beginning with Freud, Western psychology has maintained a consistently negative view of religion and spiritual experience. Freud (1966), believed religion to be a "universal obsessional neurosis," and in *Civilization and Its Discontents* (1959) equated the mystic's "oceanic experience" of oneness with "infantile helplessness" and a "regression to primary narcissism." Psychological literature has followed this bias, describing spiritual experience as symptomatic of ego regression (Leuba, 1929), borderline psychosis (Group for the Advancement of Psychiatry, 1976), a psychotic episode (Horton, 1974), and a temporal lobe dysfunction (Mandel, 1980). In the *Diagnostic and Statistical Manual of Mental Disorders III-R*, all 12 references to religion in the "Glossary of Technical Terms" were used to illustrate psychopathology (quoted from Lukoff, Lu, Turner, 1992).

The pathologizing of spiritual experience by traditional psychology has by now been amply documented (see Grof & Grof, 1989; Walsh & Vaughn, 1993; and especially Lukoff, et. al., 1992). The effect of this on therapeutic treatment has been to try to stop these "pathological" symptoms as soon as possible. Thus hospitalization, the use of anti-psychotic medication, and a mind set among treatment staff that viewed such experiences as "sick" are what has been offered to individuals in this state to help them. The result of this treatment is that a potentially growthful step of consciousness gets derailed, invalidated, and submerged in a sea of medication and shame, leaving the person unable to integrate the experience.

SPIRITUAL EMERGENCE VERSUS SPIRITUAL EMERGENCY

Spiritual teachings view the emergence of spiritual experience into daily consciousness as the culminating point of development. The function of religion and all spiritual seeking is to come into increasing contact with the Divine, in whatever form it may be conceived. Transpersonal psychology affirms this movement of spiritual seeking and places the highest value on the realization of our spiritual nature. Spiritual experience is viewed as desirable and spiritual seeking is seen as natural, healthy, and, in the final analysis, the only truly fulfilling answer to the challenge of existence.

Most often spiritual experience develops gradually, with a slow lifting of the veil between normal consciousness and spiritual awareness. Or, when this development is rapid and the person has the inner resources to assimilate it, he or she welcomes it and is able to allow the transformative power of the experience to work on the consciousness. Sudden illumination, descents of bliss, expanding into love or unity, the opening of perception to inner worlds—whatever the experience, steady spiritual practice, guidance, and purification have laid the foundation for a relatively smooth integration of the spirit's bounty.

Sometimes, however, spiritual experience erupts so forcefully that the usual integrative capacities of the person are overwhelmed and psychological functioning is disturbed. New energies, beings, planes of experience bombard the person, resulting in confusion, fear, and attempts to control what is going on. At this point, spiritual emergence becomes spiritual emergency.

There are two major circumstances in which spiritual emergency happens. The first is fairly uncomplicated though less common.

1. The person or environment has no conceptual framework to deal with what the person is experiencing. It is then usually pathologized by the person's support system, parents, doctors, et cetera. This is relatively easy to work with. Providing a cognitive framework and a supportive environment in which the person can fully experience the process is often sufficient to enable the person to assimilate what is going on.
2. There is not enough physical or emotional resilience within the self to integrate these experiences. Psychological structures become disorganized as the self fragments.

This second is more difficult to rectify, requiring such things as therapy, experiential work, bodywork, and sometimes medication and/or hospitalization to slow down the process. Although this may also be accompanied by a lack of a conceptual framework, just providing a conceptual map is not sufficient to end the crisis, for the structures of the self are disrupted and need to be repaired or transformed.

There are three major responses to spiritual emergency:

1. Integrate the experience, move forward in life.
2. Be overwhelmed for a period of time, with integration following.
3. Fixate and fail to integrate. The experience may subside, but the person remains fixated on some level, resulting in lessened or marginal adaptation.

The Chinese character for the word crisis is translated as "ki-ki," meaning "dangerous opportunity." When the rapid infusion of new energies into the system has a disorganizing, fragmenting effect upon the person, the psyche shatters along its "fault lines" (wounds, defensive structures, and less firmly developed lines of growth). Although spiritual emergency provides an opportunity for new healing and growth to occur, like the Chinese character for crisis indicates, it also poses a risk for increased psychopathology or vulnerability to future psychopathology, depending upon how the person meets the experience.

A common belief in New Age circles is that the universe doesn't give you anything until you are ready for it. While this *may* be true from a large, cosmic perspective, clearly, from the standpoint of *this* lifetime, it is not always the case. Some people are overwhelmed, get lost, and never recover. While there may be a gain in a future life, there seems to be only a loss in this life.

Although any kind of spiritual experience can become an emergency, it is noteworthy that what usually precipitates spiritual emergency is some sort of stress, a time when the person's defenses and inner resources are weakened and more vulnerable. This seems comprehensible since it may be this very vulnerability or "thinning" of the person's ego structures that allows spiritual experiences past the usual filtering mechanisms of the psyche.

Some of these stressors are *physical*, including such things as near death experiences, pregnancy and childbirth, drugs (especially psychedelic drugs), fasting, injury, or physical hardship (such as occurs during a vision quest). Other stressors are primarily *emotional*, such as experiences of emotional intensity (e.g., a personal growth weekend workshop), emotional deprivation or loss, and intense sexual experiences. The other major source of stress is *spiritual*, especially intensive spiritual practice. Concentrated practice periods, whether lasting a weekend or several months, provide a chance to enter deeply into a particular spiritual practice. Spiritual emergency toward the end of a retreat or immediately afterwards is not uncommon (Bragdon, 1988).

FORMS OF SPIRITUAL EMERGENCY

Although religious traditions have described various forms of spiritual dangers, transpersonal psychology has detailed a set of more clinically useful descriptions. Grof and Grof (1989) have depicted 10 major forms that spiritual emergency takes. It should be noted that these descriptions are phenomenologically based. That is, these categories are based on how people undergoing a spiritual emergency describe them; they do not claim that these are "objectively true."

These major types are here organized into two larger categories, depending on the major features of the experience: those that primarily involve consciousness alteration and those that primarily involve opening to subtle or psychic realms (although elements of each can be found in most forms of spiritual emergency). As our understanding of these states increases, simpler classificatory schemes may develop.

Consciousness Alterations

The Awakening of Kundalini. Kundalini awakening is probably the most commonly experienced and widely known form of spiritual emergency. In Hindu tradition, kundalini is spiritual energy which lies dormant at the base of the spine. When it awakens it rises like a serpent up along the spine, opening the chakras, or energy centers associated with particular levels of consciousness, as it passes toward the top of the head, where the crown chakra is located. As each chakra opens, new levels of consciousness are revealed. Since the consciousness of most people is fairly restricted, the opening of the chakras is accompanied by consciousness expansion and a purification of the limitations or impurities that correspond to each chakra. This purifying process seems to be the root of most of the difficulties associated with kundalini awakening, for it purifies on physical, psychological, and spiritual levels.

When kundalini awakens, either through spiritual practice or spontaneously, consciousness is "lit up" as new realms are activated. There may be ecstatic visions, widening of consciousness, periods of ego loss, subtle or clairvoyant perception, and sensory awakening. The experience of energy streaming up the spine and throughout the body is common. Sometimes this energy flow is gentle and blissful, other times it is a powerful rush of energy that is overwhelmingly intense and terrifying. In many cases, spontaneous movements, called *kriyas*, accompany this energy rush. These can involve forceful shaking, involuntary spasms, jerking, and repetitive movements, which can be understandably frightening.

Two analogies are sometimes given to help understand this process. The first is based on how a light bulb produces light. The light is actually produced from the *resistance* of the tungsten filament to the electricity flowing through it. A filament like copper that conducts electricity very well, on the other hand, produces no light. Thus the parts of consciousness or the body that "light up" from the resistance to the kundalini passing through are the areas needing purification. When the "heat" generated by this resistance "burns out" the impediments, the sensations end.

The second analogy uses the image of a garden hose whipping about when the water is turned on strongly. This same amount of water pressure in a firehose, however, would cause no disturbance. Similarly, when the kundalini has "widened" the energy channels and removed the blocks, the violent shaking and *kriyas* cease (Sannella, 1978).

These analogies frame the kundalini experience as a purifying process, promoting consciousness expansion as the "impurities" or limitations of each chakra are cleansed or removed. Sanella's research indicates that for most people in the West, when the kundalini process is allowed to run its full course it generally self-regulates and comes to an end within several months. In the Eastern traditions it may continue for years, but this appears to be rare. The person emerges more balanced and open to the spiritual possibilities of life. When the process is misdiagnosed and derailed through medication, hospitalization, et cetera, the person remains suspended midway through a purification process, which he or she may be then shamed away from trying to resume in the future.

Kundalini awakening is most often misdiagnosed as mania, anxiety disorder, or, when there are *kriyas*, conversion hysteria.

Near-Death Experiences. By now near-death experiences are well known to the public and media, even the stuff of popular movies. Elements of the experience include passing through a dark tube or tunnel toward a source of light and loving wisdom, and in this passage the person feels unconditionally accepted and forgiven by this loving source. There may be a life review and evaluation of past actions. The person understands that there is still more to be done in this life and returns to live according to this higher vision.

Such an experience can be a much appreciated wake-up call or it can be profoundly disturbing and hard to integrate. Trying to align one's life with this spiritual vision can be challenging as the momentum of one's ordinary life is confronted. The reaction of other people is less frequently one of skepticism these days. More likely it is one of reverence, and the expectation that the blessing of this experience makes one an instant saint or source of wisdom can be difficult to live up to.

Although it is rarely misdiagnosed anymore, it was commonly seen as a delusional state, especially when the person had been under an anesthetic.

Episodes of Unitive Consciousness. Though rare, mystical experiences of merging one's identity into unitive consciousness can, for the unprepared, be profoundly disorienting and make functioning in the world difficult or impossible. One person described it as losing the ego by "falling into the void" and losing along with the ego the capacities to function in a directed and focused way in the world, rendering even simple things such as ordering a meal in a restaurant out of the question. Spiritual traditions are replete with examples of saints or sages who were unable to function for periods of time while they were in higher states of consciousness and who were cared for by those around them until they were able to navigate this plane of consciousness once again. Ramana Maharshi is a modern example of such a person. If he had been in the United States when his mystical awakening occurred, he would likely have ended up in a psychiatric hospital, being given large doses of medication to bring him back to "reality."

The psychiatric establishment has usually diagnosed these as fusion states, loss of boundaries, fragmentation, or depersonalization.

Renewal through Return to Center. Spiritual emergency has provided a larger context for viewing the healing possibilities of psychotic process. The British psychiatrist R. D. Laing was one of the most popular and eloquent spokespersons for this view, and he conducted a highly celebrated experiment in the early 1960s through the Kingsley Hall Clinic in London for the treatment of psychosis without medication. The hope was if psychosis is an attempt by the psyche to heal itself, by allowing this process to unfold in a supportive context, the psychosis will spontaneously end as the different parts of the psyche are integrated into a new, more inclusive whole. Unfortunately, the number of people who actually did get significantly better was so small that it was difficult to justify the enormous expense in terms of time and money in this very labor-intensive treatment.

This experiment has been tried in a few other locations around the world. The preeminent American psychiatrist to explore this direction is John Perry, a renowned Jungian who has written extensively on this approach. Perry brings a transpersonal dimension to his work and sees the potentially healing process of psychosis as an attempt by the psyche to renew itself by activating the archetypal, spiritual energies of the Self.

In this process the common themes are that the person experiences a death, followed by a regression in time back to the beginning (his or her own beginnings—birth or inside the womb—or even the beginning of the world's creation). As this is reenacted, there is a clashing of cosmic forces—a battle between Good and Evil, or God and the Devil. Sexual opposites strive for domination, and the person may experience different sexual identities at various times. As the renewal process proceeds, the person may feel chosen for a special mission to save mankind—messianic themes, king, or savior images may be prominent. The person may undergo a sacred marriage with a mythic or divine figure as part of this transformation. As the experience culminates there may be a vision of a transformed world, with the individual selected to bring about a great revolution or world renewal. Finally, it becomes apparent that this entire process has occurred inside the person rather than in outer reality as the person returns to ordinary consciousness.

Past-Life Experiences. This phenomenon usually occurs during an altered state of consciousness (usually brought about by either psychedelic drugs, hypnosis, or breathwork), and it is the vivid experience of sensing oneself living another life in a different time and culture. The "past life," which is experienced as a distinct memory, reveals insights into present life behaviors, relationships, and feelings. As the "past life" is relived, it may be accompanied by intense emotional release and catharsis. When this process is completed, present-day symptoms or complexes associated with the past-life experience may significantly improve or clear up.

A spiritual emergency may result when this process occurs in an uncontrolled way that intrudes into the person's daily life. Confrontations with parents or friends about incidents from a previous lifetime can be viewed as bizarre when they come out of context. The emergence of these "memories" may itself trigger panic about going crazy, and resistance to these apparent memories can create further tensions.

The common diagnoses for this are delusions or hallucinations associated with schizophrenia or psychosis.

Opening to Subtle or Psychic Realms

The Crisis of Psychic Opening. The opening of such psychic capacities as subtle vision, subtle hearing, telepathy, precognition, et cetera, can precipitate a spiritual crisis for the person who has no framework with which to deal with these new abilities. While psychic experiences often emerge in many different types of spiritual experience, it becomes a problem when the emergence of psychic abilities is the central feature of the person's experience and the person cannot assimilate these new perceptions in a way that is behaviorally or emotionally adaptive. Hearing others' thoughts or seeing subtle beings can be difficult to integrate. As ordinary self/other boundaries dissolve, it can feel like the self is falling apart.

The most common diagnoses for psychic opening are delusions or hallucinations associated with schizophrenia or psychosis.

Shamanic Crisis. Shamans throughout many cultures and times have often been initiated by a journey that anthropologists have referred to as "shamanic illness." This is a dramatic episode in which typically the person goes into an altered state of consciousness. He or she travels to the underworld, where he or she experiences suffering and torture, often culminating in dismemberment and death, followed by rebirth and ascent to a higher region. Along the way the person may come into contact with power animals, "allies," as well as evil spirits. The person often emerges healed of various physical or psychological ailments. Shamanic crisis indicates the person has been chosen to become a shaman, and he or she is then ready to begin further study.

Shamanic crisis is traditionally diagnosed as either schizophrenia or depression.

Channeling or Communication with Spirit Guides. During the 1980s channeling seemed to burst on the scene with a great deal of media publicity and fanfare. Channeling involves contact with a supraphysical entity by a medium or channeler, either telepathically or while in a trance (in which case there is usually no memory of what was received). The received information is either spoken aloud or written down by the channeler. The supraphysical entities are identified variously as human beings between incarnations, more evolved beings, deities, or sometimes aliens from other star systems.

As numerous commentators have noted, just because a discarnate entity is the source of information does not insure that this being is enlightened, evolved, or even particularly knowledgeable. Hence there is great variation in the quality of information received from channeled entities. Some of it is of the highest quality, such as the Koran, the Book of Mormon, and a Course in Miracles. At the other end, some channeled information appears to be confused, rambling, and incoherent, with much channeled material somewhere in between.

The experience of these entities, whether through channeling or an encounter with a "spirit guide" who assumes a teaching or protecting function, can trigger a spiritual emergency as the person has difficulty integrating these perceptions into ordinary life. Hearing voices and seeing spirits can be interpreted as signs of "going crazy." These experiences are most often diagnosed as either schizophrenia or dissociative identity disorder (formerly called multiple personality disorder.)

Possession States. Perhaps closely related to experiences of channeling is one of the most eerie forms of spiritual emergency: possession. In possession, the person feels "taken over" by an evil entity who assumes control of his or her mind and body. Bizarre behavior and vocalizations, together with wild spasms and contortions, make for a frightening picture to those close to someone who is "possessed." The metaphysical dread that most people feel about this has been capitalized on by Hollywood, which has produced numerous horror movies such as *The Exorcist* to play on this.

Most spiritual traditions warn about the dangers of possession and have rituals designed to remove invading entities. In the Bible, part of the proof of Christ's divinity was his commanding ability to cast out the demons from people who were possessed. While phenomenological descriptions of possession have also been reported since the birth of modern psychology, they have always been interpreted as signs of mental illness, for example, in intrapsychic terms such as an invasion of the ego by the id's impulses and energies. Transpersonal psychotherapy raises the possibility of holding both the spiritual and psychological points of view. That is, sometimes we may be witnessing purely psychotic phenomena, other times we may be witnessing pure possession states, and at still other times we may be witnessing a mixture where the person is indeed psychotic *and* possessed. The implications of such a possibility are so vast that it is beyond the scope of this discussion to explore them. Admitting spiritual realities into our scientific and psychological worldview opens up immense new possibilities, which transpersonal psychotherapy is only beginning to explore.

The usual diagnoses for possession states are multiple personality disorder, conversion hysteria, and schizophrenia.

UFO Encounters. Encounters with UFOs or abductions by aliens have also become themes in movies and TV. Visitations by alien beings, being captured and taken aboard alien spacecraft, physical examinations and experiments against one's will—these themes are also familiar in other forms of psychic opening such as shamanic crisis, possession, and channeling, but here these experiences are literalized, concretized, and felt to be actually happening in physical reality. People who report such incidents often are traumatized, and many times the event is forgotten until it is recovered, frequently via hypnosis.

The most common diagnoses are delusions or hallucinations associated with schizophrenia or psychosis.

Spiritual emergency opens many questions about the nature of consciousness and "objective" reality, as well as the relationship between the two. It is noteworthy that there are similar themes in half of these types of spiritual emergency. In shamanic crisis, psychic opening, channeling, UFO encounters, and possession states, there are themes of contact with supraphysical entities (some friendly and others hostile); attack by hostile entities; being taken to another realm; violent torture, dismemberment, and death; transport to another, higher realm; and return to the earth plane either healed or still wounded from these experiences. It may be that these last five types of spiritual emergency are all simply variations of a single process of opening to subtle or psychic realms.

Aside from the personal and the collective unconscious, which psychology has explored quite extensively over the past century, if there also exist, as most all spiritual traditions claim, subtle, inner planes of reality which are coextensive with our outer, physical reality, then as consciousness awakens to the inner world, it seems quite natural that there would be considerable confusion about what plane of reality experience is occurring on. It takes many years of rigorous training for spiritual adepts to begin to find their way through many of these zones of experience. It is to be expected that spontaneous awakening to these states, particularly when paired with psychological vulnerabilities and defenses would, in an average person, create a maze of inner experience that is difficult to navigate.

People interpret their experiences according to the symbol systems available to them. Flying saucers and aliens are a symbol system that is more available to middle America than shamanic visions or archetypal forms or subtle, occult worlds. Even trying to discern what is inner or outer experience is difficult for someone who has no developed inner life and for whom the gates of inner experiencing open suddenly and dramatically. Confounding inner, psychological experiences with inner spiritual realities and outer events may well be a common stage in the evolution of consciousness.

For example, most transpersonally oriented psychotherapists would probably agree that it is highly unlikely that UFO encounters are "real" in the sense of objectively happening in outer reality, capable of being videotaped, et cetera. No doubt some sort of inner experience is occurring. But what part of this is pure psychopathology and unconscious imagery, what part is an attack by hostile entities or visitation by positive entities, and what part of it is an immersion into the archetypal realm of the collective unconscious? Is it different combinations of these for different people? As yet there are no definite answers.

How does personal wounding create more tenuous intrapsychic structure so that the individual's boundaries are more porous and open to unconscious forces and/or spiritual and psychic planes of experience? Regardless of the type of spiritual emergency, what is the relationship between these three realms? That is, how does the personal unconscious relate to the collective unconscious and how do these two interface with an openness to subtle inner planes and spiritual experience? This promises to be one of the most interesting areas of investigation to be raised by transpersonal psychology.

DIFFERENTIAL DIAGNOSIS

The questions that the clinician first asks when dealing with something unusual like this are these: Is this spiritual emergency or psychosis? Or is it something in between? For the further we inquire into this field, the less clear some of the boundaries are between these different domains.

It has been said, "The mystic swims in the waters that the schizophrenic is drowning in," which illustrates just how blurred the boundaries can be between these experiences. As a person opens to inner realms, the personal unconscious shades into the shared, collective unconscious of all humanity, and these in turn are connected in some as yet unknown way to a more fundamental spiritual consciousness. It is this confusion or overlapping of inner experience that brings about most of the phenomena of spiritual emergency.

To determine whether the therapist is dealing with spiritual emergency or psychopathology or some combination of the two, three sets of criteria need to be employed:

- criteria for spiritual emergence
- criteria for psychosis
- criteria for spiritual experience with psychotic features

Criteria for Spiritual Emergency

Grof and Grof (1986) offer the following criteria for spiritual emergency:

1. Changes in consciousness (perception, emotion, cognition, psychosomatic functioning), in which there is significant transpersonal emphasis (e.g., the types of experiences listed earlier).
2. Ability to see this condition as an inner psychological process and to approach it in an inner way.
3. Capacity to form an adequate working relationship (therapeutic alliance) and maintain a spirit of cooperation. This excludes severe paranoid states and those who consistently use mechanisms of projection, exteriorization, and acting out.

Sometimes it is fairly clear that the person is experiencing spiritual emergency, and even though the person's functioning is temporarily impaired, it is not a pathological process. There is a better chance that some observing ego is present in spiritual emergency than in a mental disorder. Many times in spiritual emergency the person is afraid of *going* crazy whereas in psychosis the person *is* crazy and lost in the experience, that is, there is little or no observing ego.

It is also important to have the person receive a medical check-up to make sure that it is not a physical problem that is being experienced. There are a number of physical diseases, from brain tumors to toxic states, that can result in psychological disturbances. When calling a physician to make an appointment for a physical exam, some people have wondered what to tell the physician about the problem or how thorough a physical to request. There are no widely agreed upon and accepted guidelines in this area. If the physician is sympathetic to the spiritual perspective, the more he or she can be told the better. However, in order to avoid alarming very traditional physicians and being met with an implacable, invalidating label of psychotic, some people have kept their complaints vague. One spiritual emergency support group came up with the informal policy of asking for a standard physical and blood work-up. If nothing showed up they proceeded with the diagnosis of spiritual emergency. If psychological and spiritual work helped, they continued working along this line. If physical symptoms persisted, then further medical testing was indicated.

It is important to contrast the above criteria with the criteria for a brief reactive psychosis, which is the most similar to spiritual emergency and thus the misdiagnosis most frequently made for spiritual emergency.

Criteria for Psychosis

A summary of the DSM IV criteria for brief reactive psychosis includes emotional turmoil and at least one of the following:

1. Incoherence or loosening of associations (thought blocking, marked illogical thinking).
2. Delusions (defined as "a false personal belief based on incorrect inferences about external reality and firmly sustained in spite of what everyone else believes and in spite of what constitutes incontrovertible and obvious evidence to the contrary").
3. Hallucinations.
4. Grossly disorganized behavior or catatonia.

There are a good number of spiritual emergency situations in which it is quite clear that this is not a psychosis. The person's thinking is clear, logical, non-delusional. He or she may be terrified or overwhelmed emotionally, may have no cognitive grasp of the situation and be physically depleted and disorganized, but the consciousness changes are readily recognizable as within the province of spiritual experience, and the person is able to focus inwardly and maintain a therapeutic alliance. Being unable to function in the world and flooded with affect are not in themselves signs of psychopathology. Affect flooding may be part of the process of purification, or it may stem from the person's lack of understanding of the process and fear of it.

Other cases are easily diagnosed in the other direction, where it is clearly a psychosis.

Criteria for Spiritual Experience with Psychotic Features

But there are some number of cases where there are elements of both spiritual emergency and psychosis, and a clear distinction is difficult to make. In provocative contributions to this field, Lukoff (1985) and Nelson (1990) propose criteria in which spiritual and psychotic experience co-exist. Lukoff suggests the following criteria for what he terms "mystical experience with psychotic features":

1. Ecstatic mood.
2. Sense of newly gained knowledge.
3. Delusions, if present, have mythological themes. Very much in line with Perry's research on the mythological dimensions of psychotic process, the eight major mythological themes are: *Death*—being dead or meeting Death. *Rebirth*—new identity or name, resurrection to god or king. *Journey*—on a mission or journey. *Encounters with spirits*—either demonic or helping spirits. *Cosmic conflict*—good/evil, light/dark, male/female. *Magical powers*—ESP, clairvoyance, psychic powers. *New society*—the dawning of the New Age, rapid societal change. *Divine Union*—God as father, mother, child; marriage to God, Christ, Krishna, Mary, et cetera.
4. No conceptual disorganization. (Delusional metaphorical speech may be present which is difficult to understand but is comprehensible. This metaphorical speech, which can easily *appear* to be disorganized, is not really a form of conceptual dis-

organization but can be understood from within the experiential world of the client in meaningful and coherent ways.)

If two of the four following criteria are satisfied, the psychotic episode is likely to have a positive outcome:

1. Good pre-episode functioning.
2. Acute onset less than three months.
3. Stressful precipitants.
4. Positive attitude toward experience.

If these criteria are not met, then a psychotic diagnosis is made.

John Nelson has made a highly original contribution to the transpersonal field with his book *Healing the Split* (1990), a transpersonal approach to psychopathology. Nelson has also grappled with this issue of how to differentiate between healthy processes that on the surface look similar to pathology and true pathology. Nelson adds that in spiritual emergency hallucinations are of a "higher order" and there is an absence of paranoia, although there may be appropriate fear. Nelson also brings in another perspective, which is how to differentiate a form of spiritual emergency that Washburn (1994) calls "regression in the service of transcendence" (RIST), or "the dark night of the soul," from schizophrenia.

Schizophrenia generally begins when a person is a teenager or in their twenties, whereas RIST can occur anytime and usually doesn't happen until mid-life or later. Schizophrenics have little insight into their process, whereas those experiencing RIST have profound insights. The feeling tone of schizophrenia is generally a bleak grayness with affect that is "shallow or incongruent with what the person is saying," whereas the affect during the "dark night of the soul," though it may also touch depths of bleakness or despair, is marked by greater intensity and fluctuates with highly positive, rapturous affect states. Schizophrenia disrupts reality testing and cognition, but a person experiencing RIST maintains the capacity for abstract thinking. Even when hallucinations occur in RIST, they are of a "higher order, and though they may advise, they never command."

These guidelines are extremely helpful in differentiating between spiritual emergency and pathological forms of regressive psychosis. But it is crucial for the therapist to have actual clinical experience with these diagnostic categories. As experience increases, the seasoned clinician becomes more skilled at grasping a presenting problem. A more subtle perception emerges of those border areas between personal, collective, and spiritual planes of experience so that progressive crises can be more reliably differentiated from regressive, malignant crises.

TREATMENT

The treatment for spiritual emergency is markedly different from the conventional treatment of psychosis. Whereas the standard approach to psychosis is to view the process as pathological and act to suppress or stop it as soon as possible, in spiritual emergency the process is viewed positively and allowed to develop naturally to its conclusion. Converting spiritual emergency to spiritual emergence means creating a set and setting that support and encourage the unfolding of this transformative process.

Education. Generally the best and most powerful intervention in spiritual emergency is education. A wise therapist or support person will first provide a psychospiritual framework for understanding what is occurring. This reframing de-pathologizes the person's experience and normalizes what otherwise appears to be an out of control "disorder." It is hard to emphasize the importance of education about spiritual emergency too strongly.

Education about spiritual emergency serves two primary functions. First it gives the person a cognitive grasp of the situation, a map of the territory he or she is traversing. Having a sense of the terrain and knowing others have traveled these regions provides considerable relief in itself. Second, it changes the person's relationship to the experience. When the person (and those around him or her) shifts into seeing what is occurring as positive and helpful rather than bad and sick, this changes the person's way of relating to the experience. To know that this process is healing and growthful permits the person to turn and face the inner flow of experiences, to welcome them rather than turning away or trying to suppress them. The person can begin to relax and "go with the flow" rather than tensing up and trying to control. By coming into better relationship with the inner flow of experience, the person can more easily maneuver within these inner realms and better tolerate temporarily painful feelings and experiences instead of trying to immediately cut them off.

Providing a Container. The next order of business is to provide a safe container for this experience. If it is at all possible, it is a great help to have a sanctuary, a retreat from the ordinary world in which to experience the profound consciousness changes that are occurring. It is preferable that this not be a hospital or some other clinical, sterile environment. Ideally this safe haven should be comfortable and quiet, warm and home-like with soft lighting, and connected to nature. Such ideal settings are not often available, in which case the person's home may need to be good enough. The idea is to protect the person undergoing a spiritual emergency from the psychic stimulation of the everyday world, which is usually experienced as painful and interfering with the inner process. It is important to feel as free as possible for catharsis and physical release, so that the person can move about, vocalize, scream, cry, or express whatever feelings come up without fear of disturbing others.

Presence. In spiritual emergency the personal presence of the therapist is key. Although some people are able to sail these waters successfully by themselves, for many people the presence of one or more wise, compassionate guides or companions on this journey can be of enormous help. The requirements of the therapist in this situation are far greater than for normal clinical work. The heightened state of awareness that accompanies the person's openness and vulnerability makes the integrity and authenticity of the therapist crucial. The slightest bit of the therapist being "off," condescending, overly alarmed, or pretending to know more than he or she actually does can send the client careening off into a veritable Niagara of fear, images of distrust, or paranoia.

Since the "being" dimension of the client is so powerfully activated, the being dimension of the therapist comes into sharp focus. Warmth and compassion combined with a degree of softness and gentleness are essential, for hardness, coldness, or insensitivity can be highly jarring to the delicate and refined perceptions of a person undergoing these consciousness changes. Additionally a certain calmness and quiet confidence serve to energetically reassure and soothe the apprehension and alarm that are frequently present. The therapist's own awareness of inner states and personal experience of opening to the Divine furnish a crucial common ground to the person's experience.

Beyond the personal qualities of the therapist there are skills and a knowledge base that are needed. Solid clinical experience with both psychosis and spiritual emergency is the first requirement. Training in both domains makes for an easy diagnosis much of the time, as well as greater appreciation of the gray areas in between. It also supports the therapist in doing whatever education the client or family may need. Access to good supervision is essential, as is knowing when to refer.

Grounding. The spiritual teacher Mira Richard (also known as the Mother), who lived in India, once remarked that the very best protection against various spiritual attacks was the body. Many times in spiritual emergency the person is relatively disconnected from the body and lost in a ferment of experiences on an inner or astral plane. Clinical experience confirms that grounding spiritual emergency in the body allows the process to proceed in a more assimilable way. Over the years a number of ways of helping the person ground the experience have been developed.

Diet. One easy and effective strategy for helping to bring the person back into the body is to eat grounding foods. This means eating "heavy" foods and staying away from etheric, "light" foods. Specifically this translates into a diet of grains (preferably whole grains), beans, potatoes, dairy products, and meat (if the person eats meat). Staying away from raw fruit, vegetables (salads), or juices is recommended. Vegetables if eaten should be cooked. Sugar and stimulants like caffeine or chocolate are better avoided.

Exercise and movement. Exercise of all kind brings consciousness into the body. The person may not be up to learning new forms of exercise, so types of exercise that the person is familiar with work best. In spiritual emergency different ways of moving the body may even suggest themselves naturally, for example, people find themselves moving into spontaneous *asanas* (yoga postures) without any previous knowledge of hatha yoga. Any physical discipline that the person can relate to is helpful in this regard.

Walking is another activity that may suggest itself, although where the person walks assumes a greater importance than under ordinary circumstances. Long walks in nature can be very centering. However a stroll along congested city intersections may be more disturbing than calming. Finding parks or less crowded areas to walk is advisable.

Physical work that is agreeable to the person is another way of coming back into the physical world. Such things as sweeping, washing dishes, working in a garden with the earth can all be grounding. Any way of connecting to the natural world promotes a more embodied focus, whether this is through working with the earth, being in nature, or just being outside looking at clouds and breathing fresh air. Another possibility for connecting to natural elements that can be done indoors is sensing the ground through mindfully standing, sitting, or lying, which brings a person back into the fundamental relationship to gravity and the supporting earth.

Bodywork. Physical touch focuses consciousness on the physical. Taking frequent showers or baths is another way of awakening sensory and body awareness. Light massage or bodywork can gently invite the person back into the body as well as reduce anxiety and tension. Some people, it should be noted, definitely do *not* want to be touched. Obviously this should be respected, for the affirming of boundaries is itself conducive to defining and grounding the self.

Medication. Medication is generally discouraged for treating spiritual emergency, but it need not be ruled out. The danger is that medication will simply suppress the process and leave it unfinished, denying the person the healing potential of a complete resolution. But sometimes the process is so forceful, the person is being shaken so powerfully, or the person's anxiety is so great, that it is helpful to slow the process down or reduce the person's anxiety without stopping the process altogether. Small amounts of alcohol or minor tranquilizers can often alleviate some of the most distressing feelings and allow the person to better assimilate the experience instead of being overwhelmed by it. This should be monitored carefully to see that it is not overdone, for some people will seek immediate relief through obliteration rather than ride the crisis out (most notable in people for whom substance abuse can be a problem).

Sleep. Sleep can be of great help to some people, especially when it was sleep deprivation that helped trigger the crisis, as sometimes happens during meditation retreats. Even if this is not the case, however, sleep has a grounding function. Encouraging the person to sleep as much as possible is helpful, for consciousness is refreshed and settled after a good sleep. The inability to sleep *can be* an indication for the judicious use of medication.

Changing meditation. Meditation is oftentimes a catalyst for spiritual emergency. Intensive meditation retreats in particular are known for occasional casualties, but also a long-term meditation practice, which can be likened to a slow, years-long drilling for oil, sometimes becomes a "gusher" as new spiritual experiences rush in when the veil is suddenly penetrated. Stopping or decreasing meditation are ways of affecting what is occurring. At times modifications to the meditation practice will emerge intuitively which the person may experiment with. When the process feels out of control, stopping altogether is suggested.

A corollary to this is to stop all anxious situations and activities that provoke the spiritual emergency. While this may seem like common sense, many times it has not become fully conscious that certain situations or locales or activities serve to intensify the inner process. Identifying provoking stimuli is helpful so that they can be minimized or eliminated.

Experiential Therapy. Therapy with spiritual emergency needs to be more experiential, to have a wider range of possibilities for cathartic expression and emotional release than the usual office set-up allows for. There needs to be a safe space to express fully whatever impulses and feelings arise—raging, crying, holding, hugging, being held, breathing loudly, dancing and moving freely, vomiting, screaming. As the psyche opens up, a whole range of basic desires, fears, traumas, wounds, and developmental arrests emerge, often with great power and intensity since many of the usual filtering mechanisms are not in place. Being able to physically act out and release the intense energies being activated is an important way to facilitate this process.

Creative expression can also help. The language of symbol and metaphor is one way that many people are able to connect spiritual experience with ordinary reality. Expressive arts modalities such as drawing, painting, coloring, working with clay, music, writing poetry, using movement and dance—whatever medium a person may be drawn to—are ways of articulating and working through inner experience. The Grofs use mandala drawings at the end of breathwork sessions as a way to synthesize what occurs. Such nonverbal means can help the person express inner experience and be a way to integrate what can never be fully verbalized.

While talking serves an important grounding and integrating function, it should not be overdone out of the therapist's own anxiety. Alternating periods of talking with periods of silence and nonverbal experiencing is important. Excessive verbalization can be a way of prematurely bringing the person down and dissipating important dimensions of the experience. Too much silence, on the other hand, can be experienced by some as abandonment or lack of caring. The therapist needs to strike an ever-changing balance between the two. As the person comes back from the experience and verbalizing comes back "on line," there will be ample opportunity to symbolize and integrate the experience.

An expanded time frame is also important. Spiritual emergency does not fit neatly into weekly 50-minute sessions. Having sessions last several hours over consecutive days is not uncommon, although once the crisis stage has passed, a more standard schedule can resume.

IMPLICATIONS OF SPIRITUAL EMERGENCY

In Thomas Kuhn's classic book *The Structure of Scientific Revolutions* (1962), Kuhn notes that when a new paradigm is about to replace an older, less useful paradigm, the new emerging paradigm calls attention to some of the anomalies that had been overlooked or not explained by the old paradigm. The old mechanistic, materialistic, Cartesian paradigm that typifies much of modern scientific thought, psychology and psychiatry is being increasingly challenged by spiritual and transpersonal approaches. As this occurs, one of the anomalies that is being brought up as inadequately explained by conventional psychology is spiritual emergency. To anyone well trained in both standard psychiatric evaluation and spiritual emergency, it is quite clear that this is a phenomenon that cannot be explained by the conventional paradigm. Spiritual emergency is a paradigm buster.

Observing the process of kundalini awakening and the profound consciousness changes occurring in this; witnessing the incredibly accurate psychic perceptions of someone undergoing an opening to psychic realms; reading reports of great precision about events that transpired while a person was medically dead; hearing of many people who have had their spiritual crises brought to an abrupt end and were then indoctrinated in the belief that their experiences were a sickness to be ashamed of by well-meaning but poorly trained psychiatric staffs;

working with someone who experienced God's grace and experiences of cosmic unity, love, and bliss, yet who's psychological functioning was temporarily disrupted and who barely escaped being hospitalized and medicated: at some point it becomes clear that all of this cannot be reduced merely to psychopathology.

The recent introduction into the DSM IV of the new diagnostic category of spiritual emergency, under the classification of "Religious or Spiritual Problem," is evidence that the new transpersonal paradigm is having some impact upon conventional psychiatry. Yet for the moment the transpersonal paradigm, as exciting and cutting edge as it is, has not yet gathered enough momentum to significantly offset the current mechanistic paradigm.

The current trend in conventional psychiatry, toward so-called biopsychiatry, is severely challenged by transpersonal psychology in general and spiritual emergency in particular. Against the materialistic, Cartesian mind-set that pervades much of contemporary psychological thinking, the transpersonal perspective argues that consciousness is not simply a result of the body. Sri Aurobindo (1971b) once remarked that although it seems like consciousness is in the body, actually the body is in consciousness. If so, then attempts to manipulate consciousness via the body and drugs will always be limited and partial, for the sources of consciousness go well beyond the body. Although clearly the body has an essential role, biopsychiatry can never yield fundamental understandings of the mind, for consciousness cannot be reduced to biology.

And if mental hospitals are full of people who are not only psychotic but are possessed as well, people whose psyches are being stimulated, pushed, and fed on by beings and forces from other planes, then we are just taking our first baby steps in coming to an understanding and treatment of what is called psychopathology and its possible treatment.

Chapter Seven

Altered States of Consciousness

Altered states of consciousness come in a variety of different forms, ranging from hypnosis and dreams to dissociative states. But what has had the greatest impact upon society as a whole, as well as upon transpersonal psychology and the field of consciousness study in particular, are those states produced by psychedelic drugs. Psychedelics are important in transpersonal psychology for several reasons, but the chief one is because with proper preparation these substances can reliably produce transpersonal and spiritual experiences of profound intensity and power. A psychedelic journey can open consciousness to vast new dimensions of experience, shattering previous conceptions of reality and revealing a new world of perception where spirit is no longer an abstract concept but a living, vivid actuality.

In some sense transpersonal psychology is a child of the psychedelic revolution of the '60s. Most all of the founders of transpersonal psychology have been influenced by psychedelics or originally became interested in spirituality as a result of psychedelic experiences. It may be no accident that the *Journal of Transpersonal Psychology* was born shortly after 1967's Summer of Love, a period of great psychedelic experimentation in virtually every part of society.

The cultural, psychic, and spiritual landscape has changed considerably since that time. Drugs have gone underground. People no longer are introduced to spiritual experiences through psychedelics in such high numbers as before. But psychedelic drug use as a method of self-exploration has remained a force in transpersonal psychology and continues to have a significant following.

It should be acknowledged that, while the original enthusiasm of Leary and other popularizers of psychedelics ignored them, there are indeed hazards to psychedelic use. Since Western society was first introduced to psychedelics in such an unstructured, undisciplined way, naturally there were many casualties and much understandable fear about such uncontrolled use. The 60s and 70s also taught us about another danger. When we open the door to psychedelic drugs, the other drugs of abuse can easily rush in. For the innocent and undiscriminating, this can lead to great pain and travail. Society is still reeling from the fallout of those tumultuous times.

With hindsight it is clear that much of this could have been prevented with proper supervision, guidance, and containment, but at the time there was no knowledge base in the West on which to draw, something most indigenous cultures possess and ritually use. For while we often think of the drug scene as something special to our culture, it is important to view it within a cross-cultural and historical context. Virtually every culture in history has had ritualized ways of using drugs to alter consciousness, and it goes back as far in history as there is writing. In the West alcohol has primarily been the drug of choice. In the East marijuana has primarily been the drug of choice. Both East and West have used psychedelic mushrooms at times, as have Africa and the New World. One exception to this is the Eskimos, who had no access to drugs until whites provided them with alcohol.

Andrew Weill (1972) posits that the drive to alter consciousness periodically seems to be inherent, much like the drives for sex, food, et cetera. From a transpersonal perspective this can be seen as part of the evolutionary drive forward toward higher, unitive states of consciousness. Although not everyone is drawn to drug use as a way to express this drive, for most of history and in almost every culture, most people have participated in some form of ritual drug use.

Most writers in this area agree alcohol and the common drugs of abuse (cocaine and other stimulants, heroin and other opiates, and depressants) are not very significant in terms of the exploration of consciousness. While every consciousness experiment with drugs ultimately has some effect on the psychic economy of the person, such drugs do not have the profound consciousness opening effects of psychedelic compounds, which is what this discussion will focus upon.

EFFECTS OF PSYCHEDELIC DRUGS

There are two major classes of psychedelic drugs that are in widespread use today. The first are the true psychedelics—LSD, mescaline, and psilocybin—for which the term psychedelic was coined. The word "psychedelic" is usually explained as meaning "mind-manifesting," from the Greek "psyche" (mind) and "delos" (manifesting). But psyche also means soul or spirit. This is significant from a transpersonal perspective, for it shifts the meaning of psychedelic to "mind and soul manifesting." The second class includes MDMA and MDA, and is sometimes referred to as the feeling enhancers or empathogens (Naranjo, 1973; Adamson, 1985), which will be considered later in the chapter.

LSD, by far the most widely used psychedelic, is a synthetic chemical that is active in extremely minute amounts (100 millionths of a gram) and produces a dramatic expansion of consciousness as a great quantity of psychic energy is released, resulting in a highly energized, at times almost electric, state of consciousness. Mescaline is the active ingredient in the peyote cactus found in the deserts of the American southwest and Mexico. Its action is a smooth, deepening and expansion of consciousness. When ingested in plant form, nausea is a usual side effect, which is absent or much reduced when the mescaline is extracted from the plant or synthesized in the laboratory. Psilocybin is the active ingredient in certain mushrooms found around the world. A relaxation response typically accompanies its consciousness expanding effects, so it tends to be experienced as the most subdued of the psychedelics. Apart from these slight variations in the level of arousal, however, the effects of LSD, mescaline, and psilocybin are roughly similar.

These three psychedelics effect consciousness as *non-specific awareness amplifiers*, that is, the full scale of consciousness—physical, emotional, mental, spiritual—is opened up, the normal filters are lifted, and consciousness extends. The depth dimension is unveiled as consciousness widens, deepens, heightens, opens within to a vast interior spaciousness.

At the physical level, the senses come alive with a whole new range of perception, which inspired Aldous Huxley to take the title of his first book about psychedelics, *The Doors of Perception* (1954 title page), from a quote by William Blake, "If the doors of perception were cleansed, every thing would be seen as it is, infinite." Each sensory modality and experience, from the bliss of sexual pleasure to the taste buds exploding at the taste of a peach, can become a world unto itself. However, the worlds of sight and sound reveal whole universes of new experience. Internal visual displays and visions of new worlds unfold with closed eyes, but the greatest wonders are discovered in beholding the splendors of the outer world, especially the extraordinary beauty of nature. And hearing discloses a realm of experience that was there all along but never noticed. Laboratory tests of auditory discrimination show that on LSD people can physically hear better, both higher and softer sounds that they ordinarily cannot perceive. Music opens to new dimensions of feeling and appreciation as the aesthetic sense is heightened far beyond what it is in normal consciousness.

This enlargement and refinement of perception is also accompanied by a deep sense of presence and meaning in this enhanced sensory field. The sensory world becomes intensely engaging, far more so than our usual cursory acknowledgment of the world around us. There is the experience of waking up from the trance-like condition we call normal consciousness into a profound sensory feast that is exquisitely beautiful, intrinsically meaningful, and satisfying.

Stanislav Grof (1985) asserts that the opening of this sensory barrier is without much consciousness significance. When LSD is used merely for entertainment, a kind of "inner Disneyland," this may be true. But when this sensory opening occurs in a context of psycho-spiritual growth, such an assertion may be a premature dismissal of this level of consciousness, for this is a dimension of experience that can be accessed without drugs and made a regular feature of normal consciousness. One far-reaching effect that psychedelic drugs have on lifestyle can be an opening to the vistas of the sense life, bringing one to more fully inhabit an awakened physical consciousness. Indeed, Charlotte Selver's work with sensory awareness illustrates how profoundly the opening of the senses can affect consciousness, and it has many correlates in meditation practices of various spiritual traditions. Coming into one's body and fully appreciating the beauty and sensory wonder that is native to our body sense may be one of the greatest teachings the psychedelics have to offer.

On the emotional level the psychedelics bring into high relief the major emotional wounds and conflicts within the psyche. Grof has charted this territory more fully than any other researcher, and a more extensive discussion is given below.

On the mental level there is a release into a vast mind space in which thought is no longer confined to verbal symbols but becomes far more fluid, flexible, and seems to operate from a more intuitive level or be informed by a more luminous source. Thought is more rapid, and there are insights into a deeper order of things as well as new connections within existing conceptions and knowledge. Creative problem solving is one use that was studied with great promise before legal sanctions ended such research.

On the spiritual level there is access to the whole range of spiritual experiences described by the perennial philosophy. There are experiences of the intermediate plane, such as clairvoyance, subtle perception of auras and energy fields, seeing different spirits, and knowledge of other forms of existence such as animals, insects, plants, and even the earth itself. There are experiences of the soul with its light, love, joy, power, and great peace, along with greater communion with the Personal Divine and the celestial realm. There are also experiences of the Impersonal dimension, of "Big Mind," of immense inner space in which consciousness is allowed to roam freely in vastness. There is also the classic cosmic consciousness experience originally described by Bucke (1923) in which there is entire ego loss and an experience of vast light, unimaginable bliss, and a consciousness of the entire universe aware of itself in an endless, ecstatic moment. Some commentators have noted that for some reason this only seems to occur once or twice for those who experience it and generally does not recur.

It is not that psychedelics magically invoke God. Rather it seems that if the set and setting (see below) support it, the psychedelic compounds somehow act to thin or lift the normally thick veil between normal consciousness and the spiritual dimension, allowing the spiritual dimension to be revealed.

Any or all of these physical, emotional, mental, or spiritual effects may be experienced. Often a person begins in the sensory realm and later begins to traverse the inner realms, but other people seem to journey to the interior spaces immediately. In order to account for the great variation in people's experiences with psychedelics, Leary (1962, 1967, 1968) first introduced the terms *set* and *setting*. *Set* refers to the psychological expectations, hopes, fears, moods, intentions, and mind set that people approach the experience with. *Setting* refers to the physical environment, as well as the interpersonal and emotional environment in which the drug is taken. The psychedic experience will grow into a person's set (how they approach the experience inwardly), and setting (whether a hospital, a home, nature, a crowded city, a rock concert, or whatever) and the other people in that setting (is the interpersonal atmosphere one of total trust and support for inner exploration or is it geared for partying or is it hostile to anything of this kind?). Thus a difficult emotional wound can be worked through to a new level of integration if the set and setting support this or it can become a frightening "bad trip" if the set and setting do not support this.

The most comprehensive map of psychedelic experience comes from Stanislav Grof, whose 30 years of studying psychedelics has made him the world's leading psychedelic researcher. A more thorough discussion of his work is offered in chapter four, so this is but a very summary review.

Grof maps out three realms of consciousness revealed by psychedelics. The first realm he describes as the sensory barrier and the personal unconscious. Here the psychedelic effect is to open the senses and to increase a person's access to the personal unconscious. He thinks that Freudian psychoanalysis has best described this realm of consciousness and finds confirmations of many of Freud's discoveries in the psychedelic work.

The second realm Grof calls the perinatal realm, and it relates to the birth process. His observations have led him to conclude that there are four basic perinatal matrices, each one corresponding to a different stage of birth and each providing an organizing schema for related psychological material.

The third major realm Grof calls the transpersonal realm. This is the area of spiritual experiences such as are described above. Although it is not necessary to work through all of one's psychological material in order to enter into the transpersonal realm, Grof notes that a connection seems to exist through the perinatal realm, as if birth provides a kind of doorway into the spiritual.

Grof's map has found wide acceptance as a thorough explanation of the phenomena encountered in altered state work. Although he has attempted to apply this map to consciousness in general, this wider application is problematic and has not been greeted with such enthusiasm.

The question arises, do the psychedelics produce genuine spiritual experience, or only a vivid psychic imitation, a kind of astral analogue? Grof has shown that the phenomenological reports of psychedelic experiences seem to be identical with the classical mystical literature. But opinions are split on this issue, with experience with psychedelics generally being the deciding factor. Those who have experienced the psychedelics tend to think of the experience as intrinsically valid, whereas some of those who have not tend to dismiss the experience. This holds even when those trying the psychedelics are religiously trained seekers. An example is the famous Good Friday experiment in which Walter Pahnke administered small capsules to 20 Protestant divinity students before a church service on Good Friday in 1962. Half the capsules contained psilocybin and half a placebo. The majority of the psilocybin group reported experiences that were indistinguishable from classical mystical experiences. In a 25-year follow-up study the experimental subjects unanimously described their Good Friday psilocybin experience as having had elements of, "a genuine mystical nature and characterized it as one of the high points of their spiritual life" (Doblin, 1991, p. 13).

What may be even more important is the effect of such experiences, which generally is a radically altered worldview and an activation or renewal of spiritual interests and possibilities. Whatever the "true" nature is of psychedelically induced spiritual experiences, the *effect* of a spiritual awakening after the drug experience is beyond dispute.

MODELS OF WORKING THERAPEUTICALLY

A number of ways have developed for using psychedelic compounds in psychotherapy. Unfortunately, since psychedelics were made illegal 30 years ago, these models were either developed in the 1950s or else have emerged from underground experimentation. Since the mid-60s there has not been an atmosphere in which a wide range of therapeutic methods, open discussion of results, and ensuing dialogue could be freely carried out. As the FDA gradually eases the impediments to such research, however, this much needed exchange may once again begin to happen.

Low Dose Therapy

One of the first ways to use psychedelics in therapy was to simply give a small to moderate dose to a psychotherapy client and to do regular therapy with the person. Originally called psycholytic therapy, this approach was popular in Europe in the late 1950s and was gaining support in the United States in the early 1960s, up until psychedelics were made illegal. One of its great advantages is that because it utilizes low or moderate dosage levels, communication between therapist and client is not a problem. Also, the experience is not so "far out" that it is hard to remember afterward. Since there is easier access to the material which had been uncovered in the psychedelic session, the post-session work is considerably facilitated.

Classical psychoanalysis and Jungian analysis were the two major therapeutic modalities used with low-dose therapy, as these were the main two clinical approaches used in the 1950s. Predictably, the Freudians reported a higher incidence of childhood memories in their clients and the Jungians reported more transcendental experiences among theirs. The Freudian clients reported considerable therapeutic improvement after reexperiencing these childhood experiences, and the Jungian clients reported improvement after theirs. What is interesting is that when the Freudian clients reported transcendent visions, there was no accompanying improvement. This led researcher Charles Savage to note at the time, "Because the results are so much influenced by the personality, aims, and expectations of the therapist, . . . where there is no therapeutic intent, there is no therapeutic result. . . . I think we can also say that where the atmosphere is fear-ridden and skeptical, the results are generally not good. . . . (F)ew drugs are so dependent on the milieu and require such close attention to it as LSD does" (quoted in Yenson, 1988 p. 40). With our increased understanding of psychotherapy and the much greater variety of therapeutic approaches available today, we can only speculate about what might emerge were this experiment to resume.

High-Dose Therapy

This approach, originally called psychedelic therapy, holds that improved functioning results from a transpersonal or mystical experience, such as encounters with death-rebirth or ego-transcendent type of experiences. The major emphasis is not on the facilitation of therapy, as in the low-dose model. Rather the focus is upon an experience of the numinous, which then brings about improved functioning. This was originally pioneered by Humphry Osmond and Abram Hoffer in the 1950s in their work with chronic alcoholics. Giving a single large dose of LSD or sometimes repeating this over three or four sessions, these two researchers discovered that the greatest improvement came in those alcoholic clients who had mystical experiences. The spiritual experience caused a major reorientation to the person's life, which in turn led to therapeutic improvement. While the experience of an intense, transcendent experience can be powerfully life changing, this approach has the obvious disadvantage of not working through the person's psychological material in a more thorough way.

Programmed Therapy

Carrying the importance of set and setting to one logical conclusion, Salvador Roquet, a psychotherapist from Mexico City, developed a form of therapy in which different psychedelic compounds are given to clients in a group setting (Roquet, Favreau, Ocana, & de Velasco, 1975). The sights and sounds that the clients experience are programmed by the session leader using slide projectors, movie projectors, and stereo sound systems. After ingesting one psychedelic compound or several together, the entire group is exposed to a continuous cascade of images and music designed to evoke deep unconscious material. The session usually begins with appropriate music that accompanies images and themes ranging from chaos, war, destruction, death, and sexuality. As it heads toward resolution toward the end of the session, the themes shift to soft, serene images and sounds of nature. Usually lasting all night, the psychological material is integrated the following morning and afternoon as participants then speak and share their experiences. Roquet scheduled one drug session per month with a follow-up non-drug group session lasting eight hours and an individual non-drug session. He reported improvement in 85% of his clients.

While this approach has many advantages, such as the efficiency of working in a group session and the evocation of psychological material, its drawbacks are the inability to attune to an individual's particular state of mind and the forcing of pre-programmed psychological themes that may be out of touch with the client's actual process in the moment, thus impeding the free emergence of material that would otherwise spontaneously arise. Nevertheless, it is an intriguing contribution which many people have found useful, often as an introduction to psychedelic work.

Shamanic Approaches

Taking the lead from shamans and indigenous groups in North and South America who have ritually used peyote, magic mushrooms, and other psychoactive plants for centuries, some therapists have developed a format in which the group participants ingest a particular compound sitting in a circle and stay in this sacred circle for the entire journey. Some therapists use only natural psychedelic plant sources, while others augment the plant sources with LSD to enhance the effect. Generally it begins with brief introductions and perhaps statements of intent, followed by drumming (which may continue throughout the entire session) and prayers. As the psychedelic effects come on, however, there is little or no talk as the members becomes increasingly drawn into their own inner worlds. If there is a problem, the guide is present to help, otherwise the sacred circle provides the container for each person's inner voyage.

Here again there are advantages, especially the group setting and the absence of any pre-programmed themes to be worked with. The disadvantages lie in the direction of a less explicitly psychotherapeutic context and, because of the group setting, a less attuned therapeutic presence for each person.

Self-Therapy

One model that is followed by many people on their own, particularly after they have become familiar with psychedelic states of consciousness and are able to navigate fairly well on their own and no longer need the introductory help of a guide, is taking a psychedelic either alone or with another close person or group. The intent is explicitly self-exploration, there is great trust among the dyad or group, and the setting can be a private home, in nature, or anyplace that is well away from other people, so that the experience can be safely contained and is free from outside interference. With preliminary centering and a conscious choice of the physical setting, the psychedelic session opens into whatever realm of consciousness is ready to emerge. If there is a particular intent or issue, then whatever necessary cues or stimuli are deemed helpful are arranged, such as, pictures of childhood, parents, et cetera.

Some therapists who value psychedelic work yet do not do it for fear of legal consequences feel safer in sanctioning this kind of exploration with their clients, since it is separate from the actual therapy work. Advantages include a therapeutic or personal growth intention, the freedom to design the setting to personal preferences and make whatever interpersonal communication is needed without fitting oneself to a pre-arranged format. Disadvantages are in the lack of a trained therapist to help sail through difficult waters, although with sufficient psychotherapy experience and previous psychedelic experience, this is usually not a problem.

EFFECTS OF THE FEELING ENHANCERS

The second class of psychedelics is often referred to as "feeling enhancers," a term that was coined by Naranjo (1973) and which captures the phenomenological effects of these drugs better than any other term. This includes the very popular MDMA (also known as "E," Ecstasy, or "X" on the street), MDA (which was popular in the 70s but now has been mostly replaced by MDMA), MMDA, and a host of other MD . . . series of compounds. Although there are differences between the variations of feeling enhancers (for example, MDA tends to evoke past material more readily while MDMA is more present centered), they all have a similar effect. This discussion will center on MDMA, for it is popular and readily available.

Whereas LSD and the true psychedelics open up the entire range or spectrum of consciousness, the feeling enhancers act very selectively and open up one particular band or level of consciousness, namely the heart and feelings. There is minimal change in the rest of consciousness. Mental functioning remains basically normal, hallucinations or sensory distortions are not usually present or are minimal, but the emotional realm of experience is greatly amplified. This only minor change in the rest of consciousness has the great advantage that, since there is not such a great difference between MDMA consciousness and regular consciousness, there can be greater recall and integration of what emerged during the session.

Because MDMA and the other MD . . . series of drugs are psychedelic variations of an amphetamine base, there is a stimulating effect to them and, at least for the first number of trips, an exquisitely blissful physical feeling often accompanies these experiences. This physical effect tends to fade with repeated MDMA use, although not entirely. This physical effect is largely responsible for its street name, Ecstasy.

A number of metaphors have been used to describe its psychological effects. One is that MDMA is like giving an anesthetic to a person's neuroses. It puts the defenses to sleep, so there is greatly heightened emotional awareness and insight. Another description is that MDMA eliminates or greatly reduces fear and anxiety. This allows feelings below the surface to be felt and experienced. A third metaphor describes the effect of MDMA as opening the heart chakra. As the fourth chakra opens, there is an amplification of the usual barriers to an open, spacious heart. The normal issues and feelings of ordinary consciousness that act to close the heart and restrict the flow of love can be experienced and gone through to a wider, more deeply loving and centered space that emanates from the heart.

The rare "bad trips" on MDMA can be seen as lack of skill in navigating this passage to the inner heart, a refusal to acknowledge, deal with and work through the negative emotional patterns, wounds, defensive postures that make up so much of ordinary ego existence. Thus the lack of a psychotherapeutic orientation or willingness to explore one's inner shadow is the biggest potential psychological hazard this class of drugs presents.

Because feelings, especially positive feelings, are so enhanced with MDMA, and because our feelings are so linked to other people, MDMA is a much more social drug than LSD. Indeed, MDMA has become something of a party drug and a regular feature at raves. Since interpersonal fears are so much reduced and the joy of being with other people is so heightened, it is obvious why this would be so. However, this can become one of the biggest distractions with MDMA. While having a good time and using MDMA recreationally is one possible use for such a drug, from a psychotherapeutic perspective it can also be a wasted opportunity to explore the depths of one's own psyche or to explore the realms of intimacy with significant others. It should also be noted that taking MDMA alone in a non-social setting can also be powerfully revealing, and it is in individual and couples therapy that MDMA holds greatest promise.

WORKING THERAPEUTICALLY

MDMA was not used legally for long enough to develop the variety of treatment models that came out of research with LSD. Between the time it was rediscovered by Alexander Shulgin, Ph.D., and introduced into the psychedelic drug scene as a legal improvement over MDA in the late 1970s until its becoming illegal in the late 1980s, it was used informally in many settings. Psychotherapists were particularly attracted to it because of its power to open up the psyche to feelings and affects in a relatively mild, controllable way. Also, as noted above, since MDMA consciousness is not so very different from normal consciousness, it readily lends itself to working afterward with the psychological material that emerged during the session. Mostly MDMA has been used in individual psychotherapy, couples therapy, and informally for self-exploration and group exploration.

Since the length of the MDMA trip is so much shorter than with LSD (2–3 hours vs. 8–12 hours for LSD), it can fit more easily into a typical psychotherapy structure. Many therapists have had clients come during a regularly scheduled hour or scheduled a double session while the client was experiencing the peak effects of the drug. Other therapists have preferred a more informal structure of inviting the client to their house for an afternoon or evening and making themselves available periodically and whenever the client requested it. These formats work equally well for individual or couples therapy.

Profound depths of feelings, wounds, and psychological trauma can be readily accessed with MDMA, which makes it a psychotherapeutic drug par excellence. It has also successfully been used with specific client groups, such as cancer patients, drug addicts, and the dying. MDMA can be used to feel with great intensity deep emotions and to express these emotions simply and clearly or dramatically and cathartically. Periods of nonverbal experiencing often alternate with verbal expression and exploration. And because the overall consciousness is so similar to ordinary reality, this material is easily remembered and worked through more fully in the days and weeks afterward. The coming-down portion of the journey, like with LSD, is often a time of integration, a time for gaining a larger perspective of what was experienced during the peak.

Some of the most dramatic effects of MDMA therapy have come from work with couples. Couples who are in trouble, who have accumulated secrets or hurts, or who simply have drifted apart and are no longer very intimate with each other find that MDMA can create a degree of intimacy that allows the distance to be bridged enough to begin facing the issues and feelings that have separated them. This shift into greater depth of communication may make it seem as though years of therapy can be accomplished in a single session. However, it is probably more accurate to say that the window of opportunity which MDMA provides can uncover material that may have taken years to unearth, but the working-through process will still take the necessary months or years that any system takes to accommodate healing and growth.

GUIDELINES FOR USE

With the legal sanctions against psychedelic use, the ethical issues of therapists using psychedelics in therapy work with clients are very murky. To be sure, some of the ethical issues are clear, for example, it is obviously illegal for a therapist to provide psychedelics to a client. This has not prevented an underground therapeutic community from doing so, but it remains a huge risk for any therapist. For those therapists who do not wish to jeopardize their licenses by illegal actions, there are a host of other ethical dilemmas to consider. To name just a few: If a client comes in high on a psychedelic, is it ethical to work therapeutically with the person, or is it more ethical to refuse to work with him or her? Certainly a very good case can be made that, in terms of client welfare, the most therapeutically beneficial choice would be to work with the person and provide a safe, psychologically facilitative environment rather than to refuse service and abandon the client.

What if the client tells the therapist in advance that he or she will be coming high to a session? Should the therapist agree to this or refuse? Is offering information to a client who is beginning to experiment with psychedelics helpful or can this be construed as encouragement? Where does support for a client's growth-steps become encouragement for illegal activity? Is support for psychedelic experimentation ethical or unethical, or does it depend upon the client's intent? These are thorny ethical dilemmas that confront therapists. As yet there are no clear-cut ethical standards from which to operate. Although client welfare is the overriding concern, what in these circumstances constitutes client welfare? The answer depends upon an individual therapist's beliefs and life experience.

Although there was a great deal published about psychedelics in the '60s, today there is a paucity of material to guide an interested explorer or therapist. However, with the benefit of several decades of experience and much informal exploration by the culture at large, there are some definite guidelines that can optimize a psychedelic experience and minimize the hazards. These guidelines have been developed over many years of working with psychedelics in a variety of settings. My own background includes spending a decade working in the drug treatment field, where I worked in sessions and on hotlines with many clients who were on a variety of different psychedelics and in a variety of different emotional states; in hospitals with clients on extremely high dosages, who were often brought in by the police; at numerous rock concerts as part of a medical team, with concert goers who were having bad trips; with individuals and couples when some psychedelic substances were legal. These guidelines are put forward to help therapists who may encounter clients experimenting with psychedelics.

What any guidelines boil down to are attempts to stress the importance of controlling the set and setting as much as possible, so that there are the fewest possible chances for toxic influences to disturb a psychedelic journey.

1. Controlling for set involves preparation or purification at different levels: mental, emotional, physical, and spiritual.

    Mental preparation includes obtaining knowledge about the various realms of psychedelic experience where one might travel and knowledge about the effects and duration. The more a person knows about psychedelics the better. A positive expectation toward the experience is important, as is an exploratory attitude toward what might emerge during the session. Perhaps the most significant factor is a person's intention in taking the substance. The willingness to enter into negative, scary, painful states is essential to safely navigate the psychedelic seas. Otherwise one becomes merely avoidant of unpleasant affect states, which is a formula for disaster. Taking a psychedelic for recreation, fun, or escape can create a very different relationship to one's inner experience than does an intention of growth or self-exploration. There is nothing wrong with recreational use. After all, in almost all cultures recreational drug use is permitted; it is only the type of drug permitted that varies. But it is here that the hazards of psychedelic use are most likely to occur. A serious psychotherapeutic or growthful intention is the best insurance there is for it to be an expansive, liberating journey.

Emotional preparation includes taking time to center oneself before the session. This may mean spending time in the weeks and days before the session reviewing the possible issues or directions one wants to focus on, tuning in to one's emotional state as the time nears, and making sure it all feels right. Advance planning and anticipation of the journey can allow the issues one wants to explore time to "cook," as well as to arrange for any special arrangements such as photographs, special music, mandalas or religious objects, et cetera. Some fears and anxiety are almost inevitable in the beginning, until a person has confidence in being able to sail the psychedelic seas, so it is unrealistic to expect to be without these. But in addition it is important to feel safe in the physical and interpersonal environment.

For the first few journeys it is important to have a guide, someone the person trusts as fully as possible, to act as ground control and a source of reassurance and guidance if needed. Obviously no one should be a guide who is not thoroughly familiar with the psychedelic terrain. Trust in the interpersonal atmosphere is crucial for a good experience, and fear poses the greatest peril to it. If the guide is not a trusted friend, it is important that the person spend time with the guide before-hand, to get to know him or her and feel comfortable.

Controlling the physical set means making sure the body is in good form for the experience. Practically this translates into being physically healthy. Taking it while sick or recuperating or taking other medication is less than optimal. Also, when a psy-chedelic's effect begins, consciousness tends to roam around the body, and some people experience some nausea. The best safeguard against this is to take psychedelics on an empty stom-ach. Fasting is best, but to have eaten nothing for at least six to eight hours beforehand will greatly reduce potential nausea and extra body "noise." Appetite is usually suppressed during the session, but in the coming-down phase food can be exquis-itely delicious.

Spiritual preparation involves as much meditation, prayer, and spiritual practice beforehand and while coming on as feels right. Entering into a psychedelic space is greatly facilitated by a meditative preparation. Indeed, the meditative skills of non-reactive attention to whatever arises, trust, and devotion are enormously helpful in taking the inner journey.

2. Controlling for setting is the other variable. It is best to do this in a place that provides a safe container for the experience. There is a big difference between LSD and MDMA in this regard. With LSD it is important that there be protection from outside influences. Other people, especially if they may not be sympathetic to a psychedelic atmosphere, can be extremely distracting or fear inducing. Ideally it will be a place where a whole range of emotional expression can occur without both-ering anyone. Even if nothing dramatic happens and the entire session is silent, it is good to know that the freedom exists where anything is possible. This may be in isolated nature or in a person's home. With MDMA a wider range of interpersonal contact can be allowed, but even here it is best to be discrimi-nating about what interpersonal energies one exposes oneself to.

3. When the psychedelic effect begins, regardless of whatever "program" or issue may have been hoped for, relaxing and going with the flow are important. What decades of experience have taught us is that whatever emerges is important and in

some way right for the person's process. The inner movement of the psyche can be trusted to go where it needs to. Psychotherapeutic skills are of great help here in learning to surf one's inner experience, riding the feelings and thought waves to whatever shore of the psyche they may wash up on.

4. Checking in with the guide or with the fellow travelers from time to time is helpful to not feeling too isolated, even if it is a brief contact and signals that further nonverbal time is desired.

5. Coming down is the time for review of the journey and a time when things begin to come together. What didn't make sense at the time begins to make sense now in light of the larger whole of the entire trip. Verbally sharing the lessons and insights is crucial for bringing them back into regular life. It helps to symbolize them and store them in memory, so that they can be accessed in ordinary consciousness.

6. To bring the lessons into regular life more fully, taking time the next morning to talk with someone and again go over the significant events and lessons of the voyage is of great help. The psychedelic journey can easily dissipate into thin air, leaving hardly a trace. To consciously remember and bring to mind the previous day while it is still fresh in memory is important.

A Note on Working with Bad Trips

The fear of a "bad trip" has prevented many people from experimenting with psychedelics, but it is a fear that is greatly exaggerated. Even in the heyday of psychedelics, bad trips were never estimated to be more than 1 to 2% of the total trips taken. But they do sometimes occur, especially if there has not been much planning or thought for the circumstances under which they are being taken. There are two main ways of working with bad trips. But before reviewing these, it should be understood what a bad trip is.

While under the influence of a psychedelic, a stimulus, either environmental or within the person, may trigger something unpleasant, scary, painful, dark, or forbidden. This may be an image, feeling, thought, or inner state. The person internally turns away from it or pushes it away. However, under a psychedelic the usual defense mechanisms of the person are not operating. And since there is so much more energy in the psyche than normal, when something is pushed away it doesn't just go away. It gets bigger. This causes the person to turn away or push it away even more forcefully. And it gets BIGGER. As the person avoids this scary state, he or she becomes more and more anxious and scared. The more the person doesn't look, the bigger it gets. Until finally it becomes so big it overwhelms the person, and the person freaks out. Panic, running away, feeling terrible, frightened, at a loss, seeking relief at whatever cost—the person is in the grip of a bad trip.

Treatment for a bad trip is simple and extremely effective. There are two options, depending upon circumstances.

The best and preferred method of dealing with a bad trip is to work with what is coming up, to turn and face it. What the dreaded image or feeling needs is attention, not avoidance. Avoidance feeds it. Attention dissolves it. The therapist's job is to be a reassuring, soothing presence that gives permission to the person to stop running from it and let it be there. The idea is to stop furiously paddling upstream, to just let the fear or paranoia or whatever the bad feeling is in, and to explore what it is. Just float downstream and be carried wherever it wants to go. What can be learned from it? The therapist is an allowing presence who coaches the person to stop resisting and go with it.

What happens when the person can tolerate the feeling is that it washes over and through the psyche. This may take a few minutes or it may take longer. But the research of Grof and so many others confirms that by going into it, the person sooner or later emerges into a new, often blissful state of integration and wholeness. Staying in contact with the person, letting the person verbalize as much of the experience as possible, calmly saying in one form or another to the person that this experience, too, is okay, is to be accepted and learned from, conveys the message to the person that it is safe to be with what seems so frightening.

The second method is less preferred, but when time is of the essence (e.g., at a rock concert where there are more people freaking out than therapists to work with them), it often works just as well. The crux of this method is simply to shift the person's attention. For example, a person comes in highly agitated and fearful. Gently guide the person to lie down on a cot and gaze at the ceiling. See what images can be seen there or what the different patterns form. Or perhaps look at a candle, or listen to some different, soothing music. Direct the person's attention to some other sensory object and stay with it.

This simple shift of attention works very often, especially when the circumstances of the bad trip may be environmental. Getting into a different setting can get the person back into a good place. While the first method is optimal, circumstances do not always support it. This second method can work, especially when deep psychotherapeutic work is not the goal.

Another circumstance is when the person comes down before there is a chance to work through the difficult material. Grof found that when this happened the person remained fixated at some level in this space, and he would give another dose as soon as possible in order to go back and finish working through the issue. As the person did this, they then broke through to a new synthesis.

Precautions

There are no known physical problems associated with LSD, mescaline, and psilocybin. The early scares of brain damage or chromosome damage have been extensively researched by now and thoroughly refuted. MDMA, however, may have neurotoxic effects. Initial research with monkeys shows damage to the serotonergic nerve cells in the brain, and although it appears that the cells do repair themselves over time, the exact nature of this in humans is currently unknown. Hence, caution is advised in this class of psychedelics at present.

The main hazards for psychedelics are psychological, namely, entering into painful psychological material without the inner or outer resources to successfully work it through. It is important for anyone taking psychedelics to be prepared to confront difficult feelings and areas of their psyche. If either the inner attitude (set) of the person or the outer situation (setting) do not support this, psychedelics should not be taken. The optimal situation is when both the intention and the situation are aligned in supporting this.

Age is also a factor. It is important to have a developed ego structure, meaning that it is better to wait until the person is at least 18 or so. While many young people do psychedelics before 18, there are more casualties when an adult ego structure is not yet developed.

It should be noted that with some rare individuals, there are some issues or areas of the psyche that may require a good number of sessions before the material is worked through. This can seem like a continuous hell with no relief in sight, and it may not be worth it to the person to keep plugging away at it. And psychedelics are clearly not for everyone. Obviously no one should take a psychedelic without full consent and interest. For many people psychedelics are of no real interest. For others there may be biological reasons for not taking them. Some people's chemistry just does not work well with psychedelics, and this needs to be respected.

LIMITATIONS OF ALTERED STATE WORK

There are several limitations to working with altered states of consciousness. The first of these comes out of the work on state-dependent learning. What some early researchers discovered is that if you give a rat LSD or cocaine or alcohol or some other consciousness altering drug, and then teach this rat to run a maze, when the drug effects wear off the rat forgets how to run the maze. Give the rat another dose of LSD, cocaine, alcohol, or whatever the drug was, and the rat again knows how to run the maze. This effect became known as state-dependent learning. That is, learning is encoded in ways that are specific to the state of consciousness in which it was learned. Change the state, and you change the access to the memory.

So even though there may be a depth of experience and insight during a psychedelic session which seems cosmic and life-changing at the time, upon returning to normal consciousness the experience or insight can seem ethereal, hard to remember or put into practice, and with time may fade away altogether. For this reason spending time at the end of the session and the beginning of the next day going over what happened are important for bringing back the learnings of the experience. While high-dose sessions have their own value in opening the person up to new realms of experience and in producing transcendent states which can profoundly alter the course of a person's life, state-dependent learning research points to the value of psychedelic experiences which are closer to normal consciousness, such as MDMA or low-dose LSD sessions, for these can be more easily integrated into regular life.

A second limitation to altered state work is that it by-passes the ego and its defenses (to use classical psychoanalytic language). This is the standard psychoanalytic critique of hypnosis, and it holds here as well. Freud began his career by using hypnosis, but he abandoned it when he realized that its therapeutic effects were only temporary. What he understood later in life, after he had developed his theory of psychoanalysis, was that hypnosis acted directly on the psyche so that certain feelings and events could be remembered, but the ego and its defensive structure was by-passed in the process. When the person was not in a hypnotic trance and the ego and its defenses were in full strength, symptoms returned. The real work, Freud recognized, was with the ego and the working through of the defensive structure.

This is also the case with psychedelic work. While much important psychological material can be accessed with the use of psychedelic drugs, it is because the usual defense mechanisms of the ego have simply been by-passed. But so much of psychotherapy is with the ego that to exclude this is to exclude most of the therapy process, which is the working through of the resistances. This again points to the value of low-dose sessions and the importance of bringing the learnings of the session into regular therapy for a full working through. With some of the psychedelic literature, the enthusiastic implication seems to be that if a client just takes enough LSD, all wounds will be healed and all neurotic problems resolved. This hardly seems the case. Indeed, it is possible to work through an issue in a cathartic, dramatic, and seemingly permanent way only to find one week later that the issue is as present and alive as ever. Although *some* work can clearly be done via psychedelics, it is not clear how much can be done in an altered state and how much needs to be done in regular consciousness.

A third critique of psychedelic work comes out of self psychology. In self psychology the key to growth is the development of new self structure. But new self structure is not built in psychedelic work. The gradual accretion of new self structure is a slow process which occurs within the therapeutic relationship via transmuting internalizations, and it is the result of sustained empathic inquiry and many, many disruptions and restorations of the empathic bond. That is, in most contemporary psychoanalytic approaches, the self develops over time within a relational, intersubjective field. This continuous, longer term relational matrix is not present in psychedelic therapy, and there is no reason to believe that psychedelic therapy produces new self structure. Psychedelic therapy evolved before relational theories such as self psychology even existed, so of course it does not address the therapeutic concerns raised by such theories. It is interesting to ponder what a self psychologically informed, intersubjective approach to psychedelic therapy would look like and what clinical data it might generate, but this will have to await further research.

The fourth limitation to altered state work is simply that altered states, no matter what kinds they are, produce skewed maps of consciousness. It was believed at one time that psychedelics are the equivalent in psychology to what microscopes are for biology or what telescopes are for astronomy. But it is now clear that psychedelics generate consciousness-specific maps that do not have clear and obvious relevance to ordinary consciousness. Some of what the psychedelics teach us about consciousness and reality is profoundly important and relevant. Other aspects of altered state maps seem to have little bearing upon regular life. Thus, far from being the microscopes and telescopes of consciousness that were once hoped would show us the undistorted truth about the nature of consciousness, psychedelics are a kind of lens that obscures as well as reveals, and as yet there is no universal agreement about the significance of some of its views of human consciousness.

IMPLICATIONS

Transpersonal and spiritual experiences can reliably be produced when we follow certain preparations. This is an astonishing, revolutionary fact.

This knowledge has been used by some cultures to initiate its citizens into a deeply spiritual and reverent approach to life and work. It has yet to be absorbed by the field of psychology or our society as a whole. Although psychedelic substances have been banned, and their use was relegated to the fringes and outskirts of society, this knowledge and power is still there, waiting to be used intelligently in a supporting context of spiritual seeking and psychological exploration.

Ram Dass has told the story of asking his guru what the significance of LSD was. His guru replied that the West was so materialistic that God had to take a material form to be revealed here.

The psychedelic experience poses a serious challenge to the dominant materialistic, scientific worldview. It shatters the materialistic paradigm. While it may seem paradoxical that a completely material substance opens to the spiritual realm, it is also part of the larger Mystery that no opening to the Divine is excluded by Spirit.

The anthropologist Joan Halifax has made an observation about shamans from different cultures. Younger shamans seem to be fascinated by altered states of consciousness and psychedelic plants, whereas older shamans tend to value being very clear, present, and focused in this consciousness. Transpersonal psychology began with a strong interest in psychedelics. As it matures it seems to be undergoing a shift similar to what many shamans experience. Although the altered states that psychedelics induce are still an important aspect of transpersonal psychology, they are no longer so central to the more recent trends in the transpersonal field, which tend to be more focused on exploring the sacred in ordinary, daily living.

For a shamanic path or to explore the intermediate plane, psychedelics may be of use. But to really enter and live in the realms of soul and spirit—the domains of the Personal Divine and the Impersonal Divine—at this point it seems clear that it is necessary to leave the psychedelics behind and earnestly pursue a spiritual path. For this reason it has been said that psychedelics are a door, not a path. This may be overstating the matter somewhat. Psychedelics clearly do have much potential, not only for spiritual opening but for psychological growth and healing, although even here there are limitations. Perhaps it is more accurate to say that when psychedelics are used as a path, it is a rather short path. For ultimately it is our normal, daily consciousness that needs to be worked with and transformed.

Chapter Eight

Selected Topics in
Transpersonal Psychotherapy

BIRTH AND DEATH

Birth

Anyone who has participated in the birth of a baby can attest to the shattering intensity of the experience. It is as if some mysterious force of great immensity accompanies the entrance of a new human being into the world, a force that has the power to melt the hearts of everyone present. It is no wonder that a transpersonal perspective takes birth beyond merely a physical process and views it as a psychological and a spiritual event. Truly, birth is a miracle.

While traditionally birth was seen as beyond the scope of an adult's memory, in the past few decades therapists using altered states of consciousness have made the birth process accessible to exploration in new ways. Although it is far from clear to what extent actual birth memories are recalled and to what extent fantasy and imagination play a part, nevertheless there have been remarkable confirmations of events that were later corroborated via attending physicians, nurses, hospital records, et cetera. Combined with recent research techniques of medical science that permit investigation into the experience of newborns and prenatal existence, a new field of prenatal and perinatal psychology has emerged. These investigations paint a picture of the prenate and neonate as vastly more awake, aware, discriminating, and tuned into the physical and interpersonal environment than ever previously thought. We now know that Margaret Mahler's description of the first month of life as an "autistic" phase represents a major misreading of life's beginnings.

What is noteworthy in this new field of prenatal and perinatal psychology is that it is strongly transpersonal and spiritual. So many of the therapists and researchers in this field view birth with awe, respect, and reverence. The therapists especially tend to see the fetus and neonate as making a transition from spirit to matter, with consciousness at this stage still aware of its spiritual source as it moves toward identification with and immersion into body consciousness. When people do rebirthing, regression work, or somehow enter into a reexperiencing of the birth process, entering into spiritual states is a common feature. Birth is a gateway into the spiritual. Also frequently reported is an intense awareness of the parents and their relationship, the mood and feeling state of the mother, and the family's receptivity or lack of it to the newborn.

The true significance of birth in a person's psychological development is presently controversial. One factor that makes a difference in people's perspectives on this matter has to do with personal experience. Those who have explored their own birth via regressive work are generally more open to this area than people whose exposure is purely theoretical. Some rebirthers and related therapists view birth somewhat like a prima causa of later psychological difficulties, but such enthusiasm may be too extreme. Certainly tracing the full complexity of difficulties in the adult psyche to birth trauma becomes so reductionistic that such a position is hard to justify. That birth does have some effect, depending upon circumstances and later life experience, seems far more plausible, but the parameters of this effect are not yet known.

Here we enter into a realm of human experience where fact and fantasy may intermingle, where the boundaries are not sharply demarcated. For example, what effect will there be when the mother-to-be feels rejecting of the fetus, thinks to herself that she does not want this baby, yet goes through with the birth and raising of the child? In regressive work, the adult child may tune in to the exquisite psycho-spiritual and telepathic sensitivity of early fetal life and feel devastated by these thoughts and feelings of the mother. What part is memory and what part is fantasy informed by later childhood experience? Researchers have shown that a fetus' heart rate increases when the mother simply *thinks* about smoking a cigarette, so from a transpersonal perspective it is not a difficult jump to admit the possibility that the prenate is telepathically sensitive. How do perception, memory, and projected fantasy interact, and what is "really" going on in a regressive experience?

While the exploration of birth trauma is still seen as something of a fringe movement even within the transpersonal field, it raises important theoretical and therapeutic issues. Some of these are: what the consciousness of an infant or prenate may be, what the effect of birth trauma is on later development; what impact the emotional state of the mother has on the baby in utero and immediately after birth; the reliability of different methods (breathing, hypnosis, psychedelic drugs) for producing true regression; and the extent to which true regression is attained, as opposed to an enhanced fantasy level produced by the altered state, or even some combination of the two, that is, memory inspired fantasy.

A transpersonal perspective radically changes how we view birth. Rather than seeing the infant as a crying, wriggling protoplasmic blob who only needs some physical and emotional needs met, a transpersonal lens brings birth into focus as a sacred event and the newborn as a conscious being in touch with spiritual states of consciousness who is simply without a developed instrumentation for self-expression at the moment. This is not to make the pre-trans mistake and assume that the infant is enlightened. It is simply to say that even without egoic, self-reflexive structures the newborn may well be in touch with spiritual states of consciousness that perhaps far exceed what the parents are in touch with. This certainly has profound implications not just for the birth process (the conditions of delivery, how the baby is treated in the first minutes and hours after birth, etc.), but for parenting and child-rearing as well. These implications have only barely begun to seep into the larger culture. At the very least this shift in perception must inspire far greater seriousness and respect for the beginnings of life than now exists.

Death and Dying

As Becker noted in his classic *The Denial of Death* (1973), there is immense denial around death and dying. It is so frightening that for almost everyone it is avoided at all costs. It was the contemplation of death that inspired Kierkegaard to articulate the human response to death as dread, angst, and the urge to escape from this awareness. The existential movement was founded on this central insight into the powerful human temptation to avoid confronting this most basic fact of existence and to cope with the horror of death through distractions of all kinds.

But the dying process can also provide a window into the transpersonal. As Grof (1985) has pointed out, both of the terminal points of human existence (birth and death) intersect with the spiritual. The dying process releases powerful energies that can be transformational for both the dying person and those around him or her.

Psychotherapy with the terminally ill and dying was virtually ignored until Elisabeth Kubler-Ross brought dying out of the collective closet a few decades ago. Since then it has become a subspecialty in itself, with a rapidly growing literature, conferences on the topic, and training programs to work with the dying. What is equally fascinating is that this also is a field that is overwhelmingly transpersonal and spiritual in its outlook.

As all writers on the subject of dying note, death brings life into perspective. It clears the air of all minor clutter and allows a person to see what really matters. It is a chance to finish unfinished business, especially to feel more emotionally complete with important relationships. As this occurs, loving relationships with others, along with the spiritual questions of life's meaning and what happens after death, come into the foreground. Steven Levine (1982, 1987) has written eloquently on this subject, showing how dying is a crisis that allows for great psycho-spiritual change.

Anyone who has experimented with the psychosynthesis technique of disidentifying from the body, originally inspired by the Hindu sage Ramana Maharshi, knows that this is much harder to carry out than it might seem, for disidentification is not just a mental decision. In sickness, for example, we see just how strong our identification with the body is. But the immanence of death allows this identification to loosen. As the body fails and death approaches, the self relaxes its tight identification with certain physical and mental images and can begin to let in other possibilities of who we really are.

A transpersonal perspective of death sees it not just as the ending of the body but as a change of consciousness. Although different spiritual systems see what happens after death quite differently (for example, is there reincarnation or not?), all spiritual systems assert that death is not the end of consciousness. A spirit within transcends death. For both client and therapist such a belief system can help in accepting death and reducing fear. This allows the client to more fully inhabit the dying space instead of recoiling in fear and anxiety. It also lets the therapist be more present with the client in the dying space, a space that can powerfully affect the therapist as well. Not everyone experiences this, of course, but there tends to be a quality of consciousness in the dying that pours out on those around them, allowing them to participate in these transformative energies.

This is a clinical area in which the lack of a transpersonal orientation can be a major disservice to the client. Not to honor the spiritual, transcendent significance of dying maintains a very limited view of this immense event. For not only can much psychological work be accomplished in a short period of time but the imminence of death vastly expands the possibilities for spiritual experiencing. As death nears, consciousness opens to new vistas. The intensity of emotion, the vulnerability, and the presence of the sacred all combine to make dying an opportunity for great evolution, the final step of growth in this life.

SPIRITUAL BY-PASSING

In addition to the enormous good that spirituality has brought to humanity, in the form of organized religion it has also brought a great deal of pain, both psychological and physical. Beginning with Freud, psychology has made a daunting critique of religion and the devastating effects it has wrought on the human psyche. While this criticism has served to undermine religious teaching for many people, it may well be that in the long run this critique will turn out to actually have been quite helpful to spirituality because it shows us that so much of destructiveness of religions throughout history have been a result of *psychological* distortions operating in a spiritual guise. Some of the most obvious negative consequences of religion that psychology has exposed are discussed below.

Religion has been anti-sexual, and the painful consequences of repressive sexuality are by now quite well documented, extending beyond the sexual arena to constrict all expressions of human feeling and warmth. The persecution of "witches" by the Catholic Church is the most dramatically destructive example of this; an estimated several hundred thousand women were tortured and killed by sexually repressed priests who projected their own sexuality onto the women "witches" and accused them of being associated with the devil because they were "sexually tempting." Western society is still reeling from centuries of sexual repression. Most religion has been anti-body, seeking to attain spiritual liberation at the expense of the body and earthly life; the denigration of the body and the earth-denying religions have had massive repercussions for the appreciation of a full bodily-sensory life as well as for the earth's ecology. Most religions are anti-feeling, at best exalting love and compassion but tending to disparage all other feelings; repressing anger, hate, and other negative feelings we now know result in even greater destructiveness when they are then expressed unconsciously. Many religions are anti-intellectual, the Dark Ages in the West being the most dramatic example. Most religions are anti-spiritual, claiming a monopoly on truth and work to suppress other forms of spirituality. While providing a hopeful, optimistic worldview and holding up the ideals of love and truth to strive toward, religion has simultaneously crippled every aspect of psychic life—the mind, the heart, the body, even spirit itself.

These cultural and historical movements still have great effect upon the collective psyche. When they are given individual form in a particular client we now view this through the lens of how personal psychodynamics interact with spiritual practice, something that has come to be known as _spiritual by-passing_. Spiritual by-passing is when a person cloaks defensive avoidance in spiritual ideas. It is a phrase that enjoys increasing currency these days and is a helpful way to name a phenomenon that therapists see every day. Originally coined by John Welwood (1984), historically it is related to the notions of spiritual materialism and rationalization. Spiritual materialism, a phrase introduced by Chogyam Trungpa, is where the self wraps itself in spiritual garb but continues its activities unchanged. Rationalization is the more traditional term for the defense by which the ego protects itself from forbidden impulses and feelings. Spiritual by-passing takes spiritual language and concepts to "reframe" personal issues in the service of repression and defense, a kind of transpersonal rationalization.

While often characterized as amusing or simply misguided, spiritual by-passing may be a much more ubiquitous and universal phenomenon than is generally recognized. The examples below give some idea of the various forms it can take.

1. "I don't want to express my anger because I don't want to hurt the other person." This statement made by a student in a group process class couched his avoidance of anger in the high spiritual terms of *ahimsa* (non-violence) and "right speech," and it provided a rationale for staying out of the often intense interactions of the group. The feedback that his anger was actually being expressed anyway through his biting sarcasm, a certain coldness, and aloofness was startling feedback to him and gave him an opening to experiment with being more clear and direct rather than expressing his anger indirectly and unconsciously.

2. "I don't want to dig up the past. I want to let go of it. It can't be changed anyway. I want to live in the here and now." This common reaction by clients entering psychotherapy hides a dread of facing childhood wounds behind the laudable goal of being more present-centered. After years of repression it can be difficult to see how the past is not really over but is and very much alive in the present in the form of unfinished business or incomplete *gestalten*. While it is true that the past cannot be changed, our *relationship* to the past can change dramatically as the wounds heal in the working-through process. Related to this is:

3. "I just want to forgive X and move on." Forgiveness is certainly both spiritually and psychologically healthy, but to try and force it, without having worked through the pain, hurt, anger, and grief is like putting a Band-Aid on an infected cut—it will continue to fester. When hurt and anger are worked through, forgiveness happens. If forgiveness is imposed, it is "letting go" in the service of denial. Whether the issue is childhood physical or sexual abuse, a recent fight, or anything else, forgiveness is a by-product which, if it does come, comes only as the working through progresses. Then forgiveness is an authentic

response from the depths rather than a top-down program that keeps the true feelings buried.

4. "I'm becoming more and more detached from my expectations and needs for others as I focus on my spiritual path." True spiritual detachment needs to be differentiated from dissociation and disavowal. While detachment does come on the spiritual path, gradually and with much inner work, all too often this word is a cover for dissociating from our true needs or disavowing the importance of other people for our emotional health. Many times therapy uncovers destructive family of origin patterns in which withdrawal was the client's best option for survival. The spiritual ideal of being detached from the world and beyond the need for human relationships can have a strong appeal for people whose early wounds leads them to defend against intimacy and their needs for others.

5. "I want to practice loving kindness toward people and devote myself to compassionate action in the world." The balance between attention to inner development and outer action is one of the most delicate aspects of psycho-spiritual growth. The shadow side of universal love and compassionate service is codependence. In focusing on others, it is easy to lose ourselves and stop paying attention to our own needs and self. Resentment and burn-out follow closely when the values of love and compassionate service function to negate personal needs.

Looking for the lesson too soon can also produce spiritual by-passing. While from a transpersonal perspective all of our life does have a meaning and larger purpose and seeking to discover greater meaning is commendable, to focus on trying to discover the lesson too soon can also be a way of avoiding the pain we are in. Often the lesson is *in* the pain, darkness, and confusion, not away from it. Many times the lessons become clear only in retrospect, perhaps years or even decades later, after the whole story has had a chance to unfold.

A more entrenched form of spiritual by-passing is generally seen in working with fundamentalists of any religion. Fundamentalism can be the form that a rigid character structure takes when it cloaks itself in a fixed belief system. The psychological literature amply documents how psychotherapy can move a person from, for example, belief in a harsh, punitive, Old Testament–style God to a more accepting, loving image of God as the character defenses relax and are worked through. As the therapy unfolds, gradually the person finds less repressive ways of following a spiritual path.

New converts and people who have recently experienced a spiritual opening are perhaps the most striking examples of spiritual by-passing. As people try to incorporate a new spiritual worldview into their lives, a certain amount of wholesale introjection and spiritual by-passing can even be viewed as a developmental stage as they try to accommodate to a new vision of how they "should" be and want to be versus how they are.

Working with Spiritual By-passing

In spiritual by-passing we choose a spiritual approach to match our psychology. It is the use of spiritual content for psychological purposes, in the service of neurotic conflict. Because it is so entwined with a person's whole psychological make-up, it can be difficult to tease out as a discrete element.

Transpersonally oriented therapists are in a unique position to work with spiritual by-passing because they can hold and value both sides of the dilemma that the client is facing. Traditional therapists can easily disparage or slight the spiritual framework within which the by-passing is contained. Because a person's spiritual beliefs are often so central, intimate, and so precious to a person, directly challenging them or confronting them can be therapeutically risky. It can alienate the client from the therapist, puts the therapist in the unfortunate position of implicitly asserting that the client's beliefs are somehow wrong or bad, and removes the therapist from the empathic vantage point of trying to understand from within the client's worldview. The very labeling of a client's belief or spiritual practice "spiritual by-passing" tends to have this effect.

A sensitive exploration of the issue, on the other hand, increases the empathic bond and keeps the therapist within the client's world. Gently exploring if anything else is going on in the client's experience can help change a spiritual should into a life dilemma. For example, a therapist might check to see if in trying to maintain a positive attitude toward a newly diagnosed cancer there are any other feelings that it would be important to acknowledge. This can help reframe the issue into the best strategy for keeping a positive attitude, whether this comes by pushing feelings away or by including all feelings.

Much of the time, what is needed is for the therapist to simply see the spiritual by-passing and work with it indirectly through the entire process of psychotherapy. As the defenses erode and the deeper needs and feelings of the client emerge in the safety of the therapeutic space, the by-passing changes automatically as the entire psyche shifts.

It is always helpful to ask if our spiritual beliefs and practices enlarge our world, expand our possibilities, increase our self-esteem, support us, help us to connect with others and nature, and nourish us. Or on the contrary, do they shrink our world, diminish our sense of self and self-esteem, limit our contact with others and the world? When spiritual beliefs shrink a person's world, it is likely that spiritual by-passing is occurring. However, there cannot be too rigid a rule about all this.

It is important that a purely psychological standard of mental health not be adopted wholesale. A transpersonal perspective holds both the psychological and spiritual within it. Spiritual traditions speak to a higher and ultimately more satisfying state of being than the psychological. It may be that a temporary shrinking of ego activity is in the service of spiritual growth and causes no permanent harm. All spiritual traditions would agree that there is more to the good life than simply the pursuit and satisfaction of desire. They remind us that however psychologically healthy this pursuit may be, it leaves us spiritually unnourished. When the satisfaction or repression of desire clogs up the subtle organs of perception, there is little possibility for spiritual experience.

This makes the issue considerably more complex, for what may be very healthy from a purely psychological perspective may, from a spiritual perspective, be quite unhealthy and distracting. While it is important to be cognizant of the potentially repressive and damaging effects of spiritual practice on the psyche, as inner development proceeds there may be equally significant, spiritually damaging effects of "healthy" indulgence. What if the distractions of satisfying an emotional need result in spiritual costs? A transpersonal perspective brings into view not only the dangers of spiritual by-passing but the possible dangers of psychological fixation as well. For example, a period of minimal social contact and no sexual involvement may be a great help to a person's inner development. Additionally, we must consider the possibility that it may even be psychologically healthy as well, perhaps leading the person to feel better about his or her inner resources and enhancing self-esteem.

When it is both spiritually and psychologically healthy, that is ideal. But there may be times when there is a trade-off, when it is spiritually beneficial and psychologically costly. Then the issues become harder to evaluate. How to know whether the potential spiritual benefits outweigh the psychological costs? There is no external yardstick by which to measure such things, for at one point in a person's evolution the answer might be one thing and at another time for the same person the answer might be just the opposite. It may be that only as a person tries such experiments and learns from mistakes that a consciousness develops that can discriminate wisely.

Beyond this it is important to see how understandable spiritual bypassing is in anyone's life, given the defenses we all have along with our aspirations for a more spiritual life. Of course our ego and neurotic "stuff" will wrap themselves around our spiritual beliefs, just as with anything else in our life, generating worldviews and using spiritual rationales to enforce emotional positions.

Discerning when something is psychologically healthy or repressive, when it helps or hinders spiritual growth, and when it is either/or rather than both/and requires a high degree of self-awareness. The concept of spiritual by-passing may be of most value when we see the subtle and not so subtle ways it comes to most everyone on the spiritual path.

ADDICTION AND RECOVERY

Yet another area that strongly bears the transpersonal stamp is the addictions field. While an alcoholic or addict was long considered untreatable and viewed as a "moral failure" during the first half of this century, Alcoholics Anonymous lobbied for the disease model for decades. Finally the mental health field came around to putting chemical dependency in the same category as schizophrenia and other mental disorders. But from the beginning of the addictions field, it has stood outside the mental health establishment because of the spiritual emphasis in recovery.

Ever since Alcoholics Anonymous was founded, it and the 12-step programs that followed have had a transpersonal focus for healing and recovery. This is due in part to the influence of pioneering psychologist Carl Jung upon the forming of AA. In the early 1930s Jung had told one of his former patients who had relapsed into alcoholism that it was hopeless to pursue further psychiatric treatment. Jung further told him that the only other hope he might have would be if he could become the subject of a spiritual or religious experience. This then happened, and this man had a major influence on the founding of AA. Jung wrote years later about this man, "His craving for alcohol was the equivalent, on a low level, of the spiritual thirst of our being for wholeness, expressed in medieval language: the union with God. . . . You see, 'alcohol' in Latin is _spiritus_, and you use the same word for the highest religious experience as well as for the most depraving poison. The helpful formula therefor is: _spiritus contra spiritum_" (Jung, 1975).

Jung indicated that alcohol addiction was beyond the reach of psychotherapy, and AA, although somewhat psychological for its time in the 1930s, has remained essentially a spiritual cure rather than a psychological one. However, today we know that alcoholism has far more psychological aspects to it than Jung thought and that psychotherapy is generally more effective and necessary to recovery than was previously believed. Transpersonal psychotherapy allows us to integrate the many varied psychotherapeutic approaches to addiction, while simultaneously honoring Jung's great insight and allowing for recovery to be put into a spiritual context.

One of AA's powerful discoveries is that in the depths of despair, when the alcoholic or drug addict feels most hopeless about ever changing and "hits bottom," there is an openness in which the person can experience the redeeming power of spirit. By reorienting one's life so that this spiritual light can increasingly guide daily life choices, the person is led into a path of recovery. AA maintains that full recovery is not possible without some kind of spiritual transformation. This is a strong statement, but from a transpersonal perspective we can go further to say that there can be no lasting spiritual transformation without a psychological transformation as well. It is here that transpersonal psychotherapy is a natural match with addictions treatment. A transpersonal perspective of addiction and recovery also brings out the drawbacks of any treatment program that is too exclusively spiritual (one form of spiritual by-passing). Transpersonal psychotherapy seeks a balance between spiritual and psychological working, providing a larger framework than AA alone.

For example, when a person stops drinking or using drugs, inevitably there is a big void left in the person's life, a void within and a void in his or her relationships. Even if the person is married or in a relationship, a lot of distance has crept in, since the possibilities for true intimacy with an alcoholic or drug dependent person are very limited. This inner and interpersonal void needs more than spirit to fill it initially. While ultimately and ideally spirit would be entirely sufficient to fill this void, for the vast majority of people, the spiritual connection to a deeper level of Being is not complete enough. A deeper contact with oneself and other people is necessary to fill this void, and for this psychotherapy is important. Even when the contact offered by continual AA meetings do provide respite at first, this must transfer into bringing people closer into one's heart, building ongoing support systems, finding real intimacy, et cetera. While some people are able to use AA in this way to create such a lifestyle, all too often AA alone fails to do this, for it does not have the psychological theory and technology to work through interpersonal blocks, intra-psychic defenses, and the earlier wounds behind these defenses.

AA's insight that a spiritual change is crucial for recovery is clearly valid for most people, whose need is to have a higher light to live by than the pale reflections of the material world. But all people do not have the same needs. A transpersonal perspective lets us see that this is a psycho-spiritual shift, and for some people a purely psychological approach such as Rational Recovery is all that is needed, a fact that is difficult to explain within the pure AA model.

Similarly, the disease model itself is under increasing attack from many quarters. Many people do not fit the standard disease model of an alcoholic. For example, research has shown that abstinence is not the only possible goal for recovery. Some people can adopt controlled drinking as a goal and successfully achieve it. This phenomenon cannot be satisfactorily explained by the disease model. The disease model has had an important impact upon the treatment field, and it has served to de-stigmatize alcoholics and drug dependent persons. By now a whole generation of alcoholics has come of age free of the stigma of being moral degenerates. But a transpersonal perspective, which incorporates the insights of existential and psychodynamic schools of psychology, must take seriously the critiques these schools have offered of the disease model.

Alcoholism may well have genetic, physical, emotional, and mental components. Indeed, with a multidimensional perspective of consciousness this would be expected. But whether it meets the criteria for a physical disease is increasingly subject to dispute (e.g., there is no tissue damage, except as a by-product of the alcohol itself). Emotional disease is also a problematic metaphor, as Thomas Szasz has so insightfully explored. And if alcoholism is a "spiritual disease," what exactly does this mean? Is the spirit sick or the ego? The de-stigmatizing of alcoholism is very important, but it is an entirely separate issue which is not dependent upon the disease model. An existential viewpoint will de-stigmatize at least as well if not better, for the disease model carries with it a new stigma, that of someone who is "sick." A transpersonal view must look seriously at the whole issue of chemical dependency as a disease. By holding both a psychological and spiritual view of chemical dependency and recovery, a transpersonal perspective can hold within it these ongoing questions and controversies without being wedded to any particular belief.

A further limitation of AA is that it comes out of a theistic belief system. This has been problematic for Buddhists and other nondualists. A transpersonal view is open to Buddhist and other non-dual spiritual approaches in addictions treatment. This may change the language of the traditional 12 steps, but it is possible to do so while still retaining the essential spirit.

A lack of definite spiritual and meditation techniques is often decried in AA programs, where there is so much hunger for spiritual practices by people in recovery. A transpersonal approach may synthesize spiritual practices from a wide variety of traditions and teach them to clients in recovery. Here again we are just beginning to adapt some of these centuries old meditation practices to direct treatment.

CLINICAL AND ETHICAL DILEMMAS

Along with the gains inherent in a transpersonal approach to psychotherapy, there are also some dilemmas that present themselves. While at present there may be no definitive answers to these dilemmas, it seems prudent to acknowledge that they exist and to begin some dialogue around the issues they raise.

Therapist Self-Disclosure about Spiritual Orientation and Practice

It is assumed that the transpersonal psychotherapist is open about his or her orientation and about holding psychological work within a spiritual context. But how far should the therapist go in revealing spiritual values and beliefs? Should the therapist tell clients that he or she is a Christian or Buddhist or whatever? Should the therapist decorate the office with spiritual art? Should the therapist hang pictures of his or her guru in the office? And what are the effects of this upon someone who has a very different spiritual orientation or worldview? The responses to such questions may vary with how discreetly or how brazenly a therapist announces his or her spiritual preferences. How a therapist answers may also depend upon to what extent the exploration of the transference is important in the therapy. This in turn raises another issue, that of how the therapist sees his or her relationship to the client's spiritual life, which becomes part of a larger issue discussed next.

To Teach or Not to Teach?

Although psychotherapy tends to eschew the role of therapist as teacher, it can be argued that all of psychotherapy is education: learning about oneself, learning about one's feelings, learning how to be more deeply connected to oneself and more intimate with others. And the therapist can be viewed as a teacher: teaching through modeling a way of being with difficult and painful feelings, teaching empathy, teaching a new set of values (e.g., feelings are key guides in life, intimacy is important, etc.).

It is an open question whether a transpersonal orientation, with the spiritual context inherent in it, is any different from a traditional Freudian orientation, for example, which regards religion as an illusion, though never directly addressing it in the therapy. That is, do not all orientations have a philosophy behind them? To what extent do the therapist's belief systems get conveyed on an energetic level, even if they are never verbalized? The question this section asks is: What is the impact when these belief systems are made explicit?

Many questions then arise: Is the therapist a spiritual teacher or even guide or guru? Where does the therapist role stop and spiritual teacher role begin? What relationship to the spiritual life of the client should the therapist have? What effects on the transference are there if the therapist enters into these areas? These are complex questions which need more attention than present space permits. This discussion will only touch on some of the main issues.

Therapist as Guru or Spiritual Guide. It is one thing to hold the client in one's heart as a uniquely precious and evolving being. It is quite another to assume the function of spiritual guide or guru for this person. Yet the disillusionment with organized religion in this culture has left a spiritual vacuum, a vacuum that many believe psychotherapists can and should fill. It is very tempting for therapists to see themselves as part of a new priestly caste, and one of the justifications of this position goes something like, "With all I have learned about human nature and all the inner work I have done, I am more advanced or further along the path than this person. My guidance would be helpful."

Aside from the highly questionable (and ultimately insupportable) assumption that the therapist is "more advanced," the belief that the therapist's guidance in spiritual matters is any more relevant than anyone else's guidance is similar to the notion that the therapist should give advice to the client since the therapist knows better than the client how to live. Aside from crisis situations, in depth psychotherapy this is an untenable position.

Transpersonal therapists must be on their guard even more than traditional therapists against the seductiveness of unexamined idealizing transferences. When a client gives over power to a spiritual authority (or therapist), the psychotherapeutic work is to examine the unconscious roots of such feelings. Countertransference feelings of grandiosity are naturally stirred up in the therapist, as are needs to be important, needs to be seen as someone who "knows," and the tendency for ego-inflation. Cults are born out of such unexplored feelings. The past few decades have shown how even highly trained and "advanced" spiritual teachers can succumb to such psychological forces.

Information-giving, outside resource identification, affirmation and support for a client's movement into spiritual areas are all well within the domain of a transpersonally oriented psychotherapy. But to take the next step into spiritual guide or guru is to cross the boundaries

of psychotherapy and to assume a role beyond what professional training provides.

Another question then arises. If the therapist is not a guru, what
about a more limited role as spiritual teacher? Is it legitimate for a
transpersonal therapist to teach the client about spirituality or the therapist's philosophy? At this point in the field the answer seems to be: it
depends. It depends upon two things: the content of the client's issue
and the orientation of the therapist. In the first instance, certain content
areas require an educational, reframing approach.The treatment of spiritual emergency, for example, involves educating the client about what
he or she is undergoing and linking this to the spiritual literature. This
normalizes and gives new meaning to what can be a confusing, frightening experience. The teaching function of the therapist is well recognized in this particular case.

The second instance is when the therapist's orientation supports
or even promotes teaching. For example, in psychosynthesis, very often
part of the therapist's work is to teach the client about the such things as
the transpersonal self and the higher unconscious. (How far the therapist goes in trying to convince the client to believe this philosophy
raises a whole other set of issues). On the other hand, most transpersonally oriented therapists come from frameworks which discourage this.
Most transpersonally oriented psychoanalytic therapists, for example,
probably would not teach a client any spiritual philosophy, much in
keeping with standard therapeutic tradition.

What if the therapist is trained as a spiritual director or teacher?
Should this person see his or her students in psychotherapy? This raises
serious issues about the nature of the therapeutic relationship. If a
client's therapist is also the client's spiritual director or teacher—someone who holds the client's spiritual life in his or her hands and whose
counsel can help the client toward heaven or hell—how free will this
client be to get really angry or feel disappointed in the therapist? Is this
kind of dual relationship justifiable or workable? The blurring of boundaries between spiritual direction and psychotherapy raises a host of difficult questions.

Apart from specific orientations, is teaching about spiritual matters a good idea in depth therapy? What are the therapeutic benefits
and risks? What effect does this have on the transference? These are
vital questions. For now it is sufficient to note that such teaching is done

by some therapists and is not done by others, but certainly this is an area which demands much more dialogue than has yet occurred in the field.

Should a Therapist "Prescribe" Meditation?

One of the most fascinating areas in transpersonal psychotherapy is the convergence between meditative and psychotherapeutic approaches to consciousness. Yet extending this into clinical practice raises a host of difficult questions. Assuming that meditation can be helpful, under what circumstances should it be used? Should it be used in the therapy or outside the therapy as an adjunct? When should it be used, for what problems, for what character structures, with what kind of container or support for the client? What are the effects of lifting a meditation practice out of one cultural environment and transplanting it into another? Are there some meditation practices which can be used fairly easily and benignly with a wide range of clients and others which involve very specialized knowledge and should only be used cautiously? What education should a therapist have in meditation or specific spiritual traditions, that is to say, what are the training implications of "prescription privileges"?

At present there is a wide range of responses to these questions. On the spiritual side some spiritual teachers applaud this cross-fertilization, supporting such therapeutic experimentation. They assert that consciousness is consciousness regardless of cultural contexts, and that these consciousness tools should be freely available to all. Other teachers are much more wary and say that nothing should be used outside of its specific, organized, religious and cultural context.

Therapists are similarly split over this issue. At one end of the spectrum some transpersonally oriented therapists refuse to enter these waters at all and suggest to their clients that they learn meditation from a spiritual teacher, preferring to keep these two approaches entirely separate. At the other end of the spectrum are therapists who are extremely casual about suggesting and teaching a wide range of meditation practices to their clients in the sincere belief that it will be helpful. In the middle are clinicians who are proceeding slowly and carefully, utilizing specific meditation practices for certain clients or certain issues. All of these are perfectly legitimate positions to take.

The perspective I would advance here is that not only is this experimentation happening and will continue to happen, but research into this area should continue in order to advance our knowledge of consciousness and healing. Western science has advanced by exploring areas that originally were religious taboos. For example, medicine advanced as people violated the ban against dissection of cadavers by the Catholic Church during the Renaissance in order to discover how the body is composed. Similarly, to refuse to explore areas of consciousness out of religious injunctions is to be guided by superstition. So psychology, and transpersonal psychology especially, must investigate consciousness in all of its aspects.

This means exploring meditation practices both within their cultural contexts as well as outside of them. Since meditation techniques cannot be patented or restricted, it is inevitable that individuals and therapists will try out whatever new consciousness tools appear to be promising. How do meditation practices affect consciousness in different cultural contexts? How does motivation affect practice? That is, does meditation with a spiritual intention produce different effects than with a therapeutic intention or no intention? How does meditation act on consciousness apart from intention and cultural context? What combination of factors most helps in a psychotherapeutic setting? How do personality variables affect this? This is a vast topic. The issue is not so much should such experimentation be done, rather it is how such research can be done responsibly and brought into the disciplinary discourse to enrich our understanding of healing and growth.

What Level to Intervene On?

A transpersonal orientation vastly expands the possible field of reality. For example, it brings in the subtle physical realms of auras, energy fields, chakras, clairvoyance, other beings and entities that do not have a physical manifestation, kundalini, et cetera. In so doing it opens a whole Pandora's box of epistemological questions which our current state of knowledge is wholly inadequate to answer. For example, is a given problem psychological, energetic, physical, spiritual? Even assuming the multidimensional nature of reality, do the energy field and blocked chakras create neurosis or do neurosis and faulty self-structure create energy blocks? Is it better to do psychotherapy or suggest a chakra balancing and energy healing or suggest medication or suggest an exorcism? What is the most effective level to intervene on? What is "really" causative? Do such questions even make sense in a holographic model of reality? Yet the therapist does need to act, to intervene on some level of the client's experience.

Should a therapist suggest:

- meditation?
- spiritual practice?
- specific teachers or paths?
- chakra balancing or aura cleansing?
- a shamanic journey?
- seeing a psychic or having a channeled session?
- a past life regression?
- exorcism?
- taking a psychedelic?
- rolfing?
- exercise?
- keeping a journal?
- reading specific books?

Where do we draw the line on this continuum? Standard clinical practice would have no problems with the bottom three. Is suggesting meditation much different than suggesting a book to read or the keeping of a journal? Most transpersonal psychotherapists would probably be open to this. But what about exorcism? Where does legitimate "homework" leave off and sheer flakiness begin? Each transpersonal therapist may draw the line at a different point.

Certainly there are some problems with more etheric intervention strategies (auras, chakra balancing, exorcism, etc.), a major one being lack of quality control. There is a danger of doing so-called "transpersonal therapy," using subtle energies and spiritual forces that are beyond the actual experience of most people. Does an energy healing actually help in doing psychotherapy? Or a channeled session? Most people with experiences in these matters would testify that a highly talented and skilled psychic or healer can effect powerful changes in working with people. But such highly effective psychics are exceedingly rare.

Even assuming the reality of subtle energies, until such processes are subject to verification, there is much room for deception and self-deception, particularly among those numerous well-intentioned but less gifted healers. There is also the danger of leaving the solid ground of accepted clinical practice and by-passing the hard work of depth psychotherapy. Working on the subtle body by doing crystal healing, aura balancing, and chakra cleansing may be fun and even useful, but it is not depth psychotherapy. Even when such energetic work is linked to depth therapy and even with the best of intentions, such linkages can easily pass over the line into New Age illusions.

At the present time, when someone says they work transpersonally, it may mean anything from a rigorous, grounded and clinically sophisticated approach of integrating clinical practice into a spiritual context on the one hand, to a very flaky, ungrounded, grab bag of New Age techniques and spiritual homilies. Modern science and psychology made their discoveries on the basis of hard evidence, throwing out faith in God and maintaining a skeptical, experimental stance. If the transpersonal movement indicates that we are now ready to admit faith in spiritual matters back into psychology, it is crucial that we keep doubt as well. Modern depth psychology has shown us how powerful fantasy and imagination are in human experience. The power of the human mind to create illusions is immense. How much of what passes for transpersonal practice is pure fantasy? The field as a whole must confront these issues at some point, but in a way that is not reductionistic or does not do violence to the spiritual perspective. This then raises yet another difficulty, our last issue.

Lack of Clarity and Rigor in Theory, Research, and Clinical Practice

While a transpersonal approach is open to examining all phenomenological realities and realms, it is important to do so in ways that are epistemologically and methodologically sound. Although most traditional psychological approaches stress a single worldview or epistemology (for example, behaviorism's exclusive focus upon scientific experiment and sensory data), transpersonal psychology is an integrative approach that makes use of all of the so-called "three eyes of knowledge"—the sensory (body), the introspective-rational (mind and heart), and the contemplative (spirit). How do we study the realms of spiritual experience in ways that do justice to the integrity of the experience and do not reduce it to outwardly measurable behavioral variables?

Formulating which approach or combination of approaches work and developing new epistemological methods is a fertile area in the transpersonal field. Similarly, a transpersonal orientation has been used as a rationalization for not becoming knowledgeable and sophisticated in traditional clinical approaches. The "Being" of the therapist is important, but as a support to thorough clinical training and experience, not as a replacement. For it is only by the integration of the therapist's being and solid therapeutic skill into a larger and more theoretically justifiable transpersonal framework that the transpersonal approach will represent a true advance in psychotherapy.

Part 4

Conclusion

Chapter Nine

Principles of
Transpersonal Practice

Because transpersonal psychology is so wide and there are so many specific viewpoints encompassed by a transpersonal worldview, it is difficult to find bases that are common to all transpersonal psychotherapists or would be philosophically acceptable to all spiritual perspectives. Nevertheless, I believe that there are certain overarching principles that can be distilled that embody a transpersonal approach to clinical work.

Although techniques can be derived from these principles, these are broad principles which do not comprise a cookbook of techniques. Techniques come in and out of fashion, and any therapy that ties itself to techniques guarantees its own rapid obsolescence. Transpersonal psychotherapy has implications for technique but is not defined by these technical implications.

PRINCIPLES

These principles are:

1. Transpersonal psychotherapy is a theoretical framework which views psychological work within a context of spiritual unfold-

ing. The fundamental assumption of transpersonal psychology is that our true identity is more than a psychological ego or self but is a spiritual being. This spiritual context, founded on the two perennial traditions of theism and nondualism, sees the psychological healing and growth of this self as part of its journey toward realizing its identity with its spiritual source.

What is the relationship between self and spirit, the personal and the transpersonal? This is perhaps the most fundamental question in transpersonal psychotherapy, for how we link the human psyche to its spiritual foundation determines our approach to clinical work. It is possible to distinguish two distinct phases that transpersonal psychology has moved through in its attempts to answer this question.

The first phase was characterized by a theoretical approach to this issue, and the proposed answer was that true spiritual work could only come after a person's psychological work was done. But with the rise of transpersonally oriented clinical practice another perspective has come into view. Clinicians have led this movement toward seeing spiritual work emerging *in* the psychological work rather than after it. A brief review of each may clarify this.

In the first decade after its birth, transpersonal psychology existed more as a theoretical entity than anything else. Abraham Maslow was the first to propose that the psychological leads to the spiritual in a single line. He saw a hierarchy of psychological motivation leading the person from lower to higher level needs, with the spiritual and transpersonal level emerging at the top. Several decades later, however, we can now see that spirituality can and does emerge well before a person reaches the top of Maslow's hierarchy. Although research has mostly borne Maslow out in showing that levels of need usually cannot be skipped, it has also shown that this is not always the case. In some cases they can in fact be skipped, and spirituality in particular can become central anywhere along the motivational path.

Ken Wilber provided a more detailed answer to this question. His answer built on and codified Maslow's theory but gave it a new twist. Wilber also took the psychological level as the first step toward the spiritual, but he attached specific psychologies to the levels of psychological functioning and stacked these psychologies successively on top of each other, producing a ladder model where specific psychological approaches follow each other capped off by spiritual work. In chapters

2 and 4 I explain why I believe this is problematic. Together, Maslow and Wilber provided the first, theoretical stage of answering the question of what is the relationship between psyche and spirit by proposing a sequential link between them. Much of the work in the initial years of transpersonal psychology derived from this model in which first psychological work is done, followed by spiritual work.

However in the last ten or fifteen years, with the rise of Jungian thought and such approaches as Hameed Ali's diamond model, Grof's holotropic breathwork, and the other transpersonal approaches discussed in chapter 4, as well as deeper exploration of such phenomena as spiritual emergency, a second answer has emerged to this question. Working from many different approaches, transpersonally oriented psychotherapists have independently come upon the view that *the spiritual emerges in and through the psychological work rather than after it.*

Certainly this is the view of Jung, who viewed depth psychological work as the entryway to the spiritual, archetypal realm. Hameed Ali supports this with his approach of seeing the ego or self as a compensation for the loss of spiritual essence, which is recovered bit by bit through psychological work. Grof's work with altered states of consciousness has led to a similar answer, though by a different route. In altered states psychological material can become a gateway into the transpersonal. Sometimes this occurs through exploring the realm of the personal unconscious and sometimes through the perinatal realm; at other times it occurs spontaneously without any intervening psychological material. And the field of spiritual emergency comes at this question from an entirely different angle. In spiritual emergency, the infusion of powerful spiritual energies into the person produces great psychological turmoil as well. Almost always in spiritual emergency the unleashing of immense spiritual force stirs up psychological material, pointing to a mutual influence and gateway—the psychological intersecting the spiritual and the spiritual touching the psychological. Thus the clinical data points to a far greater relationship between the psychological and the spiritual than the first stage of transpersonal psychology theorized.

The transpersonal reply to the question, "Who am I?" is, "A psychological and spiritual being." But most everyone in the world experiences themselves only as a psychological being. Spiritual practice is generally necessary to experience ourselves as a spiritual being—it is necessary to turn within to penetrate the veil. In turning within the first thing we encounter is the self, the wounded, defended, anxious, desiring self. Unless we deal with the self psychologically, it will tend to over-shadow what little light we may have experienced.

Without attending to the unconscious and defensive processes of the self, most people, though not all, get lost in neurotic inner configu-rations, founder on the shoals of their defensive structures and fall vic-tim to their super-egos' unrealistic expectations, creating new "spiritual" versions of their old standards. They remain as closed in their hearts as ever and either get lost in an inner maze of avoidances and blind alleys, or circle endlessly, repeating old patterns with new spiritual characters and story lines. Psychotherapy helps to sort this out. In passing through the self to find the soul or spirit deeper within, psychotherapy helps the spiritual seeker to navigate these inner spaces more skillfully than does spiritual practice alone. Psychotherapy in itself may not be spiritual practice, but for most people it helps spiritual practice enormously. Spiritual practice and emergence can begin anytime, at any level of ego organization, and psychotherapy is an aid to this spiritual unfolding—not a prerequisite for it.

In one sense psychotherapy actually is spiritual work, in that it aims at expanding consciousness. The personality "vehicle," so long as it exists, always needs some attention, refining, directing, healing, unfold-ing. It will not run on automatic for very long without its unconscious defenses coming into play. Attention required for it may lessen at a cer-tain point, but it does not appear to go away.

In this sense psychological work is purificatory but it is clearly not the only work of purification needed. In the future psychological work will increasingly accompany spiritual work, for an integrated, cohesive self can do anything more efficiently, including spiritual practice. An integrated psyche allows for less distortion by unconscious forces, greater skill in traversing interior spaces, and greater interpersonal har-mony and satisfaction, the lack of which can be disruptive to spiritual growth. But even though psychotherapy is helpful to spiritual work, it is not absolutely necessary for it.

Although we are psycho-spiritual beings, psychological develop-ment and spiritual development do not appear to be the same thing. The view that seems to emerge from more recent formulations of clinical experience is that the spiritual dimension of development may consist of several discrete and at times overlapping and interacting processes. Psychological development has some number of developmental lines, expressed variously as object relations and ego development, or stages of psycho-sexual development and psycho-social development, or self-object lines of development such as mirroring, idealizing, and twinship as well as physical and cognitive development. It is not hard to imagine that spiritual development, something at least as complex as the self, may have some number of different developmental pathways, each with varying psychological effects on the self. While there may well be a correlation between the psychological and spiritual lines of development, they no longer appear to be identical.

At one level to speak of spiritual development in any form is illusory. Nothing develops and there is nothing to attain. The fullness of spiritual experience is immediately available in its entirety. Enlightenment, *atman*, or Buddha-nature exists eternally and immutably in this present moment, and we need only awaken to it or have it revealed by Divine Grace, which can happen at any instant.

At another level or from another perspective, spiritual practice is a process of development that allows a person to approach and to manifest this level of spirit (*atman*, Buddha-nature) more and more in everyday mind and life. A sense of peace and inner stillness quiets the inattentive, distracted self as consciousness wakes up. The ego or self is gradually purified so that it may reflect or allow this dimension of consciousness to emerge more completely.

At still another level or from yet another perspective, spiritual practice brings forth the soul and its powers, progressively transforming the egoic self. The spiritual sun may rise to any height on any level or levels of our being, making for a widely varying and complex action on the outer self. When the soul or Divine Power or Shakti acts on the consciousness of the person there can be periods when spiritual development is entirely inward, without any apparent connection to the surface self, though at some point different aspects of the self may then be stimulated. Sometimes this action may be total, but more often it acts selectively and partially on certain parts of the being. There may be physical, emotional, or mental effects. Psychological issues are stirred in this process, early wounds are touched, contracted and defended parts of the self are activated, or dormant potentials are illuminated. As the self transforms, the love, light, power, and joy of the soul shines through more fully and vividly.

Similarly, psychological work may free up parts of the consciousness which may have spiritual consequences, releasing spiritual energies, opening a center (chakra), or allowing spiritual practice to deepen along a particular line. There are times when the psychological and spiritual seem to be involved in a process of mutual influence and interpenetration.

All of this points to a view where psychological and spiritual development are composed of multiple, complex developmental pathways that sometimes intermingle, interpenetrate, and overlap, while at other times remain discrete and more obviously separate. Sometimes growth is psychological, sometimes growth is spiritual, and at other times both are occurring together.

A transpersonal perspective holds both dimensions, or more accurately, sees the level of psychological growth occurring within the larger dimension of spiritual awakening. While the precise relationship between psychological life and the deeper spiritual reality is at present only barely glimpsed and far from fully understood, this does not make the fundamental dependence of psychological life upon the deeper spirit within any less real. It thus becomes possible to pursue psychological wholeness and spiritual wholeness simultaneously, not sequentially. Though at times one or the other may predominate, it is a *both/and* process rather than *either/or* or even *first one/then the other*. Holding the intentions for both psychological wholeness and spiritual development may have a synergistic effect, adding greater fuel and allowing the flame of aspiration to burn ever higher and brighter.

In this process we may find that the deeper soul or spiritual reality can express itself through this surface instrument of the self, the more so as this self becomes increasingly purified, and psychological healing provides one aspect or level of this purification. Thus, although a psychotic or borderline will probably integrate spiritual experience and insight into their everyday lives differently from a neurotic, it does not mean better or more effectively. This may depend significantly upon such things as the "ripeness" and maturity of the soul or spiritual being which supports the outward egoic manifestation. A "ripe" soul manifesting in a borderline personality may undergo dramatic and life-changing effects from a spiritual experience while a young soul manifesting in a well adjusted neurotic personality organization may quickly fall back asleep after a spiritual awakening. The psychological and spiritual lines of development mutually interact, at times may even appear coincident, but are not identical. It is not possible to reduce a person's total psychospiritual being to a diagnostic category or to a level of ego organization.

Though in one sense there is nothing which is not a manifestation of Spirit, in a practical sense a differentiation can be made between the body/heart/mind organism which dies and the spirit within which does not die. The body, heart, mind are the instruments through which our spiritual nature expresses itself. In awakened, God-realized beings, a perfect expression of divine wisdom and action is no doubt desirable, but the Divine does not exclude a wide variety of imperfect expressions. The body of a saint or a Buddha may be vital and healthy or sick and feeble—it does not effect the soul or spirit. The mind may be clear and bright or dull and senile, yet the spirit within is unaffected. Similarly, the emotional integration may be high or low, but the essential spiritual nature does not change. As sages over the centuries have proclaimed, even death does not affect the eternal spirit within. The state of spiritual realization cannot be measured by the state of the vehicle. For this reason when Arjuna asks Krishna in the *Bhagavad Gita* what is the nature of an enlightened being, what does the person act like, talk like, and so on, Krishna's responses pertain only to the inner experience of such a being, for there are no outer standards by which spiritual realization can be measured.

Because access to a highly psychologically integrated, post-neurotic "mature" level of functioning is such a recent historical development since the advent of psychotherapy in the past century, to presume that somehow all shamans, saints, and sages of other cultures and ages have somehow spontaneously achieved a working through of the unconscious defenses and childhood wounds to reach this "mature" stage is an extremely dubious claim, one that most trained depth psychotherapists would not take very seriously.

Just as religion dominated the field of human thought throughout much of western history, psychology has now become a dominant paradigm whose lens can easily annex any subject it touches. Those of us in the psychological community must be mindful of not yielding to the seductive trap of the "psychologization of spirituality," which is tempting precisely because it so strongly appeals to the feeling of having spe-

cial knowledge, greater vision, and, at bottom, one's narcissistic investment in a psychological perspective. Wilber's model falls into this trap
of the "psychologization of spirituality," as do many in the Jungian and
Washburn camp and as many other transpersonal psychologists do. But
it is important to acknowledge the limits of psychology. Psychology
does not make the world go round — Spirit does.

Although transpersonal psychotherapy sees spiritual development
occurring through and along with psychological development and
healing, it is important to recognize that it may happen *apart* from psychological work. Indeed, all the world's spiritual traditions arose from
purely spiritual striving and without access to the learnings of depth
psychology. By viewing psychological healing as one way of entering
into spiritual Being, transpersonal psychotherapy is not saying this is
the only way it can occur. Transpersonal psychotherapy simply adds
the perspective that inner, psychotherapeutic work is probably a help
on this spiritual journey for most seekers. At times the psychological
work may overshadow the spiritual work and initially make it appear a
longer journey. But it may ultimately assist the process by dissipating
some of the common psychological quagmires that many seekers
sooner or later find themselves mired in and which spiritual practice
alone is generally not so efficient at dealing with. The psychological
level, like the entire physical manifestation, is ultimately dependent
upon the deeper, spiritual ground of being. Psychological development
and spiritual development are different, even though depth psychological work may be an entryway into spirit and even though spiritual consciousness may to varying degrees uplift, purify, and transform the
psychological dimension of our being.

This spiritual, transpersonal framework is composed of a body of
knowledge and theory, and an understanding of this knowledge base is
essential, just as it is in any other orientation. Part of this knowledge
base is familiarity with a wide range of spiritual paths and practices, a
knowledge that should be much deeper than can be given in this volume. The therapist's own spiritual tradition will provide some of this
knowledge. But it is crucial for the therapist not to be parochial or too
closely tied to one particular path. A wide and inclusive comprehension
of the many varieties of spiritual practice and spiritual development is
indispensable.

A transpersonal orientation implies an openness to transpersonal content when it arises in the course of psychotherapy. This can take many different forms, from a client's need to be seen and affirmed in his or her spiritual wholeness to the emergence of spiritual or numinous experience in a client's life all the way to more dramatic manifestations such as spiritual emergency. Being able to recognize and bring awareness to transpersonal content is an important skill for a transpersonal therapist. A transpersonal therapist is also aware that there are progressive and regressive possibilities inherent in the range of psycho-spiritual experiences. Being mindful of both means neither glorifying nor minimizing spiritual experience but seeking to illuminate its significance in the person's life and functioning. It is particularly tempting for a transpersonal therapist to glorify spiritual or transpersonal experience because this is seen as the basis for real transformation and is the implicit goal of therapeutic work. Yet it is crucial to be aware of the full psychological context of the person's functioning in order to avoid mistaking prepersonal or regressive experiences for those that are truly transpersonal and progressive.

Another part of this knowledge base consists of grounding in traditional psychotherapeutic approaches and recognizing that there are behavioral, psychodynamic, and existential points of entry into a client's experience. Exploration can stop here (as it usually does with any one of these therapies) or it can proceed to any or all of the other dimensions of depth work. The more extensive the exploration, the greater the degree of consciousness which can be liberated.

The transpersonal lens holds all three of these forces in psychology together. I have explained in earlier chapters why I find the multi-perspectival way of organizing these three approaches to psychology presented in this book more clinically useful and theoretically sound than theories of successive, hierarchical levels. But whichever approach is used, the main thing is to include all three previous forces in psychology.

To summarize, this book contends that psychological and spiritual dimensions of human experience and development are different, though at times overlapping, with the spiritual as foundational. Achieving psychological integration is not essential for spiritual realization. And while spiritual realization does not bring about psychological integration, only entering into spiritual Being will provide a complete resolution to the dilemmas and pain of psychological, egoic existence. Psychotherapy can be helpful for many people on the spiritual path to prevent circling around in unconscious defenses and avoidances. Similarly, the inner deepening that results from spiritual practice can be helpful in a person's psychological work. Each can help the other, but neither one is necessary for the other. Transpersonal psychotherapy sheds light both on how the spiritual impulse can get detoured in the service of psychological defense (spiritual by-passing) and how an exclusive psychological focus can be endless (psychological fixation), unless we come upon the deeper ground of spirit.

2. **Consciousness is central in transpersonal psychotherapy.** Besides the intellectual learning of the transpersonal framework, what is required of a transpersonal therapist is to be seeking a deeper and deeper contact with Being; the therapist must be increasingly centered in his or her own depths in a dynamic quest for the Divine. For while engaging the consciousness of the client is the key to change, the true support and inner foundation of a transpersonal psychotherapy is the therapist's consciousness. The spiritual intention and aspiration of the therapist, the presence of the therapist, and the therapist's own deepening inner exploration and consciousness work provide the guiding light for the therapeutic journey.

When a therapist is committed to a religious belief system for defensive purposes, however, as an evasion of sincere inner work, this becomes simply another form of spiritual by-passing, and this defensive posture will obstruct therapeutic efforts. It is a living, sustained inward search for spirit, not a dogmatic clinging to belief systems as a solution to life that forms the inner core of this process.

Dealing with countertransference and personal reactivity requires this inner work. Years and decades of personal work and therapy plus years and decades of meditation and spiritual practice are required for a transpersonal psychotherapist. Patience, dedication, persistence— these time honored virtues eventually pay off, slowly but surely. As boring and tedious as this may sound, in the field of personal development there is no such thing as "Spanish made easy" or "transpersonal psychotherapy in five easy steps." Inner growth takes time and commitment. Then it is solid development, not founded on the sands of passing new psychological fads.

The consciousness of the therapist acts as a kind of subtle energy field that can help induct a client into a deeper experience of being. It is this which conveys an inner feeling, an energy that uplifts the entire psychotherapeutic enterprise. A mutual consciousness expansion of both client and therapist is a natural result of such a psychotherapy.

3. Transpersonal psychotherapy is multidimensional and experiential. By viewing consciousness as multidimensional, transpersonal psychotherapy is open to entering the client's world at any level, through any door. Even though the doors of inner experience swing open through different channels for different people, the central focus upon the client's consciousness implies an experiential process that involves the whole person. Emphasizing any particular level (mind, body, heart) is seen as but a helpful and easily accessible first step toward the totality of mind-body-heart-spirit. It also includes an openness to alternate modes of experiencing, such as can occur in altered states, through vision quests, or through meditation that can have great transformative potential.

So much of psychotherapy occurs with words, however. And although the therapeutic intent of all depth psychotherapy is to use words as a passageway into a fuller range of experiencing, all too often verbal psychotherapy can become mired in the verbal mind. The allure of insight, the comforting ease of "talking about," the hidden compulsion of fear and anxiety to steer clear of difficult material, all conspire to prevent the deepening of experience. But a transpersonal psychotherapy is experiential at its core. It is only the experience of spirit that satisfies the soul's quest, and only by plunging into the depths of the inner heart and feeling can the realms of spiritual being be plumbed. As in the Zen story of the master pointing to the moon who advises looking at the moon rather than his finger, words point to something beyond themselves, an experiential dimension of being. The articulation of inner experience is of great help in skillfully traversing inner worlds of feeling and meaning. Only when words become launching pads into deeper experiencing is their potential realized.

4. Transpersonal psychotherapy is heart-centered. The transpersonal brings in love and compassion as spiritual values that are actualized in the therapy office. Humanistic psychology's critique of psychoanalysis has shown us the dangers of being too cold, detached, and unfeeling in a profession that is about feelings. But this sometimes led humanistic psychology into making the mistake of going too far in the other direction, trying to cure through love, which became unbounded, merging codependence at its worst. A transpersonal view seeks to integrate the best of both worlds: doing psychotherapy with an open heart. In Hindu Tantra, the opening of the fourth chakra opens the person both to spirituality and to love. So it may be no accident that a transpersonal orientation opens up the possibilities of working from the heart more fully and directly than before.

Carl Rogers has been the strongest voice in stressing the importance of love. He referred to the importance of unconditional positive regard, for in his day it would have sounded too unprofessional to speak of love so directly, yet this is Rogers' underlying message. Rogers is a forerunner of a transpersonal view of working from the heart, with love. Only in his final years did Rogers speak more openly of the transpersonal dimension in psychotherapy. In admitting love to the psychotherapy process, it should be kept in mind that this is a love which is inwardly felt and does not need to be explicitly stated, a bounded, inner experience which imparts a different, warmer, and more compassionate energy to the therapy process. It is a love that can embrace the client in his or her woundedness and see the Divine potential within. It sees the client as a fellow seeker who, like us, is a Child of the Divine and is not so separate from us as our dividing, egoic mind would have us believe.

5. **Transpersonal psychotherapy is profoundly optimistic and hope-centered.** The transpersonal vision is profoundly optimistic. This goes far beyond the humanistic belief in human potential to a greater faith in the entire spiritual nature of existence and the Divine potential it is the sacred charge of each person to manifest in this life. Such a view can be described as hope-centered (Clinebell, 1995). This does not imply any kind of Pollyanna-ish naiveté or a viewing of the world through rose-colored glasses. Indeed, the immense tragedy, trauma, and appalling suffering of human beings encountered daily in psychotherapy practice is undeniable. Many religions even start from this basic fact of human existence—life is suffering, pain and death are inevitable.

But the world's religious traditions also see beyond this material world to a greater action that is being played out. There is a spiritual reality that underlies this material creation. There is a bliss, *ananda*, a joy of spiritual existence which religious traditions universally affirm, a pure, unalloyed delight of Being. In connecting to this greater reality life receives its redeeming and transforming significance.

This means that the therapist continually views the experience of the client as meaningful, no matter how bleak, painful, or apparently random and meaningless it may appear on the surface. It is hard to capture, but the transpersonal perspective brings into view the person's psychological process as a spiritual journey, a more exciting, inspiring view of psychotherapy being sacred work, and a deeper and more profound trust in the process. A purely psychological orientation, by contrast, seems much more limited and depressingly confining.

This demands faith—faith in the unfolding process, faith that a larger story will reveal itself, faith that a deeper significance will be discovered. This allows a therapist to be with a client's tragedy and pain in a more accepting, spacious way, not just caught up in outrage or sadness or personal reactions on the one hand and not in a closed, hardened, or defensively withdrawn posture on the other hand, but openly and tenderly, holding the client's pain in his or her heart in a way that facilitates the client's being able to be with this pain more fully. A transpersonal therapist has an unshakable belief in the client's movement toward a higher self or greater spirit, and all the wounds, suffering, and stumblings along the way have their contribution to make toward the birth of this emergent being.

6. **The transpersonal view of psycho-spiritual transformation extends far beyond the healing and growth of the self.** The transpersonal view of "cure" or healing or resolution of psychological difficulties entails all that conventional psychotherapy has discovered about the working-through process and more. For as enormously important as traditional psychotherapy is for healing and growth, as important as it is to open to the many, many layers of pain, unresolved conflict, and developmental deficits that early wounding leaves in its wake, and as fully as it is possible to work through trauma and early childhood wounding and actualize a far greater potential that each person has, full resolution and transformation occurs only by opening to spiritual Being. It is only by the infusion of spiritual energies into the psyche that a radical change occurs.

There are differences as to what Being is depending upon whether we consider a theistic-relational or nondual perspective, but there is more agreement than we might expect in these two views about what the movement into Being looks like. This movement into Being has different vocabularies to describe it depending upon the system—for example, it can be described as the emergence of the soul, an infusion of Divine grace, or the progressive manifestation of Buddha-nature. Also, there is a difference as to the final outcome, that is into self or no self (but since dissolving into no self is such a statistically rare occurrence, this is less relevant at present). Curiously, how the self becomes transformed by the emergence of Being looks very similar in theistic-relational and nondual approaches. There is a movement into greater peace, calm, a spacious and loving consciousness. Consciousness widens, becomes more refined, more interior, and has access to greater wisdom, compassion, empathy, sensitivity, and sensory and bodily awareness. The person is less reactive, more centered in a spiritual consciousness that is self-existent, intrinsically joyous, and not dependent upon outward responses to sustain itself.

The various transpersonal orientations presented in this volume are but strategies for accessing spiritual Being, using the self, its wounds and defenses, as stepping stones on this path. Some people enter more easily through the body, some by the mind or imagery, some by the heart and feeling. But all transpersonal orientations are pathways into Being. What spiritual traditions from all perspectives affirm is that there is no endpoint in sight in this voyage. The movement from self into Being is an infinite journey.

CONCLUSION

The transpersonal paradigm pushes the boundaries of the old distinctions between psychology and spirituality. Until the advent of the transpersonal movement, a sharp distinction had been made between psychology and religion, science and spirit, the profane and the sacred. But transpersonal psychology is now challenging this separation. If the roots of the psyche are spiritual, if the basis of consciousness is a spiritual reality, then this clear-cut division is no longer tenable. Spiritual emergency, altered states of consciousness, meditative experience, birth, dying—whenever the limits of the self are exceeded, spirit pours in. The boundaries are blurring. Old definitions are inadequate. We are now moving past strict divisions toward a new synthesis. From a transpersonal perspective, psychology is a psycho-spiritual field.

Although transpersonal psychology has a far wider view of the self than traditional psychology and may allow us to ask more fundamental questions, it must be acknowledged that we are still very far from having a satisfactory understanding about the nature of the self. How and why the process of internalization occurs of early object relations, how the self emerges in relation to its family or intersubjective field, what the self is and what it expresses, why is it so persistent despite some spiritual traditions' assertion that it is merely an illusion, what its function is in centralizing consciousness in the evolutionary journey—answers to such questions are still far from us.

Transpersonal psychology is in the unique position of being the only psychological approach to human experience that can be more than just integrative but fully inclusive, casting psychological life into a spiritual frame. All other attempts at integrating the various schools of psychotherapy, no matter how wide their scope, must inevitably fall short for all of them leave out an essential, the most essential, aspect of human experience: namely, that we are more than psycho-physical, emotionally wounded and conditioned selves but are spiritual beings. Our true identity, as opposed to our surface identification, is spiritual in nature, and any psychology that does not acknowledge this must necessarily be incomplete and fragmentary.

Only transpersonal psychology has a large enough container to assimilate all the rest of psychology into it and to see the theories and facts of psychological life through a spiritual lens, a lens that brings new worlds into view. Spirit supports, upholds, gives direction and meaning to psychological life. There are depths within depths, a journey of endless discovery. The inner riches of psyche and spirit are before us. Surely we are but at the threshold of discovering all that we can be.

References

Allison, J. (1971). Respiratory changes during transcendental meditation. *Lancet*, 1 (7651), 883.

Almaas, A. H. (1986). *Essence*. York Beach, ME: Weiser.

Almaas, A. H. (1988). *Pearl beyond price*. Berkeley: Diamond Books.

Almaas, A. H. (1995). *Luminous night's journey*. Berkeley: Diamond Books.

Almaas, A. H. (1996). *The Point of Existence*. Berkeley: Diamond Books.

Atwood, G., & Stolorow, R. (1984). *Structures of subjectivity*. Hillsdale, NJ: Analytic Press.

Aurobindo, S. (1971a). *Letters on yoga* (Vol. 1). Pondicherry, India: Sri Aurobindo Ashram Press.

Aurobindo, S. (1971b). *Letters on yoga*. (Vol. 3). Pondicherry, India: Sri Aurobindo Ashram Press.

Aurobindo, S. (1972). *Essays on the Gita*. Pondicherry, India: Sri Aurobindo Ashram Press.

Aurobindo, S. (1973a). *The problem of rebirth*. Pondicherry, India: All India Press.

Aurobindo, S. (1973b). *The synthesis of yoga*. Pondicherry, India: Sri Aurobindo Ashram Press.

Banquet, J. (1973). Spectral analysis of the EEG in meditation. *Electroencephalography. Clinical Neurophysiology, 35*, 143–151.

Basch, M. (1988). *Understanding psychotherapy.* New York: Basic Books.

Becker, E. (1973). *The denial of death.* New York: Free Press.

Benson, H. (1975). *The relaxation response.* New York: Avon Books.

Binswanger, L. (1956). Existential analysis and psychotherapy. In F. Fromm-Reichmann & J. Moreno (Eds.), *Progress in psychotherapy.* New York: Grune & Stratton.

Blanck, G., & Blanck, R. (1974). *Ego psychology: Theory and practice.* New York: Columbia University Press.

Bogart, G. (1991, July). The use of meditation in psychotherapy: A review of the literature. *American Journal of Psychotherapy,45 (3),* 383–412.

Boss, M. (1958). *The analysis of dreams.* New York: Philosophical Library.

Boss, M. (1979). *Existential foundations of medicine and psychology.* New York: Jason Aronson.

Bowman, P. (1987). *Phenomenological comparison of vipassana meditation practice and existential psychotherapy.* Unpublished doctoral dissertation, California Institute of Integral Studies, San Francisco.

Bragdon, E. (1988). *A sourcebook for helping people in spiritual emergency.* Los Altos, CA: Lightening Up Press.

Bucke, R. (1923). *Cosmic consciousness.* New York: Dutton.

Bugental, J. (1976). *The search for existential identity.* San Francisco: Jossey-Bass.

Bugental, J. (1978). *Psychotherapy and process.* New York: Random House.

Bugental, J. (1987). *The art of the psychotherapist.* New York: W. W. Norton.

Campbell, P., & McMahon, E. (1985). *Bio-spirituality.* Chicago: Loyola University Press.

Clinebell, H. (1995). *Counseling for spiritually empowered wholeness.* Binghamton, NY: Haworth Press.

Doblin, R. (1991). Pahnke's "Good Friday Experiment." Journal of Transpersonal Psychology 23: (1), 1–28.

Eisler, R. (1987). *The chalice and the blade.* San Francisco: Harper.

Engler, J. (1986). Therapeutic aims in psychotherapy and meditation. In Wilber, K., Engler, J., & Brown, D. *Transformations of consciousness*. Boston: Shambhala.

Epstein, M. (1984). On the neglect of evenly suspended attention. *Journal of Transpersonal Psychology*, 16, (2), 193–206.

Epstein, M. (1986). Meditative transformations of narcissism. *Journal of Transpersonal Psychology*, 18, (2), 143–158.

Epstein, M. (1988). The deconstruction of the self. *Journal of Transpersonal Psychology*, 20, (1), 61–70.

Epstein, M. (1989). Forms of emptiness. *Journal of Transpersonal Psychology*, 21 (1), 61–72.

Epstein, M. (1990). Psychodynamics of meditation. *Journal of Transpersonal Psychology*, 22, (1), 17–34.

Epstein, M. (1995). *Thoughts without a thinker*. New York: Basic Books.

Freud, S. (1959). *Civilization and its discontents*. In J. Strachey (Ed., Trans.), *The standard edition of the complete psychological works of Sigmund Freud*, (Vol. 20). London: Hogarth.

Freud, S. (1966). Obsessive actions and religious practices. In J. Strachey (Ed., Trans.). *The standard edition of the complete psychological works of Sigmund Freud*, (Vol. 1). London: Hogarth.

Gendlin, E. (1981). *Focusing*. New York: Bantam Books.

Gendlin, E. (1996). *Focusing-oriented psychotherapy*. New York: Guilford Press.

Glueck, G. (1975). Biofeedback and meditation in the treatment of psychiatric illness. *Comprehensive Psychiatry*, (16), 303–320.

Goleman, D. (1976). Meditation and Consciousness. *American Journal of Psychotherapy*, (30), 41–54.

Goleman, D. (1988). *The meditative mind*. Los Angeles: Tarcher.

Grof, S. (1975). *Realms of the human unconscious*. New York: Viking Press.

Grof, S. (1980). *LSD psychotherapy*. Pomona, CA: Hunter House.

Grof, S. (1985). *Beyond the brain*. Albany, NY: SUNY Press.

Grof, C. & Grof, S. (1986). Spiritual emergency: The understanding and treatment of transpersonal crises. *ReVision* 8 (2), 7–20.

Grof, C. & Grof S. (Eds.) (1989). *Spiritual emergency.* Los Angeles: Tarcher.

Group for the Advancement of Psychiatry. (1976). *Mysticism: Spiritual quest or mental disorder.* New York: Author.

Hoffer, A., & Osmond, H. (1967). *The hallucinogens.* New York: Academic Press.

Hoffman, E. (1988). *The right to be human: A biography of Abraham Maslow.* Los Angeles: Tarcher.

Horton, P.C. (1974). The mystical experience: Substance of an Illusion. *American Psychoanalytic Association Journal* 22 (1–2), 364–380.

Huxley, A. (1954). *The Doors of perception* New York: Harper & Row.

Jones, J. (1991). *Contemporary psychoanalysis and religion.* New Haven: Yale University Press.

Jung, C. (1975). *Letters.* (Vol. 2: 1951–1961). Princeton: Princeton University Press.

Kakar, S. (1991). *The analyst and the mystic.* Chicago: University of Chicago Press.

Kohut, H. (1971). *The analysis of the self.* New York: International Universities Press.

Kohut, H. (1977). *Restoration of the self.* Madison, CT: International Universities Press.

Kornfield, J. (1993a). The seven factors of enlightenment. In *Paths beyond ego.* Los Angeles: Tarcher.

Kornfield, J. (1993b). *A path with heart.* New York: Bantam Books.

Krishnamurti, J. (1973). *The awakening of intelligence.* New York: Harper and Row.

Kuhn, T. (1962). *The structure of scientific revolutions.* Chicago: University of Chicago Press.

Leary, T. (1967). The religious experience: Its production and interpretation. *Journal Psychedelic Drugs, 1* (2), 3–23.

Leary, T. (1968). *High priest*. New York: College Notes and Texts, Inc.

Leary, T., et al. (1962). Investigations into the religious implications of consciousness expanding experience. Newsletter 1, Research program on consciousness altering substances. Cambridge, MA: Harvard University.

Leuba, J.H. (1929). *Psychology of religious mysticism*. New York: Harcourt Brace.

Levey, J., & Levey, M. (1987). *The fine arts of relaxation, concentration and meditation*. Boston: Wisdom Publications.

Levine, S. (1982). *Who dies?*. New York: Anchor Press/Doubleday.

Levine, S. (1987). *Healing into life and into death*. New York: Doubleday.

Lukoff, D. (1985). The diagnosis of mystical exiences with psychotic features. *Journal of Transpersonal Psychology*, *17* (2), 155–181.

Lukoff, D., Lu, F., & Turner, R. (1992). Toward a more culturally sensitive DSM-IV. *Journal of Nervous and Mental Disease*, *180* (11), 673–682.

Mandel, A.J. (1980). Toward a psychobiology of transcendence. In Davidson & Davidson (Eds.) *The Psychobiology of Consciousness*. New York: Plenum.

Maslow, A. (1968). *Toward a psychology of being*. (2nd ed.). Princeton: Von Nostrand.

Maslow, A. (1970). *Religions, values and peak experiences*. New York: Viking.

Maslow, A. (1971). *The further reaches of human nature*. New York: Viking.

May, G. (1982). *Care of the mind/Care of the spirit*. New York: Harper Collins.

May, R. (1969). *Love and will*. New York: Norton.

May, R. (1977). *The meaning of anxiety*. New York: Norton.

May, R., Angel, E., & Ellenberger, H. (Eds.). (1958). *Existence*. New York: Basic Books.

Meadow, M., & Culligan, K. (1987) Congruent spiritual paths. *Journal of Transpersonal Psychology*, 181–196.

Michael S.R., Huber, M., McCann, D., (1976). Evaluating transcendental meditation as a method of reducing stress. *Science, 192* (4245), 1242.

Murphy, M., & Donovan S. (1985). *Contemporary Meditation Research.* San Francisco: Esalen Foundation.

Naranjo, C. (1973). *The healing journey.* New York: Random House.

Naranjo, C. (1990). *How to be.* Los Angeles: Tarcher.

Naranjo, C. (1993). *Gestalt therapy.* Nevada City, CA: Gateways.

Nathanson, D. (1992). *Shame and pride.* New York: W. W. Norton.

Nelson, J. (1990). *Healing the split.* Los Angeles: Tarcher.

Pahnke, W. (1963). *Drugs and mysticism: An analysis of the relationship between psychedelic drugs and the mystical consciousness.* Ph.D. dissertation. Harvard University, Boston.

Perls, F. (1969). *Gestalt therapy verbatim.* Moab, UT: Real People Press.

Roquet, S., Favreau, P., Ocana, R., & de Velasco, M. (1975). *The existential through psyschodisleptics—A new psychotherapy.* Mexico, D.F.: Asociacion Albert Schweitzer, A. C.

Rorty, R. (1989), *Contingency, irony, and solidarity.* Cambridge: Cambridge University Press.

Rothberg, D. (1986). Philosophical foundations of transpersonal psychology. *Journal of Transpersonal Psychology, 18,* 1–34.

Rowan, J. (1993). *The transpersonal.* London: Routledge.

Russell, E. (1986). Consciousness and the unconscious: Eastern meditative and Western psychotherapeutic approaches. *Journal of Transpersonal Psychology, 18,* 51–72.

Sannella, L. (1978). Kundalin: Clasical and Clinical in White, J. (Ed.), *Kundalini, Evolution and Enlightenment.* Garden City, N.Y.: Anchor Books/Doubleday.

Schneider, K., & May, R. (1994). *The psychology of existence.* New York: McGraw Hill.

Schwartz, T. (1995). *What really matters.* New York: Bantam.

Smith, H. (1976). *Forgotten truth.* New York: Harper and Row.

Speeth, K. (1982). On psychotherapeutic attention. *Journal of Transpersonal Psychology*, 14 (2), 141–160.

Stolorow, R. (1992). Closing the gap between theory and practice with better psychoanalytic theory. *Psychotherapy*, *29*, 2.

Stolorow, R., Brandchaft, B., & Atwood, G. (1987). *Psychoanalytic treatment*. New Jersey: Analytic Press.

Suler, J. (1993). *Contemporary psychoanalysis and Eastern thought*. Albany, NY: SUNY Press.

Sutich, A.J. (1969). Some considerations regarding transpersonal psychology. *Journal of Transpersonal Psychology*, 1, (1), 15–16.

Tomkins, S. (1962). *Affect/imagery/consciousness*. Vol. 1: *The positive affects*.

Tomkins, S. (1963). *Affect/imagery/consciousness*. Vol. 2: *The negative affects* New York: Springer.

Tomkins, S. (1991). *Affect/imagery/ consciousness*. Vol. 3: *The negative affects: anger and feel*. New York: Springer.

Trungpa, C. (1974). *Cutting through spiritual materialism*. Berkeley: Shambhala.

Vaughn, F. (1979). Transpersonal psychotherapy: Context, content and process. *Journal of Transpersonel Psychology*, 11(2), 101–110.

Wallace, R. (1970). Physiological effects of transcendental meditation. Science, 167 (926), 1751–1754.

Walsh, R., & Vaughn, F. (1993). *Paths beyond ego*. Los Angeles: Tarcher.

Washburn, M. (1988). *The ego and the dynamic ground*. Albany, NY: SUNY Press.

Washburn, M. (1990). Two patterns of transcendence. *Journal of Humanistic Psychology*, Vol. 30, No. 3, 84–112.

Washburn, M. (1994). *Transpersonal psychology in psychoanalytic perspective*. Albany, NY: SUNY Press

Weill, A. (1972). *The natural mind*. Boston: Houghton Mifflin.

Welwood, J. (1980). Reflections on psychotherapy, focusing, and meditation. *Journal of Transpersonal Psychology*, *12*, 127–141.

Welwood, J. (1984). Principles of inner work *Journal of Transpersonal Psychology 16*, (1), 63–73.

Wilber, K. (1977). *The spectrum of consciousness*. Wheaton, IL: Quest.

Wilber, K. (1980). *The atman project*. Wheaton, IL: Quest.

Wilber, K. (1981a). *No boundary*. Boston: Shambhala.

Wilber, K. (1981b). *Up from Eden*. New York: Doubleday.

Wilber, K. (Ed.). (1982). *The holographic paradigm and other paradoxes*. Boston: Shambhala.

Wilber, K. (1983). *A sociable God*. New York: McGraw-Hill.

Wilber, K. (Ed.). (1984). *Quantum questions*. Boston: Shambhala.

Wilber, K. (1990). *Eye to eye*. Boston: Shambhala.

Wilber, K. (1991). *Grace and grit*. Boston: Shambhala.

Wllber, K. (1995). *Sex, ecology, and spirit* (Vol. 1). Boston: Shambhala.

Wilber, K. (1996). *A brief history of everything*. Boston: Shambhala.

Wilber, K. (1997). *The Eye of Spirit*. Boston: Shambhala.

Wilber, K., Engler, J., & Brown, D. (1986). *Transformations of consciousness*. Boston: Shambhala.

Wolpe, J. (1958). *Psychotherapy by reciprocal inhibition*. Stanford: Stanford University Press.

Yalom, I. (1980). *Existential psychotherapy*. New York: Basic.

Yenson, R. (1988). From mysteries to paradigms. *ReVision 10* (4). 31–50.

Index